Alpha
Brain Waves

Alpha
Brain Waves

Jodi Lawrence

Nash Publishing, Los Angeles

Library of Congress Catalog Card Number: 72-186923
Standard Book Number: 8402-1263-1

Published simultaneously in the United States and Canada
by Nash Publishing Corporation, 9255 Sunset Boulevard,
Los Angeles, California 90069.

Printed in the United States of America.

First Printing.

Contents

Foreword

One of the characteristics of man that distinguishes him from lower animals is his remarkable ability to manipulate his external environment. Whereas other life forms have through the ages succumbed to changing environmental stress, man has learned to modify and control such forces. He can, for example, transform a burning desert into a lush green agricultural community. He can exist for an extended period of time on the ocean floor; he can take a small version of his earth's environment with him to the moon; and he can harness atomic energy for his cities. These technological achievements are primarily a product of Western culture with its emphasis on the comfortable, and even pleasurable, adaptation of man to his world. However, in his frantic quest to remake his external world, Western man has largely neglected his own internal milieu. In fact, the complex society that has been generated from this technological crush has itself created serious psychological and physiological problems for its members. At no time in the duration of man's existence on earth has he been so subject to psychosomatic disorders and a thousand nagging anxieties. He finds himself frustrated and overstimulated by tight schedules, crowds, noises, red tape, fast-moving transportation, increasing crime, pollution, and ever greater restrictions on his behavior.

True to his fashion, Western man has turned to *external* agents to relax or numb his body after this daily onslaught. Tranquilizers, alcohol, pot and other drugs enable him to exert some control, though often with distressing side effects, over his internal environment. Much as he has polluted the external world, man now threatens his internal world with these seductive chemicals that may bring some immediate relief at the cost of long-term psychological and physiological deterioration.

Perhaps it is time for an *internal* ecology program. Ideally such a program would not only allow modern man to withstand better the stresses of his culture, but it would subsequently result in a gradual transformation of the culture itself. This evolving culture would no doubt reflect the increasing ability of its individual members to interact in positive, loving, altruistic fashion, free of the frustration, hostility and aggression that have so characterized man through the ages.

One does not have to look far for attempts at internal ecology programs. The recent interest in health foods, jogging, bicycling, yoga and meditation are some examples that come to mind. It is interesting that in our modern technological society we are rewarded primarily for external goal-achieving activities. We receive raises, bonuses and status for working harder and faster, and producing more. There is little of this kind of reward for time spent in quiet contemplation or meditation. In contrast, Eastern cultures have for centuries held in high esteem the man who would devote his life to the development of inner awareness. This sort of striving has never received much emphasis in the more technological cultures because of the years of concentrated effort required, and because the positive results usually cannot be measured in terms of material benefits or goods. In recent years, however, there has been a surge of interest among Western cultures in both physical and meditative yoga exercises as well as Zen meditation. This is perhaps reflective of a change in values as well as a desire to find some refuge from the fast moving, dehumanizing technological culture we have evolved. For the first time we are becoming concerned with the development of inner awareness and the manipulation of the internal environment.

It was almost inevitable that Western man would turn to

technology in an attempt to shorten the time required to develop awareness of and control over internal processes. Advances in semiconductor electronics, physiological instrumentation and operant conditioning provided the means with which psychologists and engineers pursued the investigation of internal control. So great was the interest among both laymen and researchers that even modest preliminary results received unprecedented mass media coverage. As a result, many of these early findings escaped the crucible of professional criticism and found their way into the folklore of third world consciousness.

In 1969 researchers in the field gathered for a meeting in Santa Monica, California. They chose a name for their new area of research—*Biofeedback.*

Alpha—the brain wave rhythm which predominates when one is relaxed and alert with eyes closed—became the first and most popularized physiological phenomenon to be manipulated through a "feedback" procedure. The initial emphasis here was on increasing awareness and expanding consciousness. Somewhat later, researchers attempted to train humans and animals to control such responses as muscle tension, heart rate, blood pressure, and vascular changes. Clinical applications began to be explored. If individuals could be taught to control voluntarily one or more of these physiological responses then perhaps many of the stress-related disorders such as tension headache, migraine, anxiety, high blood pressure and cardiac dysrhythmia could be alleviated or even eliminated. Carefully controlled animal studies hinted at the potential of the technique for human use. Only cautious research would be able to provide proof of the effectiveness of these techniques. The possibility of an internal ecological control which would encompass the ability to resist maladaptive stress reactions, as well as the power to expand consciousness and effect positive personality change loom on the horizon.

THOMAS BUDZYNSKI, PH. D.
Assistant Professor of Psychology
University of Colorado Medical Center
Denver, Colorado

Alpha
Brain Waves

EEG feedback is the most exciting thing to hit this planet. What it promises for the individual is a change in the very quality of his life.

Dr. Lester Fehmi

Someday, instead of gulping a tranquilizer, one might merely reproduce the state of tranquility he had learned [through biofeedback].

Dr. Joe Kamiya

Biofeedback training could well open the door for us to the Golden Age of Man.

Dr. Barbara Brown

Biofeedback may enable man to exercise voluntary control over many of the physiological functions that had been considered to be almost totally beyond such control.

Dr. Thomas Budzynski

Part One: Understanding Alpha Brain Wave Research

Chapter 1
Listen
to the Music of
Your Mind
Alpha and Biofeedback Overall View

There is a new kind of revolution in the land. It is not happening in bloodied streets acrid with the smell of bombing. This revolution is a quiet explosion, but, in the long run, this challenge could remake the mind and body of America in subtle ways that the noisy street fighter cannot even approach.

This is the alpha brain-wave revolution, the most important innovation in mental and physical development in decades: Alpha, the key to tomorrow's promise; alpha, tantalizing us with the chance to remake ourselves in the light of our own desires as we control our own bodies without drugs, relieve illnesses caused by stress, and expand our mental powers to dramatic creative heights. The future nature of society may hinge upon the hushed challenges posed by alpha brain wave training, the wave of the future.

This is tomorrow's great debate, and the nature of society is at stake. Challenged on every side, establishment science has called for conditioning of and control over individual behavior, and the desperate and the confused have begun to follow this defense against contemporary jousting because, for the moment, no better answer presented itself; they forget, in their need, the idealistic aims of personal freedom and self-determination.

But a voice is alive in the land telling of a new flow of scientific discoveries, singing in a clear voice of a wonderful alternative to social control and processing and programming and directing and turning men into unhappy cogs in society's apparatus. With the aid of biofeedback teaching techniques, each one of us can learn to control our own bodies and our minds and our feelings, and claim our rightful heritage of individual expression and freedom.

Brand-new, mind-over-body biofeedback techniques promise a radical change in living for everyone. News of the proven breakthroughs in this new field is beginning to move rapidly across the country, hinting at the spectacular possibilities inherent in the idea of producing a nation of people who can utilize the great unknown potentials of their brains in quest of personal self-determination. Most exciting of all is the promise that the average person actually could learn to *control* his or her own brain waves. Reports of amazing laboratory successes are already challenging the ways of the past. Mind-over-body laboratory feats have been reported by respected scientists, and substantiated with laboratory proof:

> In New York City, an epileptic learned to spot the abnormal brain wave that precedes an epileptic seizure, and turned off impending epileptic attacks at will through biofeedback training.
>
> In Baltimore, men and women trained in biofeedback were able to slow the rate of their heartbeats and smooth out dangerous cardiac irregularities.
>
> In Berkeley, slow readers suddenly learned to read well after only one session of feedback training.
>
> In San Francisco, a sixteen-year-old student reached a satorilike mystical experience by letting his alpha brain waves flow after only one feedback training session.
>
> In Topeka, an uptight housewife learned to turn on her alpha brain waves and relax away migraine headaches, without drugs.

In Los Angeles, a young artist gave up LSD for self-controlled highs with alpha feedback.

In Denver, a tense schoolteacher learned to turn on alpha and deep relaxation with both EEG and EMG feedback, and could resume teaching without stress.

In New Orleans, a journalist used feedback to turn on alpha and theta brain waves, and reached a major creative breakthrough in her work.

In Beaumont, overactive hyperkinetic children learned to relax without drugs through increasing their alpha brain waves with biofeedback techniques.

Such experimental news explains the crackle of excitement in the scientific community over biofeedback and brain-wave control. From a handful of investigators, only a few years ago, biofeedback experimentation has leaped to include hundreds of research scientists in laboratories scattered throughout the United States. The promise of mind over body captures the imagination of the daring, and frightens the more cautious into warnings that all of the promises have yet to be thoroughly proven and checked.

Is "alpha" a controversial fad? Or is it part of a broader scientific insight that may have deep meaning for each and every one of us? Is it:

Electronic yoga?
A rocket to inner space?
Electronic LSD?
A charlatan's trick?
A technological placebo providing a panacea for the masses?
A hoax of self-hypnosis?

The charges and countercharges clash, and confuse everyone. The furor centers around brain-wave control achieved with "biofeedback," sometimes called merely "feedback." The word "biofeedback," is derived from *bios,* a Greek word meaning life, and *feedback,* return to the source; the effects of the return of a given process to its source. This ponderous term simply refers to the process by which you are given instant information about your mind or body using an electronic instrument, or monitor as the agent; biofeedback learning occurs as you become able to perceive the minute internal happenings of your body and mind, and learn to "feel" how to control events at will—how to turn on, or turn off, a bodily function.

Biofeedback is the brainchild of a wedding between the psychologists, engineers, physicists, meditators, and physiologists. A child of our times, alpha brain wave control was born from the Zeitgeist of "state-of-the-art electronics, psychophysiology, operant conditioning procedures, and a desire to explore inner space," according to researcher Dr. Thomas Budzynski. He predicts that biofeedback techniques, "may yet realize their greatest potential in the applied areas of psychotherapy, behavior therapy, psychosomatic disorders, education, and attitude and value change."

Biofeedback methods are already being tested for many kinds of controls, ranging from brain waves to heart rates. Alpha brain wave control, or alpha, is the most popular area of biofeedback scientific exploration, and is also the most publicized of the complex biofeedback training areas. Almost everyone has alpha brain waves, and just about everyone seems able to learn how to control these brain waves quickly by working with one of the biofeedback instruments. For many, alpha waves may be the first step toward claiming tomorrow.

Learning occurs as instant facts are received within your inner consciousness to aid you in manipulating physical and psychological processes as you wish. The control of some bodily functions, such as heart rate, blood pressure, breathing, and sensual perceptions, were believed to be automatic and therefore beyond human reach by any means other than through drugs or by use of a scalpel. Yet, we are now told that we can watch the music of our minds or listen to the symphony of our bodies, and seize the power to shape ourselves at will.

Such fantastic possibilities capture the imagination. It's not surprising that the popular press and media of news distribution (the *Saturday Review of Literature, Look, Life, Glamour,* the *New York Times,* the *New Yorker* magazine, the *New Republic, Time,* ABC, CBS, NBC, to name just a few) have leaped upon the bandwagon to announce this new scientific discovery by dedicated researchers. Unfortunately, the medicine men of our times, contemporary sellers of home-brewed cure-all potions *they* call alpha, have also jumped on that razzle-dazzle wagon and are riding along on the coattails of sincere research scientists.

From research to mass reality is a long journey. Biofeedback training and self-regulation of the alpha brain wave are brand-new sciences. Much remains to be proven before the average person can benefit from their unique insights. And for some, alpha brain wave control or other feedback skills will not help cure a psychosomatic illness because it's already too late to reverse the organic damage which may already have occurred. Defective organs and irreversibly damaged organs might not respond to feedback methods. For others, the holistic medicine and growth promised by biofeedback are too challenging. Many people prefer pills to responsibility and power over their mental and physical states.

But many people may benefit from the findings of biofeedback science, as they learn to control the involuntary nervous system. Biofeedback is a by-product of familiar electronic lab machinery like the EEG, the electroencephalogram; the EKG, the electrocardiogram; and, the EMG, the electromyograph. All of these instruments are commonly used in medical checkups to diagnose bodily changes by amplification of the information. But biofeedback machinery is more advanced, and the new factor of "loop completion" has been added. The information loop is completed by giving you instant information concerning your inner state to activate internal learning. The facts are given to you with a kind of instrumental cue: a color or a tone or a percentage of success or a temperature.

Biofeedback is an electronic mirror of your mind and body. We take transistor radios, complex rockets, and computers for granted, but these everyday electronic miracles have revolutionized electronic possibilities almost overnight. Only a few years ago, it was not possible to detect the more subtle electronic energies produced by the brain, but these recent technological innovations have opened new doors: Sensitive transducers, elaborate computers, sophisticated high-gain amplifiers—almost overnight, science has new tools which are leading to brand-new insights into the complexities of the human mind and events in the human body.

Paralleling such electronic breakthroughs are new findings about the bodily processes. Scientists have discovered that the "involuntary" processes of the body are not inevitably involuntary, and that they can be controlled with this new electronic type of learning. Experiments in this field seem to indicate new possibilities for mankind. Today, we stand on the threshold of these vast promises. Much of the professional machinery is still awkward, or expensive, or fragile, or even painful, and is not adequate for everyday needs. Tomorrow's generation will learn whether today's pioneer uses or abuses these new findings.

Three rivers of thought have met and merged into the great flood of feedback. The first river, is the technological revolution. The second river, is the national need for inner awareness sparked by Eastern influences upon our culture. The third river, is scientific challenge to the old concept of "involuntary" bodily functions. All call for the possibility of control by the mind, an age-old goal. Eastern mystics claimed such control centuries ago, but we dismissed the tales of mystics who stilled their blood pressure and were buried alive for hours, as fiction. Mystic experiences? special mind-over-body consciousness from meditation? nirvana? satori? Again, such claims were disregarded as impractical fairy tales.

East meets West today; no outpost of America is immune to the cultural innovations in clothing, religion, art, and even foods, sold as frozen Chinese dinners and available in your corner supermarket. But the most far-reaching influence of this cultural challenge is the effect it has had on personal orientation. Americans, brought up short by world conditions, have shifted from the other-directed extroverts of the 1950s to internalized individuals seriously concerned about goals, sensitivity, consciousness, and life-styles. Sensitivity groups flourish at the local Methodist church. Books on "increasing your sensuality" sell in the millions. "Do your own thing," the mass media screams at us. "Do your own thing" is all well and good, but what do you do if you have no idea what "your own thing" could possibly be? To answer this common question, we all turn inward for knowledge of ourselves.

Ecologically, internal awareness through feedback without any mechanical device may be the next logical step in evolving thought. Ecological awareness of the external environment has so inundated everyone that it stands in danger of becoming passé. Even Madison Avenue has "discovered" the ecological trip, and uses pitches claiming items to be organic or natural in order to sell new brands of shampoo and soap. And once the mass mind of Madison Avenue has discovered it, the intellectual energy of a movement is soon dissipated, and dies. We are all almost too aware of our external world, and we all know how the processes of life are linked as we interact with other living beings on this blue and green ball we call Earth—the home planet. People look inward for answers that the outside world has failed to supply.

Yet, Westerners have a tradition of wanting answers quickly, and Oriental meditative disciplines take too long for most people. Feedback beckons, with the promise of instant internal communication. This is internal ecology inside each one of us. Claude Bernard spoke of the "internal milieu," the world within ourselves. Extending this idea even further, feedback expert Dr. Joe Kamiya suggests that we think of this internal milieu in a broader fashion. Kamiya proposes thinking of the center of your nervous system, most essential to consciousness, as the "occupant" supported by a multilayered milieu all ecologically entwined and amenable to control by you through internal operant behavior.

In a thoughtful essay, Kamiya wrote:

> Western man has tended to focus on the external world, assuming the internal world to be beyond control, except for what happens to it as a result of efforts toward goal achievement in the external world. Eastern man, on the other hand, appears to have focused more attention on achievements (knowledge and control) in his internal world, assuming the external world to be largely beyond control.

Recently, Kamiya told a *Look* magazine reporter:

> I may be an optimist, but I do believe that the next step in man's evolution will be in the experiential domain.

You can experience exploration without drugs by using biofeedback training. Unlike LSD, which carries you on its chemical wings, biofeedback gives you full control of your sensations; unlike meditation, biofeedback takes only a few hours to reach the levels that take years to attain by mantra contemplation and intricate religious procedures leading to internal insight; unlike hypnosis, biofeedback is controlled by the self—it has no external savant directing you to results.

LSD does expand the mind, but sometimes the trip to one's own private adventure movie goes too far, and turns out to be a frightening horror movie with no ending. Such mind-expanding drugs cannot always be self controlled, and "bummers" are common experiences in the drug culture. But biofeedback training can expand the mind by letting you explore the richness that is already there—and you regulate your own trip! Sustained alpha brain waves give many people a serene drifting "alpha high," according to many investigators. Anxiety usually melts away as alpha comes on. Because of this high, a number of scientists are checking out possibilities that brain-wave control could free people from chemical sedatives and addictive or dangerous drugs.

To turn on your alpha, you still your mind to outside activity, and focus all of your attention on only one function. As you concentrate, you suddenly become aware of the intricate and rich characteristics you've previously ignored. As you perceive the subtle changes of your heart, or of your breathing, your perception begins to change as your ego boundaries alter and shift.

Dr. Martin Orne, biofeedback researcher, has pointed out that many of these changes may simply be due to the actual act of concentrating upon one function, and thus inducing a special state of consciousness. Special states of consciousness, he noted, occur in such simple exercises as the Kubie Mongolian discipline, where people are trained to focus all of their attention upon their breathing. Perceptual changes then take place, and altered consciousness results. Such altered consciousness, or awakened consciousness, is tremendously speeded up by the help of physiological mirrors of biofeedback machinery, instruments like the electroencepahlograph (EEG) or the electromyograph (EMG). Scientific psychology may be radically changed by biofeedback, but scientific psychology actually began with concern over one's perception. This concern led to introspection that fed the information for analysis into primary dimensions. In contrast, today's · biofeedback introspection is related to earlier psychology, but focuses upon the individual's self-discrimination of psychological states.

There is nothing new about the idea of biological feedback. At an early age, everyone learns to think—"move hand and grab that"—and is able to make the hand move to pick up the desired object. This event is both visual and muscular feedback to the central nervous system. The only new element in biofeedback is the occurrence of instant information, and the added perception that accompanies such use of the external monitoring instrument.

It takes three things for biofeedback learning self-regulation of any kind of brain wave or bodily function to take place: Monitoring of the physiological activity must be continuous and

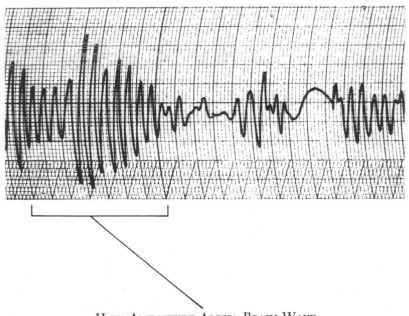

HIGH-AMPLITUDE ALPHA BRAIN WAVE

sensitive enough to spot instant by instant alterations; physiological facts must be given back to you quickly; and you must want to learn how to do it. It doesn't matter whether your motivation stems from curiosity or from deep physical needs, but you have to care about turning your own possibilities on.

Alpha brain waves, the principal concern of this new science of biofeedback, have always been present in our brains. Most of the time, most of us generate alpha brain waves mixed with the other distinctive waves of the brain. Training by feedback methods only amplifies what is already there, and lets you know how to sort your alpha from your beta, theta, and delta waves.

The four kinds of brain waves—alpha, beta, theta, and delta—are really descriptive tags for different wave speeds. Brain waves are measured in Hertz units (numbers of cycles per second). Delta brain waves are the slowest of all, 0 to 4 cycles per second, and are most prominent when you're so deeply asleep as not to be dreaming. Theta brain waves, 4 to 8 cycles per second, seem to be related to drowsiness, creativity, and the dream portion of the sleep cycle. Alpha brain waves run 8 to 13

δ DELTA 0.5 TO 3.5 CYCLES

θ THETA 4 TO 7 CYCLES

cycles per second, and are generally connected with a relaxed, yet alert, mental state, or shifting consciousness. Alpha brain waves are often seen in profusion in the EEG's (electroencephalograms) of the brain patterns of skilled Zen monks and other Eastern meditators. Beta brain waves are the fastest, running 13 to 26 cycles per second, and even faster in cases of schizophrenia and other related mental disorders. Beta is linked to mental concentration, anxiety, certain kinds of problem solving, attention, orienting, and the jangled state most people feel from coping with the concerns of the everyday world.

Think of your brain waves as rhythms. They move in wave-like ripples of electrical energy, currents that crest, recede, and crest again (see below). Since science argues about whether alpha is 8 to 12 cycles, or 9 to 12 cycles, or even 9 to 13 cycles per second, it helps to think of alpha as an area, rather than a specific. These are measurement devices, the logical way social scientists try to pin down the elusive.

Biofeedback uses many tools—EEG to measure brain waves, EKG (electrocardiogram) to graph heart processes, GSR to measure skin responses, and EMG (electromyograph) to check

α ALPHA 8 TO 13 CYCLES

β BETA 14 TO 30 CYCLES

muscle tension—but most original research deals with EEG reports on the brain and EMG records of the relaxation of muscle tension.

The special alpha experience comes from sustained and strengthened alpha waves. It takes complex EEG machinery to measure both the particular brain-wave state you are in, and how strong it is. When you remember that there are billions of cells in your brain, you realize that even an EEG is giving you only a partial picture of all the complex things happening in your mind. How strong your alpha brain wave may be is measured in volts, just like the electrical supply for your toaster or TV set. Electricity in the home measures between 110 and 120 volts. The electrical energy generated in your brain by alpha waves usually measures only 20 to 150 microvolts. This is millionths of a volt, smaller than the electrical voltage of your toaster!

Early EEG machines also picked up background noise, those electrical fingerprints of our environment, mixed in hodgepodge fashion with the electrical energy of the brain waves. But, new instruments can filter out this background noise, sort out different EEG brain waves, count them, and even give special information, like the relative strength of each wave. To date, the EEG machines still use mechanical pens to record specific brain-wave records, and a large part of the brain's activity picture may be missed because the pens can only move so fast. Even more surprising rhythms could be taking place that were too minute for present instrumentation to detect.

Electricity, in your brain or in your home, is probably a mystery to you. It is generally taken for granted, except when a raging thunderstorm causes the power to fail, or when a flashing spark from a defective connection startles us. Webster tells us that electricity is "one of the fundamental quantities in nature, consisting of elementary particles, electrons, and protons. Electricity is characterized by the fact that it gives rise to a field of force possessing potential energy and that, when moving in a stream (an electric current), it gives rise to a magnetic field of force with which kinetic energy is associated." Electricity is basically a conversion of power occurring when one form of physical matter is converted into another.

In your brain, electrical energy seems to occur as information is transformed, in very much the same way as electrical activity occurs in a computer. According to Dr. Barbara Brown, information in the brain is handled like a gigantic multidimensional computer, with intricate processing, coding, distribution, verification, and evaluation.

A typical EEG machine, used to detect the particular electrical energy in your brain, sparkles with buttons, dials, and controls. A few tiny plastic or metal electrodes are attached to the scalp with a plaster and kind of salt paste. Long delicate wires carry the electrical information to an EEG machine which acts like the amplifier in your stereo system, and then transfers the message to writing pens which draw your mind's patterns upon continuously moving graph paper.

The pens of the EEG machines record as bioelectric shifts occur. They swing up when the charge is negative, and down when it is positive, to trace a series of up-and-down strokes upon the graph paper sliding underneath. Although these pens are a convenient way of measuring, they do not replicate nature. The zigzag waves that they record are not, in actuality, a solid block of movement. Instead, the electrical energy of the waves generated by your brain alternates, just as does the electrical current in your home. When you are awake, the electrical "voltage" in your brain is usually low, irregular, and changing quickly. As you relax, your voltages change and may rise, while the speed of your brain waves begins to lessen.

Using the machinery of biofeedback, which is like an EEG machine with the added feature that you can get an instant check on your particular brain patterns, a feedback loop, or circle of information, is drawn as you get these facts. (The simplest, direct feedback we all know is a mirror into which we preen at our own reflections and our eyes follow our images as we shave or brush our hair.)

But biofeedback acts as a mirror for things we cannot see with the naked eye, opening a universe for exploration. A toothache is a feedback that you cannot see. The ache is invisible, but it exists and sends sensory stimuli to your brain. A real feeling of pain results. (Other feedbacks you take for granted are falling asleep when you're tired, sweating when you're hot, eating and digesting food when you're hungry, and hitting a golf ball with a golf club.) Biofeedback merely takes one or more signals of a physiological function, converts the information in that external feedback device to let you perceive this internal fact in your external perceptual world. And this is when "it." happens. As you perceive it, you get the "feel" of it, and have a chance to control it. Consciously, you may not know how you do it, but you can "feel" how to do it. Such control can be as sophisticated as the willful firing of just one or two of your millions of muscle nerve units, a feedback phenomenon already demonstrated in studies by Dr. John Basmajian.

Cues, like a sound or tone, signal what's happening as your mind or body actions are translated into sensory signals helping you to learn how to control the internal action. With such nonverbal learning, Dr. Elmer Green has taught people to control their finger temperatures over a ten degree Farenheit range while at the same time reducing the skin temperature of their foreheads. Rather than being a spectacular parlor trick, this learned skill promises to cure migraine headaches. It works by enabling you to decrease vascular congestion, regularize the vascular supply to the brain and head areas to eliminate migraine headaches without drugs.

"Biofeedback is no more a fad than the microscope," pioneer researcher Dr. Joe Kamiya points out, and uses the concept of a thermometer as an example of a beautifully accurate piece of feedback equipment.

Although many scientists are reserving judgment about biofeedback techniques until more data is available, most are excited by its possibilities. At the annual meeting of the American Psychological Association, held in a 45,000-square-foot exhibition hall, it was reported in *Science* magazine that the most crowded exhibits were the booths demonstrating brain-wave biofeedback machines.

Because of this interest, the A.P.A. heard the report of E. C. Brown, T. J. Erwin, and R. T. Putney, of Atlanta's Georgia State University. This study examined relationships between meditation, biofeedback, and increased alpha-wave density, and used a control group with no feedback for reference contrast.

The report stated that "all subjects increased in alpha density during the experiment," except for the control group. Increase in alpha density due to biofeedback was not completely confirmed, but they did find that "biofeedback had some effect." They also cautioned that meditation had some of the same effect as well.

Other psychologists, like Dr. Thomas Mulholland, add their cautions to the overenthusiasm about alpha brain wave control. "The response of the occipital alpha rhythm is a time series, not a singular response," he points out, "and alpha and no-alpha events are not functionally equivalent. Their position in the time series must be taken into account." The alpha brain rhythm is not a solid block like a wall of bricks, and intervals of little or no-alpha are often sprinkled between the alpha spurts. The most reliable feature of the occipital EEG seems to be the way alpha and no-alpha times fluctuate or alternate. Our description of the physical occurrence of alpha is a convenience, just as we measure space in inches, and time in minutes. When we talk about alpha, we have to remember that many other factors are also involved—the location of the electrodes for the recording, the wave frequency, the amplitude and the duration of the rhythms—including such external factors as how heavily you smoke. In a 1969 experiment, Dr. J. A. Ulett and Dr. T. M. Itil showed that heavy smokers had less alpha and more fast high-frequency beta waves than nonsmokers. Yet, smokers who avoided cigarettes for twenty-four hours before a test suddenly showed a significantly decreased brain-wave frequency, and lots more alpha.

With continued enhancement of alpha brain waves, it is suspected that perceptual changes occur and cause states of altered consciousness and the "alpha experience." Alpha consciousness that arises from enhanced alpha wave production is a complex sideshow in the intricate land of our minds.

Inside each of us is a private universe. Fifteen billion or more cells compose the brain and, like the stars in the galaxy, brain cells are arranged in bunches and groups. These "cell galaxies" are called cortical areas in your brain. The cells we are most aware of are those of the cerebral cortex, which retain stimuli like higher universities of knowledge, while the other cells can be compared to through stations and paths of information as primary as a fictional elementary school.

Many layers make up your brain, almost like a fresh walnut. A skin envelope surrounds it all and your skull acts as a protective shell. Under this is the inner skin of the soft membrane which covers the hardish matter of the brain. The exquisite kernel of dura mater lurks inside all this like a kernel of consciousness.

The cerebral cortex is one of three areas of your brain: the brainstem, the cerebellum, and the cerebral cortex. Both brainstem and cerebellum are called "white matter" areas, because of the white color of the axons covering them. The cerebral cortex is mostly grayish in color, from the gray appearance of the neuron bodies.

The cerebral cortex cells are those which make you conscious of your self and the world, of thinking, feeling, speaking, dreaming, loving, enjoying life and learning. Each individual cell is an "I" of the persona, while "we" is the totality of the

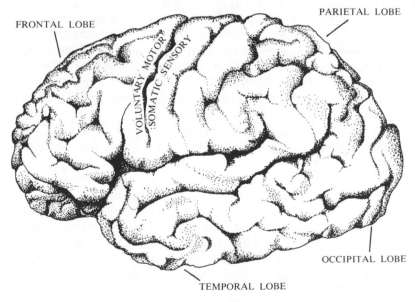

VIEW FROM LEFT OF BRAIN

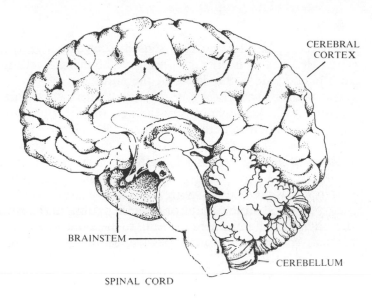

SECTION VIEW FROM LEFT OF BRAIN

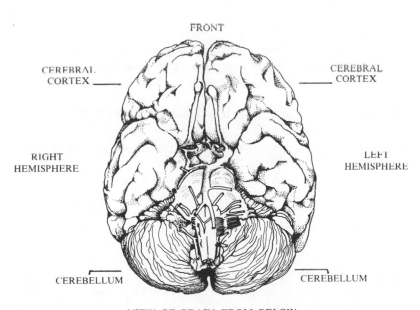

VIEW OF BRAIN FROM BELOW

cortical cells. The "I" you first sensed years ago is, in reality, a gigantic electrical concert performing as the minute cells in your brain fire and fade in the dance of the mind.

Your brain is actually a pair of brains, with two independent "hemispheres" like separate continents, on the right and left. Generally, one hemisphere is dominant. Women tend to have a more even balance between hemispheres than men. Paul Bakan's controversial hemisphere study offered certain characteristics for the left and right hemisphere dominance. He suggests that the left hemisphere deals with the rational, objective, active, tense, verbal, abstract, euphoric, and sympathetic qualities, while the right hemisphere is said to be concerned with the preverbal, spatial, emotional, passive, subjective, relaxed and depressed qualities.

When someone is best described by one set of adjectives over another, Bakan proposes that the corresponding hemisphere is probably the dominant one. How to test it? He suggests that you ask a person a question, and then watch his eye movement, called CLEMs, or conjugate lateral eye movements. According to the theory, the analytical verbal person will ponder, and glance upward and to the right, in opposition to his dominant brain hemisphere, the left hemisphere. The emotional subjective person will move his eyes upward, and to the left, as he thinks about the answer to your question, signifying dominance of his right hemisphere. Bakan noted that people with right hemisphere dominance generally produce alpha brain waves more easily than people with left hemisphere dominance.

The base of these two hemispheres in your brain is connected with white matter, like a network of tissue bridges and girders. Each hemisphere is divided into areas scientists call lobes, and each is enveloped with supporting membranes, the three meninges. These meninges are tough fibrous membranes made of dura mater and a softer pia mater, all protecting your brain. The areas called lobes are the frontal lobe, in the front of your brain; the parietal lobe, on the top of your head; the occipital lobe, behind the parietal, about where the back of your head rounds out to its furthest peak; and the temporal lobe, connecting the occipital to the frontal lobe. Your brain is like a coiled shell, or a ram's horn; and its growth spiraled in that sensuous curve, as you developed from single cell to full-blown human being. Consisting of about 70 percent water, your brain is a tiny computer that weighs only about three pounds. (The size of your brain means nothing, because geniuses like Raphael, Dante, and Bach had smaller than average brains.)

Cell is piled upon cell in your brain, like building blocks. The large ones are like pyramids in shape. Nerve cells and motor cells make up the rest of the structure of your mind. The motor center, made up of motor cells, sends currents of information coursing to your muscles. The area of sensation reception lurks just behind the motor center at the top of the brain. Sleep is turned on by a complex center in the depths of the brain, and is

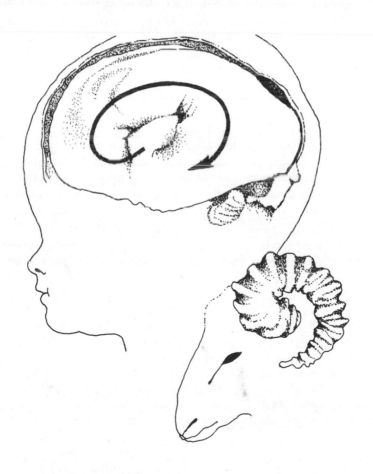

caused by slowed blood flow, calcium liberated at the ends of nerves, and an organic chemical compound called acetylcholine produced by nervous excitation. Natural sleep is body sleep, while drug-induced sleep is brain sleep, as your cerebral cortex and will and consciousness are blocked chemically by the sedating drug.

Scientists link the lobes of the brain with specific functions, and you should know from which part of the brain you're recording brain waves. Alpha waves are most likely to occur in the occipital lobe, which is linked to visual impressions, abstract thinking and conceptualization. Your frontal lobe is the reflective contemplative area, and your temporal lobe, center of word and sound formation, is thought to be most prominent if you're an auditory person, one who learns most quickly through a lecture rather than through reading a book. The visual person is thought to have more dominance in the frontal lobe, and the abstract thinker more prominence in the occipital lobe.

No two brains are identical, and your own private brain computer features an ever-changing cellular pattern of firing, as individual cellular action varies in every person's patterns. Different cells have different rhythms and, when we say someone is "in alpha," there may be many other rhythms going on in other cells away from the recording electrodes; occipital-lobe alpha is usually strong and may hint at a disuse in the seeing and visualization function of this area. Yet Akira Kasamatsu and Tomio Hirai's EEG brain-wave recordings of skilled Zen monks showed strong alpha waves in all lobes of the brain, unlike the average person who is strong on alpha in only one area without training. Because of this evidence, some researchers have suggested that mental training increases the brain's power over visual attention, valuing, body senses, memory, and verbalization.

Some people generate a mixture of alpha and beta brain rhythms during most of their waking hours. Others generate mostly alpha, and some generate no alpha at all. In some studies, the high-alpha producer has learned to suppress alpha, and improve attention spans. In other cases, the low-alpha person has learned to turn on alpha brain waves and help himself relax. All of these varied brain-wave patterns are a montage of electrical energy.

Why do electrical-type energy waves occur in your brain? Why are some alpha, some beta, and so on? Scientists are not certain, but postulate that energy brain waves come from the difference in potential between individual cells or cell groups. With inner knowledge through biofeedback training, some investigators propose that this electrical energy activity of neighboring cells could be made more synchronous, and perhaps more effective.

Your brain cells are composed of neurons and they vary in size depending upon their function. A neuron looks like an uprooted tree with its bulblike body, intricate roots, and narrow trunk spreading into branches toward the end. The main trunk body of this neuron is the axon which catches electrical pulses at the tip of its branches and carries them to the root of the structure. As the body fires a new pulse, it is carried out through the branches to the axon tips of other neurons, and an electrical current is generated, called a synapse. It may be this synapse that we sense when we attach electrodes to our scalp and an EEG machine tells us alpha brain rhythms are present.

The alpha brain wave is not just a letting-go of anxieties, but in some way is a creative coming together of rhythms. Dr. Edgar E. Coons, a physiological psychologist at New York University and a talented musician, was trained to produce alpha waves by pioneer researcher Dr. Lester Fehmi. Dr. Coons called the experience one which "makes me feel as if I'm floating about a half-inch above my seat."

Artists, musicians, and athletes are prolific alpha producers. Introspective sensitive people tend to be high in alpha waves. It has been claimed that Albert Einstein was a strong producer of alpha waves, particularly when he theorized. Creativity and alpha ability may be linked, and creative people are intrigued by alpha brain wave control.

Under Dr. Fehmi's tutelage, David Rosenbloom presented a concert of his brain waves, using biofeedback. The performance was given at the Automation House in New York, where Rosenbloom fed his thoughts into a computer, and then to a synthesizer. Another musician, La Monte Young, has his own use for alpha. He keeps a strong individualized tone for the alpha brain wave running in his Manhattan studios on which he can home in, and claims that it improves his creativity. In Fullerton, a college-credit class is given in biofeedback training, so that people can learn to train themselves to relax and lose tension. In Chicago, an alpha-and-the-arts course is set up to train people to enhance brain waves and expand creativity.

It seems that alpha brain wave control can give us many gifts—enhanced creativity, relaxation from anxiety, better ability to meet the world's stresses, control over psychosomatic ills of the body, the capacity to learn and absorb information faster and better, and a chance to know our innermost selves— but alpha is not the cure-all or be-all for all desires and for everyone's needs.

For some people, "alpha is a downer," according to Dr. Maurice B. Sterman, and "it's not a panacea for all ills." It is also not a way to read someone else's mind, although some confused people hope for this kind of aid from alpha. A prospective buyer wrote to Tim Scully, owner of Aquarius Electronics, one of the first in the portable feedback machine field. The man wanted to buy a portable alpha wave detector apparatus and asked Scully for "information on an electronic type of brain wave snooping device . . .[that] works on the same principle as the electroencephalography machine . . . the way this machine works is that the operators of this snooping device listen to your thoughts and dreams, and play to someone else's ears in sound. They can use this machine, and transmit their voices to people in mid-air on the street. They can transmit your thoughts in voice in mid-air to people in buildings for harassment purposes." The letter writer concluded with a request that Scully ignore any letters or phone calls from others about him.

Scully turned down the man's request and points out that alpha control has reached fad proportions and such misconceptions are common. But alpha machines are not mind-probers. Alpha instruments are still a far cry from the "lapsometer" described so skillfully by Walker Percy in *Love in the Ruins.* The lapsometer enabled the fictional character, Dr. Thomas More, to peer into other people's minds, and read their thoughts.

Alpha brain waves are a natural and common occurrence. Biofeedback equipment is not a "snooping device," and it will *not* help you spy upon the world's private thoughts. It may let you probe the workings of your own brain and gain specific insights as your consciousness alters and you travel upon the rainbow of your mind. It may even help man fulfill the prediction by Reinhold Niebuhr that, "The chief source of man's dignity is man's essential freedom and capacity for self-determination."

Chapter 2
Consciousness:
The Constant Dance
of Change
Alterations
of Consciousness and Mind Expansion
Perceptual Changes

Altered consciousness is a different state from your normal consciousness. Contrasted with your normal sense of reality, altered consciousness states affect many levels of perception. Often changes in perception happen without your knowledge or consent, as outside factors seep in upon your senses.

Your normal consciousness is really your base line, or home base, and acts as a reference point. But normal consciousness often gets so pushed and shoved by everyday events that it becomes battered and unrecognizable, and you no longer know where you stand. If you sip a glass of golden chablis, you'll feel your arms and legs begin to soften with relaxation as tension disappears; if you have too much to drink, you swear you can see the room spinning around. As your boss criticizes you, you may feel tension tightening your muscles, clenching your stomach, and sharpening your senses. If you push yourself through twenty-four hours of work without sleep, you'll suddenly notice how everyday sounds rub your senses raw. And, as you begin to float off to sleep, you sometimes sense amorphous images rippling behind your shuttered eyelids. Such alterations of your consciousness are really subtle shifts in the way you sense the smells and sounds and tastes and sights all around you.

Most people believe that the normal state of consciousness is the way they feel in most of their waking hours. Probably, what feels normal to you is how you think "normal consciousness" feels to everyone else. But this almost universal assumption may not necessarily be true.

Dr. Charles Tart points out that, "A normal state of consciousness can be considered a resultant of living in a particular environment, both physical and psychological. Thus, the normal state of consciousness for any individual is that which has adaptive value within his particular culture and environment." So far, this is not a startling thought, but then Dr. Tart adds, "Many primitive people believe that almost every normal adult has the ability to go into a trance state, and be possessed by a God. The adult who cannot do this is a psychological cripple. How deficient most Americans would seem to a person from such a culture!"

Exactly what is your consciousness? If you've never thought about it, consciousness may be only your realization that you are "you." But, if you've wondered about your self, you begin to feel that consciousness is a shifting mass like the sands of the Gobi. Actually, you get contrasting feelings with each aspirin you gulp, pain you feel, or martini you sip. Brain-wave training holds out the tantalizing possibility of shaping your consciousness into an organic whole so that you can fit into any setting.

Brain-wave control is thought to open the door to the joys of awakened consciousness. The Oriental world of meditators seems to know more about awakened consciousness than the world of the West. The Sanskrit language has twenty words for types of awakened consciousness, according to Frederick Spiegelberg, a scholar of Sanskrit. Perhaps because we do not pay as much attention to sense changes, the English language is poverty-stricken when you search for words to describe consciousness alterations.

We don't have twenty words for "awakened consciousness." Most of us, if pressed, could only list a few words. For all kinds of consciousness, Dr. Stanley Krippner managed to identify nineteen perceptual levels differing from the "normal" waking state. In the *Journal of American Sociology, Psychology Dentistry* and *Medicine,* 1969, he named: *dreaming, sleeping, hyperalertness, rapture, hynopompia, lethargy, hysteria, fragmentation, trance, regression, hypnotic dream, meditation, daydreaming, stupor, stored memory, internal scanning, coma,* and *expanded consciousness.*

You've probably experienced many of these shifting perceptual levels without even trying to alter your consciousness. Each state or level holds its own feelings, and its own potential insights. Without even being aware of it, you may have stood on the threshold of richly complex experiences solely through your altered perceptions.

Many years ago, in the proper time of stiffened collars and confining Lillian Russell types of girdles, William James sounded a cry for freedom of perception.

> Our normal waking consciousness . . . is but one special type of consciousness . . . all about it, parted from it by the filmiest of screens, there lie potential forms of consciousness entirely different. We may go through life without suspecting their existence; but, apply the requisite stimulus, and, at a touch they are all there in all their completeness. . . . No account of the universe in its totality can be final which leaves these other forms of consciousness quite disregarded . . . yet they may determine attitudes, though they cannot furnish formulas, and open a region, though they fail to give a map. At any rate, they forbid a premature closing of our accounts with reality.

Today, we are exploring inner space. We are cautiously curious as we search inside ourselves for answers to the chaos of our external universe. We cannot answer man's eternal "what is the purpose of life" question until we first know ourselves. Brain-wave control and biofeedback techniques might help us find such answers. Men have set off into the exploration of the universe, but it is turning out to be a rather bleak place after all. Slowly, we are beginning to wonder if humanity might not really be alone in the vastness of space and only the earth be peopled with our own kind. Because of this fear, many people now search inside themselves for the knowledge that, in other times, they received from outside and higher Authority.

Altered states of consciousness can vastly expand our horizons, but most of us don't have the tools to open those doors to perception. It isn't this way for everyone. In a northern California experiment, doctors reported that anesthesized patients could recall exactly what the doctors had said during surgery while the patients were supposedly unconscious. Even more startling, many were able to read correctly numbers and letters traced on the tops of cabinets high above their vision. They claimed they did this by "leaving their bodies."

In another experiment, by Dr. Elmer Green and his wife Alyce, a swami, drifted into EEG-recorded deep sleep as the Greens read material to him. Later, when the swami was awakened, he could recall, exactly, 85 percent of the phrases read to him. Unlike you or I, this man was aware of his mind's wanderings and could will himself to remember exactly what happened while he slept.

Such expanded mental strength seems to have become a national goal, replacing the old push for enhancing the G.N.P. Encounter groups overflow with newcomers. Greenwich Village "dealers" have no problem finding buyers for their latest chemical mysteries. Maharishi Mahesh Yogi chants his meditative message to sell-out crowds. And even the intellectuals ponder and wonder about conscious existence. The Nobel Prize-winning scientist, Sir John Eccles, a pioneer explorer of the brain's mysteries, said, "I can explain my body and my brain, but there's something more. I can't explain my own existence. We should not pretend that consciousness is not a mystery. People are looking for packaged answers. There are none."

The answer may be that each and every one of us must search until he finds his own answer. Brain-wave exploration and feedback techniques allow each of us to search within ourselves. Our Western heritage tells us that consciousness is either normal and, thus, good, or changed, and, thus, pathological. For decades, Western scientists studied only the pathological changes. Studies of the mentally deranged provided masses of material, but everything else was ignored. The scientific community ignored any possible positive effects from the altering of consciousness, and answers are sadly lacking for all of us. But, suddenly, biofeedback presents us with new possibilities, possibilities that may seem somewhat ominous to Westerners because it's unexplored ground in the Western world.

But answers are demanded.

Self-knowledge will help you cope with a chaotic society.

Consciousness control will help you handle life's challenges without having to live a schizophrenic existence. R. D. Laing tells us that Western society is schizophrenic. Consciousness is a perceptual adaptation to internal and external stimuli, and the normally conscious adaptation to a schizophrenic society would be to live a split existence. But people want answers that work from moment to moment, answers that have an overall unity and worth. People want to "feel," but they also want to be able to control how they feel.

Knowledge of our internal states can give us one type of control of consciousness, and may be a first step in shaping our perceptions to our needs. The intricate map of the brain's energy often reveals hints of subjective states. These "brainwave correlates" might show us a way out of the contemporary dilemma. Through biofeedback training of such energies as the alpha waves, it is possible that some conscious states may be turned on at will.

Although no one really knows what the conscious states actually are (you can't see altered consciousness under a microscope), scientists are studying them, and people are learning to use biofeedback to arrive at the level of consciousness they want.

How can we study consciousness, without knowing exactly what it is? Dr. Charles Tart suggests this analogy:

> Some people do not really know what an automobile is, in the sense that they have no idea what, if anything, is under the hood, and how it works. Nevertheless, they can learn how to drive the car, how it handles under various conditions, etc. . . . We can find out what some of the ways consciousness works are, how it organizes itself, and what the consequences of these various fluctuations are. . . . I suspect that some sort of basic awareness or consciousness may be a basic thing that cannot be further explained or subdivided.

There are many ways you can tinker with your basic consciousness. The most modern way to shift your private slice of reality is to use biofeedback. You can use EEG feedback to turn on your alpha brain waves and, perhaps, rest from the jangly state of beta waves so common in most people's lives. If your life is a constant storm of anxiety, overloaded with beta rhythms, the addition of periodic waves of the slower, restful, alpha might refresh you and help your spirits bloom.

Perhaps such rest periods are necessary for the brain. Many people seem to function at beta most of the time. According to Hebb's studies, each of us must have a myriad number of stimulations and changes, or we will have "mental aberrations." That seems to be a little far-fetched, but periods of alpha rest could have a less grandiose therapeutic value. If you shuffle the same papers back and forth each day and then gobble down the same TV dinner every night, you may be heading for problems because of the monotonous repetition of your life. Or, if each day of your life seems like a grey duplicate replay version of the day before, you might want to consider consciousness alterations to enrich your perceptual life.

Drugs, or liquor, are not the only answers. There are so many ways, scientists have found, that you can change your perception of reality. Some ways are extreme, while others are simple tricks upon your mind.

Basically, there are five ways to remake your own reality. Psychologist Dr. Arnold M. Ludwig outlines the possibilities: Reduce your motor activity and/or external stimulation; increase your motor activity, or external stimulation; increase your mental alertness; decrease your mental alertness; or turn to an outside "agent" to effect your body's chemistry or mental well-being.

What does all this mean to you? Let us play with Ludwig's first guideline, reduction of motor activity or external stimulation, and see what happens. Sit very still. Try not to let a whisper of movement occur. Close your eyes and stop up your ears. Take three or four deep breaths. Now, open your eyes and stare at the nearest object without blinking. Don't let your eyes flicker as you stare. Now, continue staring until you begin to feel the sense of colors and words beginning to drift away. Silently, think of the following words:

I exist, therefore I am . . .
   I exist, therefore I am . . .
      I exist, therefore I am . . .
         I exist, therefore I am.

Could you feel your perceptions change as your senses began to shift? This exercise in altering consciousness works because you actually redo your patterning of sensory data. What you've done is use repetitive monotony as you drastically cut down your body movement and sense intake.

If you've ever wondered how solitary confinement might affect you, you've just sampled a small measure of such insular reality. Confined life-styles bring about a special kind of consciousness alteration through decreased environmental cues. Think of the lonely sailor at sea as he stares at the waves for hours. After awhile, he begins to retreat to a stillness within himself. Or, imagine the feelings of a salesman on the road, as he feels miles of asphalt under his car as he travels over dark highways. In time, he begins to find his mind wandering from the road and strange sights begin to appear. Or, picture yourself as a tired young housewife who continues to clean, wipe, and scrub after everyone that moves within her domain, until her mind seems dulled and draggy. Even patients immobilized in body casts, and elderly men seeing the world through the mist of cataracts upon their eyes, come to wonder at such changes in "how things are." Island-fever in the island-bound; kayak disease in Eskimos long at sea; break-off phenomena in high-altitude pilots—these are all types of altered consciousness due to reduced stimuli.

Toby feels the world spinning and sound begins to disappear as she reaches orgasm. She loses touch "with reality" and no longer knows quite where she is. This is another common form of consciousness alteration, but this is caused by increasing stimulation to the senses and adding more activity and emotion until an overload shifts reality.

Our ideas of reality drastically jump to other levels when we are emotionally aroused. Overloading the senses makes perception melt from one level to another. When we are extremely tired or mentally exhausted, arousal takes longer, but, when it happens, the arousal causes unbelievably intense shifts in the senses. Sex is only one road to this sort of consciousness change. Strobe lights, extra-loud rock music, the "third degree," standing in the middle of a mob, a religious revival—every one of these emotionally charged group settings could actually affect your senses and give you the ecstatic feelings of a trance state.

Staring at the homogenized offerings on your television set all evening long can also affect your conscious states. Long concentration upon just about anything—studying for a test, fervent and passionate prayers, solving the problem of that lagging sales area after thinking about it for days—can give you focused hyperalertness that leads to peripheral hypoalertness. What happens is that, as you concentrate, you confine all of your energies to one specific area. And, as all your senses flow upon this one pinpointed area of interest, the outside world is shut out of your mind. You no longer hear or see or smell the world about you.

Aesthetic and mystical experiences seem to come when cutting down attention to the outside world. Decreased alertness, and a relaxation of the critical faculties associated with the beta activity of most of our waking lives, lead to a more passive mental state. Still your mind, and listen to the music of your thoughts. As you cut out external intrusions, you begin to feel your consciousness rise to new levels. This kind of change is similar to the insight moments of satori, the autohypnotic trances of Indian mystics, and the relaxation of daydreaming.

Sometimes, your perception of life can be speeded through space to hallucinatory lands, thanks to somatopsychological factors. These factors are various outside agents which play havoc upon your body's chemistry or neurophysiology. It can happen deliberately, because you swallowed a tab of LSD, or accidentally, because you have a high fever.

Fever, fasting, hyperventilation from rapid deep breathing, or sleep deprivation, all can make you "see things in a fog," or "hear strange sounds," or even, "see the walls of the room wave as pieces of the past come floating back." External factors like anesthetics, psychedelic drugs, narcotics, and many approved medically prescribed medications can actually work upon your senses and give you a rainbow of new feelings.

Whatever the method, altered consciousness results. Some changed mental states are of value, while others may be dredging up negative sensations. Dr. Arnold M. Ludwig described the many kinds of altered consciousness as "final common pathways." He warned that, "In some instances, the psychological regression found in altered states of consciousness will prove to be atavistic and harmful to the individual or society, while, in other instances, the regression will be 'in the service of the ego' and enable man to transcend the bounds of logic and formality, or express repressed needs and desires in a socially sanctioned and constructive way."

Deliberately altering your consciousness is a gamble. You might have a delightful experience and gain new knowledge as you relax tensions and conflict. The experience might give you a new view of life that could help you handle every day better. Or it could be a dangerous game that suddenly reveals a nightmare beyond your control, a bad dream that simply won't stop. A rainbow of consciousness, colors signifying joy, or colors warning of terrible associations—all sorts of shades and hues of feeling occur in each of us. In a way, it seems like a game of Russian roulette.

"We are in a series of, or continuum of, altering states of consciousness," commented Dr. Jean Houston, of the Foundation for Mind Research in New York City. "I'm not so sure we really can distinguish between normative and altered, or different or bad or good states of consciousness."

Dr. Houston knows a great deal about consciousness. She began her investigative work with a study of the effects of drugs like LSD, and she wrote a book called *The Variables of Psychedelic Experience.* According to Dr. Houston's studies, there are four stages of ascending drug reality.

First, comes the sensory enhanced level, as you begin to be aware of "very intensive sensory experiencing." Music takes on a new life. Food has a richness of taste. Incense has a marvelous odor. The pictures on the wall become symphonies of color upon color. Next comes a recollective analytical level, and then a third or symbolic level of abstract awareness and reorienting of symbolic patterns. Finally, there may be a level which resembles religious or mystic kinds of experiences.

When Dr. Houston left drug research, she turned to consciousness states induced by other means. She found that "most people could not change their mental state simply by meditating or reflecting." To meet this need, she turned to the deus ex machina concept and invented some remarkable machines.

One of her most dynamic inventions is a machine called ASCID (its full formal name is Altered State of Consciousness Induction Device). As Dr. Houston describes it, her machine is ". . .a God coming out, it's a machine they can get into or put on." ASCID works, and it works fast. Deep changes occur anywhere from a few seconds to twenty minutes after making contact with the device for 80 percent of her subjects.

How does it work? Once upon a Gothic time ago, would-be witches suspended themselves in a mechanism called the Witches' Cradle. This contraption was really a bag hanging from a tree. Neophyte witches jumped into the bag and swung until they could "go south with the devil." Within a short time, they actually believed that they had done so, and "returned" to report their experiences with the devil.

ASCID works with a similar swinging motion to induce visual images. Body-image changes and perceptual alterations are also common with ASCID. Dr. Houston speculates that the machine works because it may stimulate the inner ear and the cardiovascular system. Let us step into ASCID with a student volunteer. You will both be restrained with bonds, to keep you from falling out of the eight-foot swing of the womblike machine. Soon, as the machine begins to move, you will feel as if you're flying. Your eyes will dim, and a mist will seem to float about you. As the mist begins to clear, you may find yourself anywhere, in any time at all. The student has his own vision. He believes he is in a psychedelic forest and he begins to race along to get to school before the school bell rings. All of this is a mechanically induced hallucination. With machines like these designed by Dr. Houston, people experience all the effects of consciousness alteration, without drugs. Such technological hallucinations could rid people of drug hangups. They might be used for expanding inner knowledge and enhancing creativity through controlled consciousness alterations.

Another of her machines is the AVE, a sophisticated mechanical environment that is capable of bringing on intense emotional, erotic, or euphoric experiences and other peak sensations. AVE is the salutation that the angel Gabriel gave to Mary when he brought the good news about the birth of Jesus. AVE is also an abbreviation for Audio Visual Environment, the unabbreviated name of the machinery.

Dr. Houston's AVE is a sophisticated audio-visual experience that surrounds you with a screen. You wear earphones, and experience a sound/visual bombardment of the senses that is programmed for a certain kind of experience. For most people, after about thirty-five minutes of melting into this environment, mental changes begin to take place. As their state of consciousness alters, they begin to project a problem or a creative design.

In one instance, a frustrated novelist sat down for an AVE experience. Soon, she began to see the characters in her novel come to life before her eyes. "They" moved and spoke and acted out scenes she had written. Then "they" began to move in new ways. "That's it," she thought, "that's the way I should have written that section." And so it went, as her characters wrote their own dialogue and solved her writing problems for her.

Conceiving original creative ideas is common in states of altered consciousness. This happens because, suddenly, one is in a new world, seeing with new eyes. Perceptions dance through many levels, and nothing seems quite the same. In altered consciousness, logical opposites breathe side by side, yet an overall unity gives one a unique sense of understanding. Time can lose its usual meaning as minutes stretch into the feel of hours passing. The realization of the self may even melt to a shadow.

Such awakened consciousness intensifies emotional sensations. Fears become more primitive and, often, pantheistic. Sensual pleasures ripen and increase to out-of-bounds proportions. The boundaries between you and others come crashing down as you feel depersonalized. Perhaps, your sense of your body begins to surprise you with new images. You might feel light as a breeze, or heavy as a rock; or your senses might join together in a different combination as you see the color of the music you are hearing; or, perhaps, you might be able to taste the feel of the chair's fabric.

Instant truth is common in awakened-consciousness states, regardless of whether the altered state is due to drugs or prayer or meditative exercise. These sudden insights are called "Eureka" experiences. William James spoke of the "depth upon depth of truth" revealed in altered consciousness, and how these knowing revelations usually "fade out, or escape, at the moment of coming to."

Many of these colored perceptions can be painted at will by biofeedback-trained people, who simply turn on alpha brain waves. Studies have shown that many altered-consciousness experiences are characterized by a high percentage of alpha brain waves and, sometimes, the even slower and more elusive theta brain-wave patterns. It may be possible to turn on special conscious states as you wish either for your own pleasure or to learn more about yourself for therapeutic reasons.

There are many stages with which you might wish to experiment. The twilight stage between waking and sleeping holds the promise of a rich store of imagery. As your ego, or sense of self, begins to weaken, images flow and ripple and race before your eyes, almost like a private showing of a motion picture. In the drowsy realms of this hypnagogic state (state of drowsiness preceding sleep), many changes occur which are very much like the low arousal state of EMG feedback. However, for the average person, drowsiness races close behind the images, and you soon lose your grasp upon that rich storehouse of material. With feedback, you might be able to avert such drowsiness, and draw upon these individual images at will.

As you pass into sleep, your brain rhythms begin to change, first from predominantly alpha to a fragmented alpha stage, to low amplitude theta, and finally into delta. As you shift from one brain rhythm to another, many changes occur in your body and in your mind. A change in the ego sense is an important and noticeable change, according to researcher Dr. David Foulkes. He found that the sense of the ego and feeling of contact with the external world begin to fade as willed control over thinking slips slowly away. Firm images become incomplete scenes or bizarre meaningless patterns. And sometimes, both ego function impairments occur at once. This ability to see images is not common to everyone. Personality differences have a great effect upon the individual's ability to visualize or see images before falling asleep. Foulkes claimed that rigid people with repressively structured lives are "less able to let go" and fantasize, less able to express their inner feelings and thoughts than people who are more relaxed and open in their attitudes.

Another twilight-stage expert, Dr. Budzynski, writes that, "Those high on fantasy tended to be more tolerant of shortcomings in themselves and others, and less dogmatic in their beliefs." Budzynski speculates about the possible positive changes in personality that might occur if uptight people were trained by biofeedback so that they could turn on more images and more sleep-onset fantasy material.

Many things happen as you begin to fall asleep. Along with the slower energy of your brain waves as you move into alpha rhythms, rapid eye movements, called REMs, still flicker and tell of activity. The waking ego remains intact for awhile. "I'm still in charge of the show," one subject commented on this stage. In the second phase, called SEMs, eye movements slow down. The sense of self, or the ego, begins to change as the alpha waves continue in the brain. Finally, as the third stage is entered, the waking ego is completely destructured, and the still pictures of hypnagogic imagery begin to flash upon the theater of the mind. In the fourth state, there are almost no rapid eye movements, a function called NREMs by psychologists, and the sleeper is no longer aware of where he is. This stage is important to some esoteric religions. According to Dr. Charles Tart, "Certain occult magical procedures" use conscious control of this hypnagogic state between waking and sleeping as an introductory discipline. Tart suggests Western man might also want to investigate such stages and use them as a doorway into "another world of experience," in addition to the usual role as a pathway to sleep.

M. Bertini, Helen Lewis, and Herman Witkin have designed a special sensory deprivation technique that might just make such uses possible. This technique induces drowsiness and stimulates imagery, recording the effects by having the volunteer subject talk about what he sees and feels while a tape recorder takes down his words. Highly emotional material is read to the volunteers and shown to them before the experiment begins. *Ganzfeld glasses,* made up of halves of ping-pong balls over which a diffuse red light plays, are placed over the eyes to restrict the vision to a homogeneous, unvarying visual expanse. The monotonous sound of staticlike white noise induces drowsiness as it is fed to the subject through earphones; it also deadens the noises of the outside, as well as distorting and weakening the sound of the volunteer's own voice.

And what happens? Sometimes lost scenes and feelings from childhood come to the surface. At other times, abstract contemporary images people the mind, lending the volunteer new insight and self-understanding. A medical student, who was first shown a film, was recorded as he went into a trancelike state. Here is part of what he said:

> Green bottle . . . interesting green bottle . . . I just fell inside. I keep falling inside the bottle. I can't tell whether I have any clothes on or not. What am I gonna do in the green bottle? I can't get out. I only keep scratching at the walls. That's silly. Why don't I do something? I'm gonna get out of the bottle. Ridiculous. Looks kind of like W's bottle. Say, what happened to that? Did he give it away? . . .maybe I'm trapped in his wine bottle. Now I'm up in a pink cloud. . . .

Later, the medical student confided that as a child he had worried about confinement, and thought about being in a green bottle. Many of the other symbols were quickly identified and helped explain his analytical associations to the student. "An associational flow relatively removed from ordinary conscious control" is the way Bertini, Lewis, and Witkin describe this induced experience. A rich variety of thoughts rise up easily to the consciousness. Some people remember feelings from childhood. Others have thoughts and images woven about their present life. Such free association is important to therapists, but it could also give the average person a rich harvest of self-insight.

Introduce biofeedback of alpha wave information, and image production can take place even faster. The Greens, in a paper coauthored with Dale Walters, spoke of their alpha and theta feedback system that can be used to turn on great amounts of hypnagogic imagery.

Drowsiness is usually a partner of this stage of low-level brain waves, but Dr. Elmer Green devised an ingenious mercury-switch finger ring to help alert people when they are getting tired. This device works so well that another psychologist calls it "Green's subliminal dredging machine." Picture yourself lying flat upon your back, with your arm bent at the elbow and jutting up vertically. When you begin to be sleepy, your forearm wavers, moves a bit, and then begins to tilt. But, with Green's invention, a chime will suddenly ring to jog you back to consciousness.

This arm-balancing tactic might be effective even without the Greens' mercury ring. Dr. Tart suggests using arm balancing to avoid loss of images due to sleepiness. Lie still, but keep your arm up in a vertical position. When you start to doze, your arm will jolt downward, and you will be jarred back to wakefulness. This arm-balancing maneuver could help you maintain alertness, if you are interested in studying your own twilight stages.

The twilight stages might also be useful for learning. Information is quickly absorbed because during this mental state suggestibility is increased. In the twilight stage, one is less able to criticize, or to ignore, new ideas.

"I was just sleepy enough to believe what you're saying is true. I couldn't oppose what you wanted with anything else," one man told sleep researcher Theodore Barber, as he drifted in the twilight state of consciousness. Light sleep and drowsy stages may make you as suggestible as if you're actually hypnotized. Barber studied this feeling and found an intense suggestibility in most subjects. Because of this suggestibility, Barber holds out the hope that suggestions of a positive nature, given in an induced twilight stage, might help heavy smokers cut down on cigarettes, aid the obese to reduce their compulsion to eat, or even give confidence to timid people. A number of scientists have used biofeedback training to help people reach controlled twilight stages.

After the twilight stage, your brain waves slow down even more, and you begin to fall asleep. It's in this first stage that you dream. Here, your brain waves are a mixture of theta waves, the faster alpha waves, and alphoid waves, a special sort of wave that is one or two Hz cycles slower than your own normal waking alpha. Here, your eyes have REM, rapid eye movement, as your eyelids flicker, but this activity disappears as you reach the second stage of sleep.

In stage two, "spindles" appear in your brain, 14 Hz cycle waves bursting like energy explosions or sun spots upon your mind. These spindles continue on into the third and fourth stages of sleep, but your brain's energy continues to slow down until it finally reaches the deep lethargy of delta waves, from almost zero to 4 cycles per second. Deepest sleep has only these slow delta waves, and no dreams.

How long you spend in each stage varies. During an evening's sleep, you could move from dreaming, to deep sleep, and back to dreaming again many times. If you happen to be deep into a delta period when you are awakened, you may find yourself groggy, disoriented, and unable to think for moments. This happens because your brain has to move from a very slow rhythm through a revving up to the rapid action of normal waking beta waves. If you are in a dreaming stage when an outside noise startles you into awakening, your dream may even seem real to you for a moment, until your brain speeds up, and you again know where you are.

Your sleeping dream pattern is almost like the program at your local movie theater. Your first dream may be like the coming attractions, lasting about ten minutes. An intermission of deep delta sleep follows. Your next dream is longer, almost like a short subject. Then comes another deep delta stage. As time passes, these deep sleep period intermissions become shorter, as you build to longer dream time. Toward morning, the feature is shown, long dreams with complex abstract structures and visions. A few short sleep periods are mixed between your long dreams.

Dreams have fascinated mankind for centuries. All sorts of ideas about dreaming consciousness have been voiced:

Dreams are your soul wandering while you sleep.
Dreams are the Royal Road to the Unconscious.
Bad dreams just mean you have an upset stomach.
If you dream of death, it means someone is going to have a baby.
Dreams will tell you the future.
We dream because the brain is really an inefficient machine.

This diversity of attitudes toward dream consciousness reveals the extremes of opinions and controversy over dreams. Dozens of dream laboratories already exist, where scientists attempt to study exactly what happens when you dream but many questions still remain unanswered. Conflicting ideas about dreams leave this a wide open field for investigators.

Some facts are known: The number and types of dreams you have can change because of outside factors. Your dream time will increase rapidly if you've been deprived of dreams through having been constantly awakened. Mothers of newborn babies who must get up for the infant's feeding every few hours, find that they dream a good deal. Alcohol cuts down on your dreaming time. The number of dreams are also reduced by many common sleeping pills. Even the feel of your bed can affect the number of dreams you have. Post-hypnotic suggestion can decrease the time you spend in dreaming and even intrude upon the actual content of your dreams.

The sound of a sudden thunderstorm outside your bedroom can dart into your dreaming consciousness, and be transformed into the crashing symbols of a military band in your dream. Or you may feel a stomach cramp from that rich dessert at dinner and, as it disagrees with your digestive system, your dreaming mind alters that lump of pain and turns it into the "feel" of a sword wound as you fight off pirate attacks in your dream. Or the sheets become tangled about your feet, and you begin to dream that you have been tied up by bandits. All kinds of outside variables can poke their way, uninvited, into your consciousness. In just this way, noises, discomfort from your sleeping position, or a breeze blowing into an open window, can be perceived and rewritten by your dreaming mind into strange scenes. Your mind does this so that you can continue to sleep. In dreams we confront ourselves.

Dr. Montague Ullman, of Brooklyn's Maimonides Medical Center, explained dream consciousness as a confrontation between the waking familiar self and the altered conscious self.

> We have a residue of the self, the familiar self. Then we have a lot of things coming into the picture that sort of represents all those things pushed into the background by the self-deceptive process. So, we have an individual who consciously in the waking state is going along in one direction and . . , at the same time, [his] muscle effects are going along in another direction, and [his] affective effects are going along in another direction. At night, what happens is a kind of backlash . . . and you're faced with a kind of enforced truthfulness about your self at an effective level that you don't always know what to do with.

Psychic powers and ESP (extra-sensory perception) are different sorts of consciousness. You may be an ESP advocate, or you may only grant that sometimes you've been able somehow, to guess what another person was going to say; or you may not grant any credence to ESP at all. A number of respected researchers have been investigating ESP powers, among them Dr. Edward Bokert, of the American Society of Psychical Research, who wonders if these shades of consciousness might not be related to depth experiences like mystical ecstasies. (A few other researchers even tentatively link ESP insight powers in some people to alpha states, but this remains to be proven.) Dr. Bokert has tried to analyze various kinds of psychic states and, according to his analysis, the first of these ESP psychic states is intensely emotional, and characterized by a highly aroused autonomic nervous system. In this state of psychic insight, breathing speeds up and becomes irregular; the heart rate begins to vary as the brain temperature rises and the cerebral flow increases. The high intensity and excitation of this state makes it seem almost like the peak and nadir stages Abraham Maslow described for extreme emotional or mystical experiences. Bokert recorded alpha brain rhythms in this stage of consciousness. Other peculiarities of this stage are REM, with a great deal of rapid eye movement, and bursts of the slower theta waves in the brain rhythms. Because of numerous case-history studies, Bokert states that this consciousness stage is associated with ESP powers. Such consciousness is extremely emotional and you would feel either great joy or terrible anxiety.

ESP powers also seem to be identified with shifting mental periods, according to Dr. Bokert's studies. As your mind changes from one conscious level to another, as from waking to sleeping or sleeping to waking, ESP phenomena have been recorded by scientific observers. Most shifting stages of consciousness contain a high degree of alpha brain waves.

Another alpha state, the period when you are already asleep and just beginning to dream, is also associated with psychic production. In this stage, the mind is believed to revert to more primitive levels of consciousness as uncensored images spring forth and new insights perceived.

The discoveries of psychic expert Dr. Charles Honorton, of the Maimonides Medical Medical Center, seem to agree with this theory linking alpha powers and psychic powers. Dr. Honorton worked extensively with alpha feedback for long periods, and he found that successful ESP insights are related to "relaxation, mild disassociation, passivity, and a reduction of visual imagery." This is almost a perfect twin to the average person's description of the alpha state. In addition, everyone who showed relatively high alpha also had relatively high ESP scores in a test. Dr. Honorton observed that the more sensitive person is more apt to generate high alpha waves and, in ESP work, seems to be more aware of his success.

A New York City high school experiment by Honorton seems to support his claim. In this test, a teenager would sit in a darkened sound-proof room. From another room, over an intercom system, the scientist would tell him: "Relax as much as you can." A group of ESP Guessing Cards rested upon a table nearby. Before the test, the cards had been shuffled and arranged in an opaque container in a prearranged order. "Now, guess which card it is," the boy was told as he lifted each card from the container. With his eyes closed, the boy was to try to "see" each card in his mind. Time after time, Honorton saw that the boys with high alpha waves also made more accurate guesses at the cards, 6.07 out of 15 runs for all of the high-alpha producers, and a negative deviation of 4 for the low-alpha producers.

Another common way consciousness can be altered is through hypnosis. Alpha and hypnosis are not synonymous. Hypnotic trances show about the same brain waves as normal waking states. Alpha is not a state of trance, and one can bring himself back instantly, unlike being under hypnosis, where control often rests outside the individual. Hypnosis calls for a semi-surrender of willpower. The will may be temporarily put to rest in a state of alpha consciousness, but to a very mild degree. In alpha, you relax your normal intellectual activities, but you do not banish the world. Instead, you refocus upon the world in a fresh new way.

Alpha consciousness is a special state of its own, that may be described as a wonderful feeling of relaxation that, still, leaves one totally aware of everything, uncritically observing and absorbing, and serenely understanding everything about one's internal and external worlds.

Chapter 3
The Hidden Treasure
Alpha Consciousness and the Alpha Experience

The cold air in the small room felt as blue as the azure walls that surrounded her. The chair was too stiff and straight, so she slipped to the floor and sat cross-legged, pushing the wires from the electrodes dangling from her head behind her. "Futuristic creature," she smiled to herself, and crossed her arms. She began to relax as she closed her eyes and let go. Beside her, the biofeedback machine began to warble on, off, on again, to give her an instant signal about her brain waves. In another room, tracing pens zigged and zagged their crooked way over the graph paper to record the presence of alpha waves intermixed with the more frequent beta waves. The tone cue sounded intermittantly, signaling alpha. At first, the sound was irritating and almost frightening as it jumped in and out. She didn't like hearing it, but she was there to learn how to turn on her alpha with the aid of biofeedback.

She relaxed and told her tensed muscles to melt, imagining herself drifting and floating in the sea of space. As she unwound the rippling shapes and lines behind her closed eyes, the tone became stronger and longer. The sound was strong and clear. Curious, she opened her eyes to see if she could hold the alpha and keep it going with eyes open. For a moment, the tone went off, and she was surprised to find that she missed it, as she would miss a friend who suddenly disappeared. But she found the alpha again, by just loosening up and letting go. Her body felt lighter, as her senses sparkled with fresh sensation. To her, the feeling of alpha was a warm flowing forth of Presence, especially across the top of her head. "Alpha feels like a prayer cap," she smiled.

This is alpha consciousness, the special experience that comes from turning on alpha brain waves. Alpha consciousness flows from awakened sensitivity to your own internal cues. Subjectively, you "feel" your alpha. Subjectively, you learn how to turn it on by working with an external monitor—a biofeedback machine with its cue—to tell you what's happening inside your mind. The wonderfully intricate mechanism of your mind works with quicksilver speed as you feel the alpha and quickly perceive what internal processes to use to enhance your alpha brain waves. Alpha consciousness is a catch-all term, to help communicate in words some measure of understanding of the meaning of the "alpha experience."

Alpha is so controversial, that some scientists refuse to admit there even is such a thing as alpha consciousness; others frown and say that alpha consciousness or special alpha states may exist, but they want to see more laboratory proof before they attest to the existence of any such thing as special alpha states; and still other scientists point to massive records of experiments made on volunteer after volunteer who all experienced alpha consciousness and reported their feelings to the experimenters.

Such controversy is not unexpected. These diverse reactions are linked to the prevailing notion in scientific circles that private experiences, like mystical revelations, either simply don't occur or cannot be studied. The public study of private subjective experiences is only just beginning. This "show me" posture is faintly reminiscent of the attitude taken by Western science for decades, refusing to believe that Zen meditators did attain unusually remarkable mental states and ignoring reports that the yogi master could actually perform fantastic no-pain feats. Now, lab proof is being provided, and scientists are just beginning to wonder if a reevaluation might not be necessary. EEGs, and EMGs, and EKGs, recorded from Oriental meditators, are showing that Eastern masters really do reach fantastic heights of control.

To many alpha converts, alpha consciousness is a reality that they do not question, because they've experienced it themselves. They speak sincerely of the tranquil state of alpha consciousness that they have felt. They openly confide their excitement from enhancing creativity with alpha. They tell how they manage to relax away the tension of stress with alpha states. They may even look at life a bit differently than other people, because the alpha converts speak vaguely of their identification with all living things, of their organic sense of unity and sense of flowing with the energy of the universe. The "alpha" that they're reaching for is the alpha brain wave, a particular rhythm that occurs between the faster beta and slower theta brain waves on the scientist's measuring scale. Alpha is a gentle electrical type of energy of eight to twelve cycles per second. Brain waves are probably produced by neural processes, the electrical activity of the brain, but even this fact has not been proven concretely as yet.

Wherever they come from, alpha brain waves are common in most people. Alpha varies from person to person, and seems to have different peaks for different people, and arises in areas of the brain particularly characteristic of each person. You flow from level to level as you shift consciousness from waking to sleeping and your brain waves slow down. Your own characteristic alpha might be recorded at nine cycles per second, while your father's alpha might be recorded and turn out to be ten cycles per second. This particular peak or home spot of alpha frequency level will probably remain consistent, except when you shift conscious states. But the strength or amplitude of your alpha could grow immensely.

Alpha is alpha is alpha. Or is it? If you've never had experience with meditation and have never tried biofeedback, your alpha probably would range around ten to twenty microvolts in strength. Many people actually generate alpha waves all the time. They can saunter down the street, absorb the music at a rock concert, or turn the pages of a book, and be producing great quantities of alpha waves. They don't even know they're "doing alpha," but it's happening.

A few people have only rare ripples of the alpha rhythm mixed with the faster beta of their normal waking hours. Their most usual alpha production is brief, slipping in just as they drift off to sleep. For such people (5 to 10 percent, perhaps), the pleasures of alpha consciousness can only be unlocked after long sessions of feedback training. Yet, such people might benefit most from the unique and restful experience.

Alpha consciousness is believed to come as your alpha state grows stronger and you become better at turning on your alpha. As you nurture and strengthen your alpha, perceptual changes and thought realignments may occur. Because you've turned on the feeling state, you have the chance to experience a wealth of physical and psychological pleasure. Some strong alpha producers speak of the alpha high, or call alpha consciousness a drug-free euphoria, and a journey into the paradise of inner space.

Learning to turn on alpha is easy for most people. The biofeedback device is necessary because you need the cues of a color or tone to let you "feel" exactly where you are in a sort of instant learning. Eyes-closed alpha is the most common and, for many people, the cue of a tone seems to be the best way to begin and produce lots of occipital alpha quickly. With practice, you might run your twenty microvolts of alpha up to eighty microvolts. Usually, alpha seems to peak after four or five sessions. It seems to take a good deal of practice before exceptional or extreme consciousness changes happen.

Such changes may be due to chemical shifts. Some chemical alteration may occur after biofeedback learning, although researchers don't yet have all the facts. They do wonder what role proteins may play in mental storage. RNA alterations might be a factor in learning. After biofeedback training, the brains of animals have been cut into and examined. Large quantities of increased amounts of RNA, the genetic material that directs protein synthesis in your body, were found in the brains of the feedback-trained animals. RNA is also thought to be directly connected with the life process as the material that makes up a new life. A wildly speculative explanation for this finding was made by one researcher who links brain-wave control to strengthening primitive parts of the brain, thus revitalizing the life spark.

Whatever the explanation, physiological and psychological changes do accompany feedback training. Mind and body control does bring mind and body changes, although the effects may not be lasting.

Green, Green, and Walters, worked with all aspects of bio-feedback, including EMG for reducing muscle tension and EEG for enhancing alpha waves. In 1969, they reported that feedback subjects experienced many mind and body shifts including body-image changes. A feeling of disembodiment occurred in those who could reach very low levels of muscle tension, in deep relaxation. Increasing hand temperatures with feedback, gave most people a general feeling of tranquility, while turning on high percentages of alpha waves brought a poised non-drowsy state of mind and seemed to aid the recall process. Feedback-enhanced theta brain rhythms and low-frequency alpha waves brought dreamlike images and a state of almost semiconscious reverie.

Psychologically, alpha consciousness may be a different dimension in pleasure. Dr. Marjorie Kawin-Toomim, who runs the Toomim Laboratories specializing in alpha work in Los Angeles and New York City, describes alpha consciousness as a pleasant, relaxed and rewarding experience. She points out that "Learning to know and control parts of one's being, previously mysterious and apparently involuntary, is exciting. With feedback, individuals are able to discriminate the kind of thoughts, feelings and attitudes which represent an easy flowing with the environment and with their inner selves, generally making life more comfortable."

The first plateau of alpha consciousness is characterized by its own brain-wave pattern. An EEG recording would show slow alpha waves, with even slower theta waves. Along with this brain-wave pattern, may be a slowing down and calming of the autonomic nervous system. This quieting of the nervous system may account for some of the psychological changes reported in alpha states. In 1969, Dr. Edward Bokert studied EEG records of people producing strong high-amplitude waves of slow alpha mixed with the even slower theta waves and added all sorts of instrumentation to further monitor this alpha state. He recorded and later reported that metabolism decreased, temperature and blood pressure dropped, respiration rate was lowered, and muscle tension fell to low levels as the alpha was produced.

This slowing down of the autonomic nervous system lowers the cortical excitatory level, so that less anxiety is felt because usual defenses and barriers are relaxed. This physiological change may account for the often reported psychological changes said to accompany high alpha states. When you are more relaxed, you do not feel as excitedly aroused and can openly devote your full attention to everything around you. You don't need to focus upon just one thing or event for defense. As your normal emotional feelings and barriers are suspended, you can drift to a different relaxed plateau of thinking and sensing.

This is deautomatization, a different way of sensing existence in the world. Psychological researcher, Dr. Arthur Deikman, suggests that deautomatization might possibly come from a synchronizing of the brain waves. He says this state may have great value as it acts to clear the mind of worn patterns of perception and give us fresh new room where we can examine preconceived realities. A new creative atmosphere is composed and new insights are common.

A partial explanation of this phenomenon was given by researcher Dr. Eleanor Criswell, who said, "If we reduce cortical activity and still the mind, we are allowing more primitive brain structures to have more free play . . . more unification."

Other scientists claim that biofeedback lets the brain know what's happening and, perhaps, develop a synchrony in the firing of cortical neurons around the area where the electrodes are placed.

Stilling of the mind (whether it comes from standing on your head, reading a book of poetry, or sitting cross-legged as you meditate) is thought to encourage, somehow, the cortical neurons to fire more synchronously like the instruments of a symphony orchestra playing together harmoniously. Alpha training stills the mind in much the same fashion as meditative

exercises. Both events limit your perceptual field. Both practices reduce the number of stimuli that enter your brain. Biofeedback works as you focus upon the repetitive monotony of
the feedback tone or light, and search inside yourself for passive
awareness.

What else happens when you "do alpha?" Your style of
thinking may change radically. A noted alpha researcher, Dr.
Lester Fehmi, called the alpha state one in which there is
"enhanced ability to attend, have presence, awareness or attention." Another biofeedback researcher, Ed Wortz, studied
both meditators and high-alpha producers trained with feedback. He found a great similarity in time sense alterations. The
perception of time is distorted, and hangups about time disappear. Hours may seem like minutes, and minutes may feel like
hours.

Other senses can also dramatically change in alpha states.
Vision may be deeply affected. The intensity of lights and the
richness of colors may suddenly become apparent.

A psychiatrist, familiar with meditation and a veteran of a
number of LSD experiences, tried alpha consciousness in the
Greens' intricate laboratories at Menninger's clinic. They
reported his impressions, "He . . . was aware of lights, colors,
things that he was seeing." The man seemed to be in a deep
trance and told them that his body felt very, very, still. "It
could be compared to a state of paralysis, but (exhibited) none
of the discomfort or concern that would go with such a state."

Perhaps because of his past experiences, the psychiatrist was
able to sink even further than alpha in his relaxation. His brain
waves slowed and drifted with long trains of theta waves, lasting
twenty or thirty seconds at a time, giving even more profound
sense changes.

The psychiatrist was one of three visitors to the Greens' lab
who had expressed interest in "trying alpha" with the Greens'
feedback machinery. The other two visitors had slightly different reactions to "doing alpha." One was a man from India,
who had practiced Raj Yoga for forty years. The second, was an
American scientist who had practiced Yoga for about thirty
years.

The Greens saw the EEG pens trace a level of about eight

cycles per second as the Indian began to meditate. He easily turned on his alpha and later told them that he had succeeded in stilling his mind and had reached a "state of awareness without thought." He called it a "state of knowingness, rather than a state of thinkingness," and compared it to a "state of consciousness that differed from the content of consciousness."

When the American yoga expert relaxed, the Greens saw that the electrodes picked up his brain rhythms as bursts of alpha and theta waves, ranging from eight and a half to seven Hz cycles, lasting as long as half a minute. The alpha experience was not pleasant for him, and he was disturbed by going into it and pulling out of it. He described his subjective feelings during alpha as "awake-dreaming." This awake-dreaming was full of images that were "very vivid scenes, people and so forth," and the visions moved rapidly and quickly disappeared.

This sort of image-filled mental stage is marked by concentration without tension, a characteristic alpha feeling. It seems to be similar to the state of mind Aldous Huxley turned on at will for creative image-gathering and which he called "alert passivity," and turned on for inspiration, before he wrote such novels as *Brave New World.*

What does alpha consciousness feel like? Is there a special sensation connected with alpha? "Well, it's a kind of a very alert sort of relaxation," a lanky blonde student explained. Another, a Fine Arts major, calls alpha "a groovy kind of floating." "It's sort of like pot," an engineer explained, "But the difference is that you never feel drugged with alpha and you can come down the instant you want to."

Dr. Joe Kamiya is probably one of the most celebrated alpha experts in America, and his long experience experimenting with alpha control makes his description of alpha states especially pertinent. To him, alpha is a passive relaxation, and an attitude of just letting things happen. He points out that alpha is not just a kind of relaxation which leads to drowsiness, like lying down to rest and nap. Instead, alpha is a specialized relaxation with a certain kind of focus of attention that increases awareness.

Zen disciples examined by Kamiya claim that the alpha state is much like the beginning stages of their meditative experiences, but that their advanced meditative consciousness is "a more floating state, a disaffected feeling, more mindless than calm, and relaxed, with great powers of concentration for some, and heightened awareness for others."

Although feedback techniques let people know perfectly well if they're producing alpha (or theta) brain waves, everyone seems to have trouble describing the alpha feeling. This difficulty results because alpha is a subjective state, an emotional and sensory feeling. Most of Kamiya's volunteers liked the feeling of alpha and spoke of the alpha state as pleasant. Attempting to explain, some volunteers called alpha a drifting tranquility or a feeling of letting go, and even, flowing restfulness.

Alpha researcher Dr. Barbara Brown invented a unique card-sorting technique to help gauge people's subjective reactions to various brain-wave states. Primarily, she was interested in learning if different brain rhythms had various subconscious associations.

Working with twenty-six volunteers, she rigged complex machinery so that various waves triggered different colors. Alpha waves triggered blue or red lights. Beta waves turned on red or green lights in the dark study chamber. Theta waves switched on green or blue lights. After each feedback session, the volunteer shuffled a deck of word cards and chose the particular words that best described the colors they saw and the accompanying brain wave state.

Most people describe alpha as a pleasant feeling, a sensation of well-being, tranquility, and relaxation. Some also picked up increased awareness of thoughts and feelings, and reviewed personal experiences to explain how alpha felt.

In contrast, beta was explained by most people as worry, anger, fear, and frustration. A few people described beta feelings as tension, alertness, excitement, contentment, warmth, hunger, or surprise. Theta, nicknamed the creative wave by some observers, was described in this experiment as memory of problems, uncertainty, future planning, switching thoughts, solving of problems, and daydreaming.

In this first test, the color blue was described as calm and peaceful before the feedback training. Red was a feeling of anger, irritation, or impatience to most people. But when Dr.

Brown changed the lights so that alpha triggered red, people's feelings about the color red suddenly changed. After linking alpha brain waves with the red light, they described the color red as calm. This would seem to prove that there is a subjective association between brain waves and feelings toward concepts like color.

"Blank mind" is the way other people have described the feeling of alpha. Researcher Dr. Johann Stoyva reports that many people found alpha devoid of visual imagery, but that it was a tranquil and peaceful feeling without the involvement of any strong emotional feelings. Dr. Stoyva adds, "In my own alpha training experience, I have noticed that any twinge of emotion causes alpha to go away. For about half of my subjects, the mental state associated with alpha is a feeling of content-free consciousness. For me, personally, the inner visual field during alpha was like a flowing grey-black film, with a luminous quality. A blank mind sensation."

Not everyone likes the feeling of alpha or the alpha state. Dr. Maurice B. Sterman, noting that alpha occurs spontaneously when people cease to process, taped the reactions to alpha at UCLA (University of California at Los Angeles). Many volunteers learned to turn on both alpha and the sensorimotor area with the aid of biofeedback. Most did not care for alpha.

"Kind of a downer," one student whispered. "I was angry and disappointed," a girl confided, revealing she'd expected much more from the experience. "I don't like having to give myself up, and not having self-control," a psychology major complained.

Another volunteer described alpha to Sterman as, "It reminds me of Seligman's learned helplessness. You give up your will to learn." Sterman describes this student as bright and well-adjusted. Dr. Sterman asked the student if he would like to work with alpha again. "No!" the 25-year-old graduate student answered intensely, no room for argument. "It wasn't fun. If I thought at all, I didn't hear any bells."

A middle-aged professor tried alpha and found that the alpha state angered him because he felt that he'd left his body and been semi-disassociated. He learned that, as he gave up his conscious will, he could achieve alpha. But to do so created a conflict in him. As he "sent [himself] out," he had negative feelings and images about "giving up my self."

"I thought I was going to sleep," an experienced Yogi meditator told Sterman in a cool voice. "I found that I was away. (In sensorimotor area work), I knew what I was looking for, and I had the feeling of having performed a task. Today [in alpha work], I had no idea what to go for, and I felt adrift." He found the feeling of alpha neutral, being neither agreeable nor disagreeable. It just existed.

This disassociated feeling is not uncommon in alpha, but it does not happen in every experience. It was reported in one session at the Veteran's Administration Hospital in Bedford, Massachusetts. In the experimental chambers, one man tried alpha feedback and later told the scientists that he felt as if he were floating in space far beyond any manmade barriers of time or place.

What does all this mean? Is alpha good? Is it bad? Or is it merely blah? Most alpha scientists are agreed that alpha can be whatever you want it to be. You tend to get what you put into the experience, and, if you really like the idea of alpha, you will probably easily succeed at turning on your alpha.

Most people who especially want to turn on their alpha consciousness are able to do it almost immediately. Dr. Fehmi found that highly motivated people had no difficulty learning self-regulation of their own brain waves. Dr. Fehmi has recorded EEGs from artists, musicians, and students; in each case, everyone who was excited by the idea of brain wave control did very well. Mostly highly motivated alpha pilgrims make fabulous alpha beginnings. Usually, they immediately find sudden increases in the strength or length of time their alpha energy flows. Quickly, they experience a duration or amplitude jump happening simultaneously at all electrode recording sites.

This jump in brain waves is an exciting feeling. When it happens, Dr. Fehmi reports that people have described it to him as "an increase in smooth flowing energy, a release of tension, and a spreading of attentional focus."

Normal attentional focus is one-dimensional and limited. Generally, you pay attention to only one or two things at a time, and almost ignore everything else around you. But, in this kind of experience, you have a brand-new way of looking at things.

To understand alpha focus, imagine a sheet of unblemished paper. Now visualize green colored water suddenly being poured upon the paper. It flows outward. It begins to soak into the paper. The very texture of the paper begins to change as it absorbs the water. This action is comparable to the absorbing kind of perception of alpha attention.

Now, picture the same paper with a waxy covering. Pour the green colored liquid upon the paper. The liquid slides right off the paper and is gone in a quicksilver moment without affecting the look or feel or smell of the paper at all. It might as well never even have been there. This is like the normal one-dimensional kind of attention as events quickly pass by without being absorbed on any deep level.

You can get all this by not trying to get it. It wasn't that the highly motivated alpha seekers sat down and fiercely concentrated to make alpha happen. Alpha cannot be forced. Alpha seekers who have a "show me" attitude, or an intense "I've got to make it work" feeling find that alpha eludes them completely. In fact, any hard or tense concentration will actually make alpha drop below the original or normal level, called your base line. You could turn on alpha and increase it by thinking of Zen. What do you do to make alpha happen? You do nothing, of course. Now, that may sound like a Zen koan to infuriate you with it's Oriental antilogic, but that's just exactly how everyone succeeds in turning alpha on.

Some kinds of people seem to be best suited to turning on alpha. Sensitive introspective people seem to be best at producing alpha brain waves and quickly learning to control them, according to Dr. Kamiya. He points out that it is only his subjective impression, but he has noticed that anyone who has been interested in and has practiced any of the myriad forms of meditation seems to be especially good at enhancing alpha brain rhythms.

Kamiya adds that the good alpha producer is likely to be an individual who uses words like "images, dreams, wants, feelings." Kamiya continues, "I have come to the conclusion that there are a large number of people who really don't know what you're talking about when you talk about images and feelings. These people don't do well in my experiments. They do not gain a high degree of control over their own alpha rhythms."

"We have found that people who were relaxed, comfortable, and cooperative tended to produce more alpha waves than those who felt tense, suspicious, and fearful," he once wrote. Sensitivity training may be an aid to alpha. In another article, he mentioned additional characteristics of the high alpha person. He mentioned that, "People who look you in the eyes and feel at ease in close interpersonal relationships, who are good at intuitively sensing the way you feel, are also good at this [producing alpha]."

Uptight, rigid people usually find alpha an almost impossible goal. It doesn't seem to matter whether you're a quiet person or an extremely extroverted person; what does make a difference in your alpha potential is your degree of openness and empathy. Sex and age and occupation make no difference, and both men and women tend to score equally well.

High alpha producers do have one quality in common—they all tend to be more sensual and turned on to the sights and sounds and feelings of their surroundings. "They are interested in the kind of sensations in their bodies," Kamiya mentioned. "They tend to be expressive of emotion much more often also, which, I think, is also a kind of internal feedback. They seem to be, on the one hand, less frightened and anxious about the experimental situation, and, on the other hand, a little more willing to give and take in the situation."

Other alpha researchers agree with Kamiya's tentative analysis. Most people who are sensitive and sensually turned on, have little trouble learning to produce alpha at will. "I'm glad that I'm an alpha, not a dirty beta," an alpha veteran punned, quoting Aldous Huxley's litany from *Brave New World.*

A lot of people would tend to agree with him. Beta people spend their waking lives in the noisy land of beta waves and they seldom relax that faster brain energy to the slower calm of alpha. This could have disastrous effects upon the body's functioning. Uptight rigid people usually have a hard time finding the feel of alpha and letting alpha happen. Perhaps because their life patterns are so rigid and repressive, such beta people have the strongest reactions of all to alpha when they do finally manage to let it happen. To them, alpha consciousness may be extreme euphoric pleasure. But, they have to work much harder to reach alpha, and many give up along the way, complaining, "Nuts to that alpha bit. I tried it and nothing happened at all. There's probably no such thing as alpha."

It may be that there are some people who simply cannot produce any alpha at all. Schizophrenics seem to fit this category, although it doesn't necessarily mean that you're schizophrenic if you can't reach alpha. The EEG for a diagnosed schizophrenic is even faster than beta rhythms, and a long long way from the slow alpha. One of Dr. Fehmi's subjects was a hospitalized schizophrenic who was unable to produce alpha, even after he had been given forty half-hour training sessions. This is about ten times as much training as the average alpha subject receives. Fehmi also found that a number of college freshman students who had been deliberately ordered to participate in an alpha experiment for a class, found alpha impossible to achieve. In kaleidoscopic contrast, the students who bombarded Dr. Fehmi with pleas until he agreed to let them try alpha, gained control over the feedback signal almost immediately and had no trouble controlling alpha brain waves.

For the most part, set, or motivation, seems to have a strong effect. In case after case, the kind of person who cares about alpha will probably find it easy and fun. The person who puts it down as just another fad will find that his EEG probably reveals nothing but beta brain waves.

Are the special experiences of alpha consciousness real? It seems to depend upon your definition of reality. If reality is that which you perceive, then it is real to you, regardless of what someone else might feel about it. Subjective states and feelings cannot be measured and catalogued and locked in neat files very easily. Alpha is a subjective state most of all, and its reality is determined by how you feel about it when you try it. A middle-aged man, head of his own law firm, suspiciously believed that alpha researcher Dr. Thomas Mulholland, would try to fool him by turning on false tones. The lawyer had read of control experiments by psychologists and he didn't want to be mislead. When he was convinced that the tones used in the feedback were accurate, he did an about-face. As long as he heard the alpha tone control, the lawyer confided to Dr. Mulholland that it had been "a good session," and he was "really able to turn alpha on." His strongest alpha waves were on the right side of his head.

When the electrodes and feedback tones were switched to the left side, he heard less tone, and he didn't like it. "A frustrating experience . . . unpleasant," the lawyer told Dr. Mulholland. Soundless electrodes placed on the right side of his brain revealed that he was actually still producing deep waves of alpha rhythms, but without any feedback tones. The alpha was still there, but the man didn't note it because he couldn't hear it. The tone was being valued solely for itself, and was an important and effective reinforcement according to Dr. Mulholland. Again, you get what you put into the experience and, often, just what you expect to get.

Dr. Mulholland reminds us that our attitudes, beliefs, expectations and fears, our "set," can help shape what seems to happen. In controlled experiments, sometimes just the sound of that feedback tone makes some people feel successful and relaxed, although they may not be producing any alpha at all. Without the tone, even if their alpha is copious, they may brim over with feelings of failure, discontent, and tension.

A teenager wandered into Dr. Mulholland's laboratory with rich fantasies about what alpha was really like. After stripping his local library dry of all material on alpha, he had come to present himself as an alpha volunteer. In the quiet room, the boy quickly turned on abundant alpha. From another room, Dr. Mulholland questioned him over the intercom system. "I'm losing track of space and time," the boy intoned, "There's a rabbit in here so real that I can almost touch it," he added.

Dr. Mulholland was curious, so he flicked off the tone control for the feedback apparatus. The boy no longer had a cue to tell him what was happening. Although the boy's strong alpha waves continued to flow, suddenly the experience was nothing special to him. There were no more reports of fearful or hallucinatory experiences. But there had been no actual change in his alpha level, and the alpha was still there, just as prominent as before.

As you mentally relax into alpha, your muscles and tendons and joints relax too. You cut down your focus on the multitude of outside stimuli and you begin to pay attention to your own mental experiences. As Mulholland explains it, "If we stop talking, this lets us hear what the other person is saying. However, *what* the other person says is not caused by our simply not talking. By taking time out to be relaxed, yet awake, for an hour in a quiet place, people are discovering that they have thoughts. . . . Obviously, after one discovers thinking, he discovers awareness, and introspects on his thought flow. At this point, a person's subjective report on his thoughts and the state of his feelings are likely to be influenced by his beliefs, by his expectations, and by his wishes and needs."

And then, changes begin to happen. If you like the idea of alpha and you do receive the alpha signal, you may very well say it is a pleasant sensation. If you're intrigued by the idea of mystic experiences, you may be able to turn one on in your mind. If you're hung up on sex, your alpha experience may be extremely sensual. Your motivation may steer your alpha experience where you really want it to go.

This self-determination to shape the experience is remarkably similar to reports in drug studies. Dr. Theodore Xenophon Barber studied reactions to major psychedelic drugs like LSD and found a wide range of effects, in spite of the fact that all participants were given the same amount of the drug. Again, people tended to get the sensations they were looking for. Some subjects actually had no reactions at all to massive doses of LSD, because they really weren't expecting any changes to happen. Barber noted that the quality of individual drug experiences depended upon "such variables as the situation and the subject's set and personality."

Industrial psychologists have seen a similar set, and they call it the Hawthorne effect. Dr. Neal E. Miller, pioneer biofeedback researcher, reminds us that "patients and workers tend to improve when they feel that someone is paying attention to them and doing something for them." This is a sort of

Hawthorne effect. Dr. Miller continues: "Thus the magical effect of the impressive apparatus, the hope that is aroused, and a certain amount of transference to the investigator, can produce a reduction in heart rate or hypertension." So far, brain-wave studies don't have controls for a person's set, and the set will have to be considered before we can conclude that brain-wave control is the complete answer for everything that ails man.

The attitude of the experimenter can also have a great effect upon one's own subjective feelings toward the alpha experience. One lab found that they lagged way behind other experimenters in getting volunteers to learn how to control alpha. They complained about the problem, but couldn't figure out why. When other scientists visited this lab, they soon saw the reason. There was an appalling cut-and-dry feeling, an "ok-Charlie-now-turn-it-on-so-we-can-clock-you" attitude. Experimenters who have tried alpha themselves, and enjoy it; seem best able to coax positive results from other people.

Studies by Erik Peper and Thomas Mulholland reveal that most people can quickly learn how to suppress alpha waves, but find it much harder to turn on their alpha. Dim lights helped people learn to control alpha as they learned to "look" or "not look." In most cases relaxation produced more alpha, whereas tension reduced it. The low-alpha-producing people actually found that tension helped them produce alpha, while relaxation decreased it.

Alpha happens all over the brain; it is not restricted to one special "alpha spot." Most alpha researchers tend to concentrate upon occipital alpha, the alpha brain waves from the back of the head, because this kind of alpha wave is most easily detected, easiest to produce and is linked to visual attention. When occipital alpha is high, your attention will probably be low. When your occipital alpha is low, your attention will probably be much higher. When Dr. Thomas Mulholland instructed people to open their eyes in the dark, he found that occipital alpha waves decreased but returned within a few minutes. When you have your eyes open in a quiet room, your alpha waves from the occipital brain area begin at a low level. Gradually, the alpha rate begins to increase. If your eye flicker rate goes down because you are staring at something, or letting images blur, you will have a better chance of making those alpha rhythms dance through your mind.

There are a number of physical changes that seem to occur along with alpha brain waves. During alpha-training control experiments at the University of Pennsylvania, Dr. David Paskewitz rigged up elaborate electrodes and machinery to record heart rate, GSR (Galvanic Skin Response), respiration, and eye movements. (Galvanic Skin Response measures the change in the skin resistance in response to an outside stimulus.) He was curious to learn if actual differences did occur as alpha waves were produced, and, his findings were surprising. The brain waves and the rest of the bodily responses were linked together in a circle of response and feeling. Time after time, as he watched, Dr. Paskewitz saw heart rate increase in a pattern opposite to the rising alpha amplitude zigzagging across the graph-paper records. Then, after a short rest period, heart rates began to drop off gradually and return to the original states at the beginning of the experiment.

The degree of tension spotted in the GSR records also changed. At first, substantial reactions occurred as each volunteer shifted the feedback control light from red to green, indicating that he had moved from beta brain waves to alpha brain waves. But, after awhile, the GSR recording began to drop in each case. As each volunteer drifted into long-controlled bursts of alpha brain waves, the GSR records dropped to highly relaxed levels.

Many things seem to happen during alpha, some real and some only fulfillment of wished-for fantasy. Scientists tend to concentrate upon alpha from different areas of their studies, and this can lead to further confusion in understanding alpha. Different areas tend to indicate different meanings, corresponding to the particular functions each area governs in the mind. If you're trying to understand your own alpha brain rhythms, go back to that map of the mind in Chapter One, and check out which area is actually giving out that signal to the electrode you've attached.

Remember that brain-wave patterns, from the left or right hemispheres of your brain, are often quite different; and different areas signify different things. Dr. Fehmi has performed extensive studies of alpha brain waves measured from the frontal or temporal lobes, those located in the front sections of the brain. Many other studies have been based on work with the occipital alpha, from that area roughly located in the back of your head. Much of the work by Hart, Knowlis, Green, Peper, and others, has concentrated upon the occipital area.

Alpha consciousness is not an overnight phenomenon, although some people find it easy to turn on alpha right away. The deeper levels of consciousness alteration come from a great deal of experience and practice at strengthened alpha. It takes time before extreme changes occur, but the simple pleasures of alpha relaxation are not so difficult to obtain, and are often immediately available. "With further training, a deeper, more pervasive alpha experience is obtained," Dr. Fehmi explained, after he had worked with dozens of creative people bent upon using alpha to enter into states of intense creativity.

Dr. Thomas Mulholland, who has used alpha feedback methods for a decade and a half to study the human orienting response, cautions that studies on alpha should qualify where the recordings are taken from. Some brain areas are synchronized, while others are not. Occipital alpha is easy and not too intense a psychological change, while frontal alpha, or temporal alpha, could mean quite another thing.

However, with enough alpha generated from a broad number of brain areas, an alpha consciousness or special alpha state would seem to occur.

Alpha consciousness is thought by many alpha veterans to be *istigkeit,* a favorite word of the fourteenth-century mystic philosopher Meister Eckhart. Such a feeling is similar to the Being of Platonic philosophy, except that Being and Becoming are no longer separated in the alpha state, and merge to be one sense of Is-ness, of *istigkeit.*

Plato separated thought and life into separate compartments, and put down nonrational material of life and thought. Huxley, in his classic *Doors of Perception,* had an alphalike experience with mescaline and tackled Plato's rather antiseptic view of life. Huxley wrote, "Plato could never, poor fellow, have seen a bunch of flowers shining with their own inner light, and all but quivering under the pressure of the significance with which they were charged; could never have perceived [that] what that rose and iris and carnation so immensely signified was nothing more, and nothing less, than what they were—a perpetual perishing that was at the same time pure Being, a bundle of minute, unique particulars in which, by some unspeakable and yet evident paradox, was to be seen the divine source of all existence."

For many people, Huxley's naturalistic-organic view of life is what alpha is all about.

When deep relaxation feedback training is combined with alpha feedback techniques, an even broader dimension of consciousness change begins to take place. As your mind and body begin to empty of normal consciousness and tension, your body may begin to feel as if it were floating or flying.

The Greens combined feedback technologies in some of their experiments, and found startling changes in consciousness occurring.

"I felt like I was floating above the chair," one housewife told the Greens. "I'm sort of lightlike. I'm not even sitting here. It felt like I'm just detached in some way."

Another woman, who showed both high alpha and deep muscle relaxation on the Greens' monitoring machines, told them that the many sensations had deep internal effects. She said, "It seems like there was some kind of force on the inside, flowing through my forehead out . . . not a hard pressure, but you can feel it, like when you move your hand through water."

Alpha is an experience in internal looking. Many feelings occur when you stop and look inside yourself and begin to pay attention to how you feel. Oriental meditators have used "internal looking" for centuries, and they reach alpha states through their practices. Definite lab-proven alterations occur in their consciousness. If you're not willing to spend years to reach such states, a biofeedback machine might give you a similar perception of your internal state. Those cues of light and tone could act as your guide as you learned about yourself.

Time mentally just to play with the feedback signal seems to make the learning go much faster for most people. Listen to the sound. Let go. In your mind, "feel" that sense of what's happening. Let your feelings tell you how to make the tone stronger. Go with it, and see what happens to you. Feel what happens, as your attention and your consciousness begin to turn inward.

What you are doing is scanning the feel of your mind. As you look inward, you will begin to sense what is happening. This is similar to Yoga meditation with its inward-looking practices. In Sanskrit, this is called "avritti chakshus." Many of the dramatic stories about alpha experiences originate in this inner journey to the specially unique world awaiting inside each one of us.

Positive environment has a lot to do with alpha waves, just as living in a tense situation with uptight people could make you become uptight, too. People bounding about, wondering when you're going to "make a brain wave for them" will actually keep it from happening. Be alone, if you can, and sit still and comfortably in a dim quiet place where you can still your body and your mind. Ignore the electrodes dangling about. Close your eyes. Alpha is fastest and easiest when your eyes are closed. Comfort and relaxation make a difference, too. There's a good reason why those Oriental disciplines recommend the lotus posture, with its crossed legs. In this position, the body is presumed to be perfectly balanced and the muscles relaxed, as tension is more evenly distributed. But, if as a Westerner, used to chairs, the lotus posture is too uncomfortable, head for a large comfortable chair or relaxing couch where you can ignore your body's comfort.

Experimenting with phosphenes, those colored spots most people see when they close their eyes, helped one alpha pilgrim in the beginning stages. You might copy this technique when you try to turn on your alpha.

Most people find it hard to explain how they turn on their alpha, but Dr. John Sinclair had a volunteer who could describe exactly what he did to make alpha happen. At first, the volunteer tried visual techniques, then turned to image games with the phosphenes and mental imagery. As he imagined sights that suited the feeling of alpha, he quickly turned on alpha brain waves. To make his alpha waves flow, he just repeated the same images.

Many of Kamiya's alpha veterans get their alpha waves going by concentrating upon a specific body function or process, like tuning in on their heartbeats, or drifting with the sound of their breathing. Whatever the process is, they let all of their concentration flow upon the one special event. His more experienced alpha subjects reach control and say, "Ah, I've got your task, and now all I have to do is forget about you and your darn tones, and just sit here like I was waiting for a bus, and I do better than if I really tried to do it."

"Free time" seems to have a great effect upon alpha production. Instead of constant trials, Dr. David Nowlis, of Stanford University, begins with an insight time to check out what a person's usual alpha base line is. After that, there are ten to fifteen minutes of "free time." In this free time, each person mentally plays with the feedback tone and tries all kinds of thoughts and images to sense, internally, what happens. Some people choose to watch their own private light shows as they close their eyes and let the phosphenes dance behind their eyelids. This free-time period helped people learn how to produce and control their brain waves more quickly. Following each free-time period, Nowlis gave them a half-dozen runs at trying to suppress alpha, and another half-dozen runs to try to produce a great deal of alpha. Drowsiness can also interrupt your alpha waves by dragging you into theta. Increasing alpha strength is hard if you start to feel sleepy. It might help you to know that this problem is not unique. Zen meditators have this problem and constantly try to realert themselves so they can remain in the brain state they wish to be in.

Most people can suppress, or turn off, their alpha much more easily than they could turn it on, according to researchers Mulholland and Peper. They point out the anxious role of the eyes, so common in civilized man, helps to hold down alpha brain waves. To turn your alpha on, you'll have to turn off your defensive eye maneuvers.

In another alpha study, 3200 miles from the Peper-Mulholland work in Massachusetts, Dr. Jackson Beatty worked with dozens of UCLA students. He found that most well-adjusted people could control their occipital alpha when they had "appropriate strategies for producing the desired changes, but were denied any information about their success in the task, or were given no prior information about strategy, but second by second information about their success in the task was presented." People who had both kinds of information had exactly the same scores as people who had only a pro-alpha strategy, or the feedback information. This would seem to indicate that, by following the keys to turning on alpha already mentioned, you *might* have a good chance of getting alpha, even without adequate machinery. And with an accurate machine, you *would* have a good chance of turning on alpha.

And without information or feedback signal? In the Beatty study, these people showed no changes and no success.

Learning to turn off your alpha is the other side of control. Think of mathematical problems. Blink your eyes rapidly. Squeeze your eyes closed and clench your jaw and concentrate very hard to remember the name of that girl who sat in front of you years ago in Mrs. Wiggens' fifth-grade class. Pay strict attention to the phosphenes and try to analyze them. Or if you are in a dark room, open your eyes and peer closely at your hand to reduce alpha; in a bright room, open your eyes and look hard at the nearest object or persons, and alpha will slide away for awhile. Or try visually to track a moving target. Crook your finger and move it along in front of your eyes, and alpha waves will disappear quickly. Following any moving stimulus cuts alpha even faster than simply trying to look around.

Some educators tend to think that learning to turn off your alpha could help you in classes, or as you try to absorb new information. Attention and alpha have a reverse relationship and increasing eye-flicker rate cuts alpha. Maybe rapidly blinking your eyes as you study those notes for your biology exam or that stock-assets-and-liabilities sheet, could speed up your attention span.

Most studies indicate that alpha consciousness is possible for the general majority to achieve, and it offers a richness of potential mental powers. Specific use of the alpha experience rests with the individual and his own expectations and goals. Enhancing alpha states seems to offer the possibilities of pleasure, new insights and relaxed attentiveness. Ultimately, the power of alpha rests with the individual.

Chapter 4
In
The Beginning
Background and History
of Biofeedback Techniques and
Alpha-Brain-Wave Research

Sea serpents and demons of the deep leaped across the pages of ancient maps of the world, and a hideous abyss awaited the unwary at the spot where the flat earth ended. The early explorer's maps to the unknown now nestle in elegant frames against paneled walls, and gracious voices chatter on about these conversation pieces.

Today, intricate maps give us information about the exact depth of each ocean, the specific height of every mountain, and the precise location of little hamlets, from Pskov to Tucumcarie. How far is it to Bristol? Rand MacNally & Company will give you the correct information—to the centimeter.

The great unknown.

Early "maps" of the brain were just as fanciful as the first geographic maps, filled with dark omnipresent mysteries. One of the earliest guides to the mind was found in Plato's writings, and has influenced thought to this day. Plato argued for the independent reality of Ideas as the only guarantee of ethical standards, and of objective scientific knowledge; that what our senses tell us is a lower order of reality—it is only opinion. Freed from the hold of the senses, Plato found true reality in the world of Ideas, or Forms. Forms were considered a higher Reality, and the physical world, as seen and understood by the senses, considered to have only relative reality. Sensations and interpretations based on perceptual changes are fallible and subjective. Plato separated the world of the intellect and that of the senses and, from this bias against the sensual aspect of man, science, built upon reason, developed a great dislike for "subjective" facts. They followed Plato, who located the "superior rational soul" in the head and denigrated the rest of the body as "the inferior soul."

Centuries later, Marie François Bichat (1771-1802), a French physiologist, divided the responses of a person into two areas. He said that the cerebrospinal nervous system, with its "great brain and spinal cord" governed important skeletal responses. The "little brain," a chain of ganglia running beside the spinal cord, was said to turn on emotional and visceral muscle reactions. This "little brain," and the emotional and visceral reactions, were further demoted by being dubbed "vegetative." It's hard to give much weight to something that is put in the same category as turnips and carrots.

Contemporary scientific findings are overthrowing this sort of thinking. None of these emotional and visceral functions are vegetative, in the literal sense of the word. Instead, all are connected and potentially controllable, making a wonderfully complex organic unity for all reactions. Brand-new discoveries seem to show that "involuntary" responses and emotional experiences can be controlled. Add the element of control and self-regulation, and the vegetative, or inferior, tag goes out the window.

In numerous biology classes, we were taught that functions of the body were compartmentalized. How your hand moves when you think, "Lift, hand" is said to be a voluntary event. How you breathe, and how your heart works, and how your stomach digests food, are said to be involuntary. From the past dark ages of scientific knowledge, all sorts of bizarre deductions were made. Now science tells us that the conclusions we were taught are inaccurate. We really can't help but speculate if actions are truly involuntary, then how could being uptight make us get ulcers? Or nervous headaches? Or high blood pressure? One begins to wonder. . . .

A great battle rages today between behaviorists like Skinner and humanists like Rogers. It's a battle fought with words on paper, but it's a battle over the minds and actions of men, and the results seep into every aspect of our daily living from the way our children are taught to the conditions programmed like Muzak into our working conditions. The humanists de-emphasize the Pavlovian idea of conditioning, and offer, instead, the individual power and responsibility of choice—the possibilities to shape oneself.

Classical conditioning, based on the "involuntary" theory, by giving a stimulus or signal and including some kind of reward, calls forth a desired response. In time, conditioning brings forth the same reward-induced response when the reward is no longer present. Such learning is limited by the need for a reward-response relationship, and takes a lot of time. It literally programs man into acting in a predetermined manner evolved by others. Reinforcement is often necessary.

Alpha-feedback learning is a different kind of learning because it is internalized and self evolved. Alpha learning is instrumental learning through biofeedback. Such instrumental learning is entirely different from conditioning. In feedback-instrumental learning, the response, the stimulus, and the reinforcement are all mixed together. They cannot be considered as the separate entities they are in classical conditioning. Feedback learning calls for a feeling state, an EEG or EMG or GSR frequency, and a cue or control, by light or tone or temperature, to act as a personal guide. All are intertwined, or learning will not happen. Programming of the reinforcement is internalized and related to your own subjective state.

You pick up the internal cues by yourself, as you wish. No one can force you to respond, and force actually negates any feedback response. Alpha feedback demands awareness and conscious thinking to make it work for you. And, once alpha learning through feedback has occurred, it is reported to have a continuous response that evolves without the need for reinforcement in most people.

Instrumental learning is faster, and the learning is its own reward, placing the power back into the hands of the individual. Rewards are internal and subjective and they strengthen the response as you turn the alpha wave on.

Classical conditioning or instrumental learning? The behaviorists or the humanists? The repressed man or the integrated organic man? Other-directed or self-actualized? Establishment or ground-breaker to the Golden Age of man? The dichotomy threatens to rip civilized thought asunder.

But it doesn't have to be this way.

It is possible that these conflicting disciplines each have their own special applications, and each relate to different areas of thought. A marriage of the two might produce a better world for all of us, if each could lower its defenses and learn from the other.

This division in learning would not have occurred if establishment science had paid more attention to some obscure, but important, past experiments.

As early as 1874, an Englishman named Caton noticed electrical current waves in the unknown maps of the brains of monkeys and rabbits. In the *British Medical Journal,* Caton wrote of his experiments with a galvanometer and electric sensors, devices something like electrodes. He placed these electric sensors directly upon the brains of rabbits and monkeys to detect their brain reactions to such stimuli as flashes of light, and arousal from sleep.

In that same era, Thorndike experimented with instrumental learning with some degree of success. But his findings, and those of Caton, were largely ignored because science was bogged down in the Darwinian controversy.

The years passed. The rose budded and bloomed on country estates, and then the petals fell slowly to the ground as time elapsed. Wars ripped the civilized world, and the sound of cannons disturbed the tranquility. Time, and science, had other, more pressing, interests.

In the 1920s, a brilliant European, Hans Berger, placed electrodes outside a man's brain, on his scalp. Excitedly, Berger noted the EEG records that he recorded. He noticed all sorts of electrical energy and began to correlate his discoveries into maps of the mind. He wrote up his findings in 1929, and included numerous details on the actual electrical currents he noted from measuring people's brain waves. In Berger's landmark study, he told of the varieties of frequencies and amplitudes he had seen on his graphs, and tried to relate them to changes in consciousness.

Berger literally discovered the alpha and beta rhythms of the mind's patterns and attempted to see how changes were linked to conscious sensations. His subjects varied, from "normal" people to drug addicts, schizophrenics, maniacs, and epileptics. Mainly, Berger investigated the "psychophysical" mind and body nonduality of human beings. Much of Berger's highly imaginative speculations about consciousness have proven to be true in later lab testing. This genius pioneer might have shown us the way to biofeedback and brain-wave control decades ago, except for the twistings of history. Berger was abruptly "retired" in 1938 by the Nazis.

Again, research lagged. Mostly, the great thrust of science in this period dealt with practical investigation like the "secrets of the atom." But a few lone scientists continued their quiet investigation of man's internal nature and doggedly sought to learn about the patterns of man's mind and the rhythms of brain waves.

In England, dedicated men like Adrian continued the solitary quest. Adrian reported that he had listened to alpha waves from himself and others through a loudspeaker. He analyzed his own feelings about the presence or absence of alpha brain rhythms in his own brain. Shipton, Walter and Walter; Conrot and Gastaut; Howlitt, and Turton all continued studying brain rhythms through the decade. Jasper and Shagass contributed great reams of primary information, working almost as lone outposts of alpha exploration as in the 1940s, they tried to modify alpha blocking with classical conditioning methods.

Others worked in related areas. W. Grey Walter explored the unknown land of the brain, and wrote a valuable guide called *The Living Brain.* Drawing on such findings, Asterinsky and Kleiman studied EEGs, and helped map regions of the brain's functioning. All of these men were fascinated by the way alpha brain waves predominated when the busyness of the visual world was removed.

As society, following the Industrial Revolution, became, by necessity, more and more specialized, academic disciplines were also separated and, finally, segregated; the ideal of the Renaissance man, adept and qualified in multiple fields was out of fashion with the overwhelming increase of information in all scientific fields. Subject specialties were jealously guarded, and little cross-fertilization occurred. Society lost the wonderful creativity that often results from this cross-fertilization of ideas.

The myth of the involuntary-system theory continued to reign, although proof of the contrary was presented. Sometimes, the evidence was rejected because there was not sufficient laboratory proof. At other times, the facts were ignored because they just weren't scientific, although they existed in more mundane corners of life. Houdini, master of magical mysteries, performed a favorite trick time and time again. He swallowed the key to a huge trunk, then had someone lock him securely into the box. The box was hidden, or buried, or dropped into the water and Houdini would "bring" up the key, and unlock himself. This flashy trick demonstrates perfect control of the "involuntary" act of swallowing.

Another form of "involuntary" control was shown many times on theatrical stages. Famous actresses, like Sarah Bernhardt, cried on cue on numerous sparkling stages. This performance shows perfect control of the "involuntary" tear ducts. But this sort of feat was dismissed as a stunt by scientists, although delighted observers of Houdini or Bernhardt would have disagreed.

Some of the lag in knowledge was caused by the primitive nature of experimental "tools." For decades, scientists had to work with crude instruments, as they studied the very subtle workings of the brain. And then came the great technological revolution of transistors and computers and electronic wonder-machines, developments far beyond man's wildest imaginings, aptly called a "revolution for mankind" by Marshall McLuhan. We take these innovations for granted as we flip on a TV set without a second thought, but the technological revolution has revitalized science and society in our time and extended the reach of the scientist's mind dramatically. It is from this techno-logical revolution that biofeedback has evolved, and it promises humankind the opportunity to shape his or her destiny as each pleases.

And today's machinery is just the beginning. Our contempo-rary measurement devices are in the primary stages and much awaits us in the future as we build upon our current knowledge. The brain is covered by a thick semi-conductive layer, removing the observer some distance from the actual source of electrical signals. What we see is not necessarily all that there is to see. Although better than a decade old, today's measuring instru-ments are still crude, and cover only an average over the large area of the brain, because the brain cells are so tiny and so subtly productive of their marvelous energy. Implanted elec-trodes give a more direct answer but, obviously, inserting such electric sensors directly into the brain has its drawbacks.

One reasearcher compares today's techniques to the navy's radio telescope search of outer space for intelligence. The naval experiment skims over predetermined special places in the galaxy for radio signals from other living beings. The areas monitored are chosen for theoretical reasons as possible sources of intelligent signals. The choices might be completely wrong but, for the time being, it's all they have to go upon.

Biofeedback is a beginning.

The new instruments start us on the long march, and some daring and imaginative scientists are heading out into the frontiers of man's mind. From a handful of researchers only a decade and a half ago, the field has expanded, almost overnight, to include some of the finest research minds in the country. Much of today's impetus must be credited to three pioneers in the biofeedback field, who stand out as brave new thinkers in the contemporary journey for knowledge—Dr. Joe Kamiya, Dr. Barbara Brown, and Dr. Thomas Mulholland—although other researchers quickly followed to blaze new trails.

Dr. Joe Kamiya is a husky guru of electronics. As he greets you, smile-ripples crinkle about the corners of his friendly eyes. He seems sensitively aware of your feelings and extends a warm handshake of welcome to his laboratories.

Originally, Kamiya was looking at EEGs, recorded during sleep, for a government-sponsored sleep research project in the 1950s. At that time, he was associated with the University of Chicago and already had a solid background in psychological research. Again and again, he spotted the characteristic alpha rhythm zigzagging across his recordings of various people's brain waves. It was like a detective story, an elusive yet ever-present clue to something. . . . He saw that alpha was present in most people's minds, even when they were awake. As they dozed off, the alpha waves drifted away. Kamiya was curious, and began to wonder if people could control their brain waves at will.

"What does alpha feel like?" he wondered, but, unfortunately, he would have to wait awhile before he got the answer to that question. He would try operant (or instrumental, instead of classical) conditioning to see if one could control his own brain waves. His first subject turned out to be both the most remarkable alpha producer any researcher could pray for—and the most inarticulate imaginable in describing his feelings. As Kamiya was later to describe it, "He must have been sent by God to remind us of man's limitations."

This man was asked to guess his internal brain wave state when a bell rang. After each guess, Kamiya told him whether he was right or wrong. The man went from 50% accuracy, approximately the same probability as chance, to 100% correctness on his fourth day of testing. He knew his internal brain state and named it correctly 400 times in a row.

But when the man was asked to describe what it felt like, he simply could not do so.

Kamiya turned to other subjects. In his first experiments, he used a bell for each subject to signal when they felt that they had turned on alpha brain waves. Later, Kamiya turned to use of a tone for control. Gambling, he took a long shot. Using a standard learning procedure developed for experiments with rats and pigeons, he connected volunteers to EEG machines equipped with filters for individual alpha frequencies. When alpha happened, the electrodes, attached by a special glue to the subject's scalp, carried the message to an EEG machine, and then to graph paper for a record of rhythms. Kamiya began to see that volunteers could control their brain waves and be

taught awareness of their internal geography through the biofeedback mechanism; that people slipped in and out of alpha
rhythms dozens of times a minute, without even knowing it. He
found that people could learn to control their alpha brain waves
with the aid of the instrument.

Kamiya turned to other volunteers to check out his findings,
and he found that almost everyone could learn to sustain alpha.
In 1961, Kamiya moved to San Francisco to the Lanley Porter
Neuropsychiatric Institute, and soon set up an electronic system
including a Schmitt trigger and relay circuit for binary feedback
to signal both alpha-on and alpha-off. Ten people took turns
sitting in his quiet basement lab, and all shortly learned to turn
alpha brain waves on and off at will.

Next came the test of the strength of the alpha brain wave.
Kamiya used biofeedback to teach people to raise their alpha
productions. The more they practiced, the more often could
they make their brain waves respond to their wishes in strengthened quality.

A final, and even more delicate, control was now expected—
increasing and decreasing brain wave strength at will—and again
Kamiya saw it happen. Ten volunteers were soon able to control
the actual rhythm and strength of their own brain waves as they
pleased. In Kamiya's labs, many people learned to hold down
alpha rhythms, and even to cut them out completely. A few
managed to increase their brain wave strength after only four
sessions of training.

Word of Kamiya's research hit the popular press and, within
months, Kamiya was inundated by hoardes of would-be volunteers, many of whom were college students turned on to the
trip of inner awareness and meditation. The furor might have
swamped a lesser man, but Kamiya is dedicated to research. In
his gentle way, he tries to ignore the fuss, and continues his
research. He is now deeply involved in pushing man's knowledge
of subjective states even further. He would like to map a
psychological guide to subjective states, and is exploring visualization and identic imagery, that phenomenon of "photographic" memory. His pretty wife Joanne, works with him now
in an old building on a hilly street in San Francisco. The setting
is stark and unglamorous, but they are engaged in generating

their own kind of excitement. The Kamiya's are able to train volunteers to enhance or suppress alpha brain waves in just a few hours with an intricate audio feedback system and huge computers following every nuance of the brain wave.

Four hundred miles south of Kamiya's lab in San Francisco is the tranquil town of Sepulveda, California, where Dr. Barbara Brown directed her own exciting pioneer research into alpha brain waves and biofeedback training. Dr. Brown is a tiny outspoken woman whose bright intense eyes sparkle with interest. Upon meeting her, one soon senses a deep and sensitive awareness and a keen intelligence beneath her wordly manner and her short-cropped hair.

Barbara Brown is a former pharmacologist, the discoverer of a number of important drugs, who now works with the experiential physiology department at the Veteran's Administration Hospital in Sepulveda, California. Her investigations are conducted in a brick structure set placidly in the middle of dandelion-encrusted lawns far from the bustle of the city. Entering the solid edifice, the smell of cooked cabbage washes over you, and young-old men seem planted about the lobby with no purpose, and even less will to live. Dr. Brown's lab, like most biofeedback laboratories, is relegated to the basement. The elevator to the basement has a defective light, and the descent into nether regions is marked by a dark ominous glow. As you step out, you find that many rooms are locked with special keys, and husky keepers seem to be everywhere. And then you enter Dr. Brown's quarters, and the electric warmth of discovery and purpose hits you like a shock wave in contrast to the rest of the hospital. Here is order. Here is knowledge. Here is a positive feeling saying "yes, it can be" to the rest of the hospital universe. And, here, too, is a bright feminine intelligence searching for answers to some of man's oldest questions.

Dr. Brown's firm place in the history of biofeedback was attained through her studies of EEGs. Where others used a tone, she worked with a light as a cue to control. Originally, she studied EEG responses to a variety of perceptual stimuli, and related these to the strength of the recall of facts. As she worked, she began to see individual variations in responses to different colors; this gave new insight into subjective factors of perception. People who were visualizers, strong in their visual imagination, had a certain special response to colors.

"I was very curious to know that, if they did indeed have different brain electrical responses to such common things as colors, did they as well have different sets of subjective associations? And, to this end, I thought, 'How can I find out something about subjective activity, particularly this kind of subjective activity?' It finally occurred to me that I could just let the subjects make their own colors. That's how I happened into the feedback business," Dr. Brown relates.

Her studies were conducted in a quiet cubicle, as she monitored reactions in a nearby room jammed full of electronic devices. As each person kept his eyes open, he tried to find an image or feeling that would keep on a blue light, to signify alpha for as long as possible. For an hour and a half, each one sat alone in that study room, as he grew conscious of his internal feelings and learned to control his own brain waves.

Highly significant degrees of alpha-enhanced activity were achieved in the first practice sessions for most subjects. Sixty percent of the volunteers showed specific reactions in their responses to a light-signal situation, as compared to the lack of response of any in the control group, where the same experiment was conducted with other volunteers without a light signal. Those who achieved the strongest enhanced alpha seemed to narrow their perceptions and achieve a feeling of a pleasant state.

In one of her experiments, a volunteer sat in a small room. Dim light barely illuminated the corners of the chamber. He sat in a comfortable chair mounted with a speaker and a microphone to a recording area, and watched a tiny blue light, shining through a cone and enlarged in a square Styrofoam box. Little noise crept into the virtually soundproof room. Some volunteers were young, others, up to sixty years of age; some were hospital personnel, while others were curious college students. For each one, the blue light shone every time they managed to turn on their alpha waves with their eyes open. Most, quickly understood how to turn on the light and keep it on by turning on their alpha brain waves.

Noticing how quickly people learned to control their alpha

brain waves made Dr. Brown decide that such learning was more an insight learning function than a conditioning learning function. Each one was actually interacting with himself, with a new knowledge of his own internal state. Somehow, each managed to activate a special kind of brain-wave activity. The learning lasted and became a new skill even after a great deal of time passed between alpha trials in Dr. Brown's lab.

Was the brain-wave control connected to feelings in some way? Dr. Brown set up a unique experiment that let each person use his subjective state to turn on his own colors through controlled brain waves. Different kinds of brain waves turned on different light shows, and volunteers had no difficulty in turning on special color patterns unique to beta, theta, and alpha waves. This fun had a serious purpose as it demonstrated how people could control their brain waves. In about thirty minutes, most people could turn patterns on at will, and easily reproduce special designs as they were fed back unique information about their different kinds of brain waves.

Dr. Brown soon set up numerous other experiments and, time after time, saw volunteers quickly learn to control their own brain rhythms. Soon, she joined with other research scientists, and was forceful in promoting the Biofeedback Research Society, a brand-new organization dedicated to sharing feedback knowledge among researchers. She served as its first president, and speaks of "getting all the scientists together to introduce new ideas and save time as we share our knowledge." To date, she commented, the society attracts two kinds of members: older department heads who are interested in knowing what new information is being surfaced, and new investigators, who are excited by revelations in a new field.

Another pioneer, and past president of the Biofeedback Society, is Dr. Thomas Mulholland, who discovered some of the initial facts about alpha and biofeedback in his work at the Perception Laboratory at the Veteran's Administration Hospital in Bedford, Massachussetts. From time to time, other scientists, like Dwan, Evans, Runnals, and Peper, joined with him in his scientific journeys. Dr. Mulholland concentrated on occipital alpha, and began to wonder about the oculomotor (or seeing) activity, and its connection with changing EEG. Dr. Mulholland worked with a tone-control biofeedback, and saw that his subjects could voluntarily control their own alpha brain waves without eye movements. "Seeing" had been linked to brain-wave production.

In a 1969 study with Erik Peper, Dr. Mulholland found that most people could quickly turn off their alpha brain waves, but only a handful were able to turn them on as they wished. Repeated trials saw little improvement in performance, and made Mulholland wonder if feedback methods affected the dynamics of the system being studied, as motivation influenced results. This is reminiscent of Heisenberg's indeterminancy (uncertainty) principle, that the act of studying something actually changes it because it is being studied, as the atom observed in the microscope is altered *because it is being observed,* and its original condition has been interfered with. Mulholland has continued his work to learn what clues biofeedback might give us to internal states, and he has led the way in describing the relationship between brain waves and the orienting response.

Different areas were investigated at the Menninger Foundation in the heartland of America at Topeka, Kansas, by a husband-and-wife research team, Dr. Elmer and Ms. Alyce Green. They worked with student volunteers, housewives, and local businessmen to study voluntary and self-control of mind and body processes. Biofeedback was their tool as they ventured into a multitude of areas about possible voluntary regulation of the central nervous system and other involuntary regions.

Alpha brain waves was only one area of their biofeedback investigation. The Greens examined theta brain waves and were able to link this rhythm to creativity, the ability to recall past events, and the feeling of reverie. They examined EEG and other recordings of a yogi master adept at voluntary control of self. Temperature self-regulation was another important investigative area, and they often used portable alpha detectors for home training. Many of their findings were to present serious challenges to Establishment medicine and the usual treatment of psychosomatic illnesses.

Could the average person control the blood flow in his body? Could he increase the temperature of his hands and feet as he pleased? Could he cool the temperature of his forehead at will? In their compact labs, the Greens set out to find the answers to these questions.

For a month, with twice-a-week-sessions of one and a half hours, each volunteer would run through a series of muscular relaxation exercises, blood-flow control routines, and, finally, control of production of alpha brain waves with biofeedback training. Separate electrodes recorded EKG pickups for the volunteer's heart rate, and EMG for muscle tension. Alpha brain waves were detected along with theta and delta waves from the occipital area of the head. With continued work, each volunteer could easily produce alpha brain waves, even when he was talking and recalling childhood memories. At the same time, some volunteers could also control the amount of muscle tension, the temperature of specific body areas, and numerous other "involuntary" body functions.

The ability to recall is important to education, psychotherapy, and to increasing one's creativity. The Greens found that recall was remarkably correlated to the percentage of alpha production. High alpha producers were also able to recall 60% of the material read to them. This is about twice the recall ability of the average person. For a moment, imagine the possibilities of doubling your memory capacity. This is what the Greens demonstrated in their experiments.

The Greens were also interested in the specific characteristics of creativity and believe creativity is dependent upon image-producing ability and recall powers. They found that creativity is linked to alpha and theta brain wave states, and managed to teach people to enhance these brain-wave experiences.

In other experiments, they showed that the no-pain states of meditative masters could be reproduced through feedback training, and that average people could learn to control their body temperature and relaxation level enough to get rid of migraine headaches without medication. Dr. Joseph Sargent was later to apply their theories in a broad clinical situation and achieve fantastic success at "curing" migraine headaches.

Around the same time, at the Department of Anatomy at Queen's University in Kingston, Ontario, in Canada, Dr. John Basmajian was training people to fire individual motor-nerve cells through biofeedback. When you recall that there are six billion nerve cells in the brain, such minute control is really astounding.

Motor units vary in size from directing as few as four or five muscle fibers to controlling as many as a couple of thousand muscle fibers from one unit. Messages sent to a general region travel at a rate of from four to six impulses per second to as much as fifty or sixty impulses per second, but they all have one element in common: When a muscle message comes, like a director's command, every muscle fiber reacts in the same way. Each muscle fiber responds instantly by twitching for the same amount of time, about eight milliseconds. This action is due to an electrical phenomenon called depolarization of the muscle membrane.

Knowing that this identical muscle response occurs, Dr. Basmajian managed to reduce reaction to the finest, most individual denominator, the single motor unit. Subjects had electrical units implanted within a muscle by means of a hypodermic needle that left behind delicate bipolar wire electrodes to pick up electrical impulses. The sound of each individual muscle-nerve fiber traveled through the wires to an amplifier, where it was magnified many times. The sound of the "firing" helped each person be aware of his nerve action, since he could hear its sound, like rhythmical drumming.

Basmajian found that each motor-nerve unit has its own individual signature or fingerprint, again reminding us of the unique individuality we all possess. In Basmajian's experiments, normal people learned to isolate a single motor unit from the other 100-200 in a tiny area. Within fifteen to twenty minutes of feedback training, as they heard the sound of their own bodies, everyone could suppress all the units or fire single units or manipulate those units or turn them on and off easily.

This delicate individual control of single spinal motor units was proven by all kinds of people, of all ages, sexes, and class backgrounds, from manual workers to college professors. Even small children, under six years of age, learned to gain conscious control by firing individual nerve units quickly. Turning on those microscopic bodies of the motor-nerve units let them feed information, as they wished, to fibers in the miniscule motor nerves. This could mean great rehabilitation possibilities for cerebral palsy and other palsy victims, wounded soldiers, and muscularly disabled people. When one motor-nerve unit is destroyed, it may be possible to activate another to replace the function of the destroyed cell.

Electrode implantation has its drawbacks, so Dr. David Kahn developed another variety of feedback to teach nerve control. He harnessed muscle cells electronically to strobe lights through electrodes glued to the surface of the skin. The strobe light flashes illuminated a screen filled with pictures. With normal firing, the light flashes were too brief to actually see the picture on anything but a subliminal level. With control, someone could turn on the picture fully for as long as he wanted it to appear.

It is believed that much of biofeedback learning happens on a subconscious level, using areas of the mind that we do not normally know how to utilize. Kahn's work adds weight to this theory. In Kahn's labs, those pictures lasted only an instant but, somehow, subjects could see the slides and perceive the scenes. In every case, distressing scenes had no effect on "learning," and people actually decreased muscle firing rate so that they would not have to see unpleasant pictures. Pleasing scenes were another story. Enjoyable images were spotted, and quickly "turned on in every case, controlled by the muscle firing rate." On a subconscious level, people decided whether they wanted to look at a particular scene, or not.

A very different sort of study was going on, on an animal level, throughout the country, but these experiments were to provide equally surprising insights into the possible control of individual systems and the roots of pleasure in creatures.

Among the palms and the brick buildings—monuments to donor's immortality—at the University of California at Los Angeles, Drs. Maurice B. Sterman and Wanda Wyrwicka used feedback to train cats. Sterman and Wyrwicka concentrated upon both the alpha rhythm and the sensorimotor area.

Watching a localized region, they saw cats whose contentment with the pleasures of brain sensation even overrode their survival instincts and their wish for food. Amazingly, the cats preferred turning on pleasing brain rhythms to bowls of milk, even when they were hungry. In another experiment on the sensorimotor rhythm area of the brain, feedback-trained cats were able to avoid dangerous convulsions from a toxic drug. What changes had occurred in their minds? Somehow, the feedback training had increased their ability to withstand bodily shocks. Untrained cats were given the same toxic drug and quickly sickened and died with shivering convulsions. Such seizure-avoidance control intrigued Dr. Sterman, and he went on with his sensorimotor investigation. Currently, through biofeedback to the sensorimotor region, he is attempting to train epileptics to avoid debilitating seizures. To date, he reports success. Perhaps such training may help make epileptic seizures a malady of the past.

In related experiments, Dr. Tassarini used feedback training, in 1968, to help people control the occurrence of epileptic brain-wave disorders, and Dr. Neal E. Miller has used feedback training to aid epileptics in suppressing the abnormal parox-ysmal brain wave spikes in their EEGs. Dr. Miller originally worked with animals in biofeedback training. He used these techniques to teach animals to control an amazing list of glandular and visceral responses including heart rates, intestinal constrictions, kidney functions, amount of blood in the stomach wall, blood pressure, independent of heart rate, blood flow in specialized areas of the skin as well as control of brain-wave activity. It is possible that his unique studies may open the pathways to new avenues for self control (control of self) in human beings. Before Miller's work, many scientists believed that instrumental learning (feedback learning of such phenomenon as alpha waves or muscle relaxation) was only useful for the "superior" cerebrospinal central nervous system. To control that "inferior" emotional, visceral, or autonomic nervous system, it was believed that you must turn to classical conditioning.

Miller, and various associates including Leo Di Cara, Trowill, and others, knew that past instrumental training of the auto-nomic system had been disputed because scientists credited the learned responses to simple skeletal response. Faulty methods had been cited. This is very much like the thermometer that registers a fever pitch because you washed it off in hot water before you used it.

To meet this challenge, animals in Miller's work were immobilized with curare, a South American arrow poison with a paralytic action used by Indians on war darts to wipe out their enemies by stilling all life processes. (Curare is also used medicinally as a muscle relaxant during shock therapy and in combination with anesthesia during surgery.) Artificial respiration had to be given to the animals so that they could continue breathing after the curare was administered. In such drugged states, skeletal responses alone were absolutely impossible. Again, and again, Miller managed to teach internal controls to the animals. Since they were totally immobilized, the only possible explanation for the animals' new skills was the feedback training.

Miller published reports on his work, and the old voluntary-involuntary theory began to look as though it had as much substance as a paper tiger. Animals could control their internal functions and, perhaps, man could achieve the same sort of success. Miller was to go on to test his ideas on human beings, and science might have to rewrite the textbooks.

"Biofeedback should be well worth trying on any symptom, functional or organic, that is under neural control," Miller speculates; the method might be useful for anything "that can be continuously monitored by modern instrumentation, and for which a given direction of change is clearly indicated medically—for example, cardiac arrhythmias, spastic colitis, asthma, and those cases of high blood pressure that are not essential compensation for kidney damage."

Miller's predictions may not be as exaggerated as they seem at first reading. He has had astonishing success in his experiments. Some animals actually learned to alter the thickness of their stomach walls. Others learned such fine blood-vessel control that they could dilate some vessels, constrict others, and turn one ear white and the other ear brilliantly pink simultaneously. Because of this learned control, Miller challenges the old belief that autonomic nervous systems and visceral responses operate independently of animal or human control.

To some scientists in the West, this news came as a shock, but it need not have been. British colonists had told of such control in the East, and Western scientists like Wegner and Bagchi had observed Yoga masters who could do such things as make their foreheads prespire upon command while also increasing systolic blood pressure.

Oriental meditative disciplines, like Yoga and Zen, hinted at internal controls. Dalal and Barber had studied yogis and cautiously concluded, "There is evidence to indicate . . . that the breath and posture exercises which are a part of some, but not all, systems of yoga may be accompanied by significant autonomic changes, and may give rise to enduring changes in autonomic balance with possible beneficial effects on mental and physical health."

It takes years for control to be achieved in Yoga and Zen meditative disciplines, but the mental shorthand of biofeedback training works almost overnight.

Tomorrow is a very long time . . . or is it? Tomorrow, for mankind, may be waiting at the door . . . perhaps we need only lift the latch . . . and turn on the biofeedback machine.

Part Two:
Specific
Alpha Research
Applications

Chapter 5
Stress:
The Civilized
Killer
Psychosomatic Illness and Biofeedback

Stress.

The civilized killer.

The stress of living, and somehow surviving, in our complex world stalks us all, reaching out tentacle fingers to wrap us in tension and weariness. And slowly, but oh, so surely, stress wears down our bodily universes with the crush of surviving, just as the storms and writhings of the earth eventually wear down the sharp rocks of the mountains.

Psychosomatic illness is an old-fashioned term, a put-down description for every sort of ailment from migraine headaches, tension headaches, high blood pressure, heart attacks, respiratory ailments, ulcers and colitis to mysterious pains in the back. Some psychosomatic illnesses are backed up by solid physical damage, while others, induced by tension, are still at an early stage where the organic damage is not yet serious. It doesn't matter what the cause is to the person suffering from pain, because the pain is all too real. Whether it originates in the mind of the overly anxious, or stems from an ill-functioning organ, the pain is equally real and, in time, the organic damage that can result is also equally real, regardless of its origin.

A pain is a pain is a pain.

Or is it? If, somehow, we might all have the power to cure stress-related ills through the mind, we. . . .

It is this promise that biofeedback seems to hold out, tempting us with the possibilities of new powers over ourselves. Will the promise become a reality? Tomorrow holds the answer but, for a few lucky individuals, today in the laboratories has already given them a "medicine" beyond their wildest dreams.

It seems ironic that America is providing the home for the new "medicine" of biofeedback training to eliminate psychosomatic illness, because Americans gulp down more drugs to rid themselves of stress-related problems than any other nation in the world. Have a headache? Take an aspirin. Have indigestion from eating overly preserved adulterated food? Take a relief pill. The TV waves ripple out the message: Pills for this, and pills for that. Pills to make you feel happy. Pills to make your stomach shift from acid to alkaline. Pills to get rid of that headache. Pills to take away that menstrual cramp. Pills. Buttons of pleasure or pain relief to deaden your feelings. Pills. Pills. Pills.

Perhaps the answer to the great onslaught of civilization's ills is already with us. Twenty-five million people in this country suffer from hypertension, the product of being uptight, nervous, and unable to relax, among other reasons. Like many family physicians, Dr. Martin Patterson wonders if hypertension might not be relieved if "only people knew how to relax, instead of tense up, when challenging situations come along."

Biofeedback training promises to teach you how to relax. Quickly. Efficiently. Thoroughly. And, as you relax, the terrible inroads that stress-induced illness make upon the human body might just fade away. In some daring experimental labs, dramatic evidence of such fading away of stress illness has been presented. Does this mean that the same thing could happen for you? It all depends. . . .

Psychosomatic illness is not new, nor is medicine to relieve psychosomatic symptoms. "It's all in your mind," is a be-whiskered homily, and physicians even have an organization devoted to solving psychosomatic ills, the American Psychosomatic Society. Eighteenth- and nineteenth-century medical literature is rich in reports by physicians trying to solve the connection between psychologic reactions and subsequent bodily illness. Today, the word "psychosomatic" is shunned by the general public as connoting a negative fact to be swept under the rug. "Stress-related illness" is a more popular way to describe that headache you get, when the traffic gets so snarled, or that mysterious ache in your side that only happens when the children are yelling too loudly. Such patterns of psychosomatic defenses against stress and challenge are believed to begin at an early age. With time, such habits become ingrained as the body learns too well how to cramp up, tense up, or throb with anguish.

In a thought-provoking essay, biofeedback researcher Dr. Neal Miller drew a connection between biofeedback training and psychosomatic medicine. "Suppose a child is terror-stricken at the thought of going to school in the morning because he is completely unprepared for an important examination," Miller says. "The strong fear elicits a variety of fluctuating autonomic symptoms, such as a queasy stomach at one time, and pallor and faintness at another; and, at this point his mother, who is particularly concerned about cardiovascular symptoms, says, 'You are sick, and must stay home.' The child feels a great relief from fear, and this reward should reinforce the cardiovascular responses producing pallor and faintness."

And when he is a grown man? And he is unprepared for his grad school orals? Or can't figure out how to pay his income taxes? Or has to cope with a demanding boss? Or . . . ? Back may come that learned response of queasy stomach and pallor and faintness in a retreat from challenge. He has learned to cope by copping out. Such psychosomatic symptoms may have been taught to him at an early age in a form of instrumental autonomic learning. Miller says these symptoms might be reversed through another kind of instrumental learning, biofeedback training.

For the past nineteen years, a neurophysiologist and physician, Dr. George Whatmore, has used external feedback (for muscle action potentials) to help patients with various functional disorders. He begins with extensive tests to be sure there is "no lesion, no anatomical lesion, no structural alterations" causing the problem. If no structural problem is present, Dr. Whatmore begins to suspect a functional problem and turns to EMG feedback. Some of these patients are so ill that they have been hospitalized because of their psychosomatic illnesses.

Tension is the culprit looked for by Dr. Whatmore. According to this physician, tension may be the cause of such varied problems as backache, circulatory disorders, depression, colitis, and skin eruptions. He blames these problems on "wrong effort, wrong energy expenditures . . . a form of misdirected effort," which he calls disponesis.

Stress makes most of us tense up habitually without even being aware that we have tightened our muscles, according to Whatmore's theory. Different people tense up in different ways, and the anxiety may not be outwardly visible. Internally, it reverberates throughout many parts of the nervous system. Whatmore searches for evidence of misdirected effort, or tensing, with electrodes placed upon muscle groups. An EMG machine picks up the muscle tension, and when it seems higher than statistical controls, Whatmore tells his patient of the tension. Often, patients are surprised to learn that they have been tensing up, or bracing.

Bracing is what happens when you tighten up to meet a challenge. Some people brace up in the throat region, and others in the arms and legs. The location of the pain or illness is not always in the same place as the tense bracing event.

Although he searches for the tension in the muscles of patients because that is most convenient and practical, Whatmore looks upon the human body as a circuit. He once described the body as a feedback circular mechanism running from the motor and premotor cortex. Whatmore said, "The interconnected collateral fibers feed 'tense up' information right into the reticular activating system, right into the hypothalmus, the limbic system, and also in the neo-cortex. . . ." He believes widespread repercussions occur from excessive excitatory or inhibitory signals being fired into the circuit.

Controversy surrounds Whatmore's theory of "disponesis," but it does suggest an explanation of how body habits could cause psychosomatic problems. The frustrated salesman may desperately want to make a sale. Before he enters the office, he braces his body as if preparing to fight, with muscle movements so minute that he doesn't realize he's on guard and ready for the fray. But the battle is verbal, and the "fight" reactions are never really dissipated with body action. If this becomes a habit, his own agitation increases, his bodily chemistry changes in constant "fight anticipation," and, perhaps indigestion, and later, ulcers, follow. (This is a hypothesis, a possible explanation.)

Some patients respond quickly to Whatmore's methods, but middle-aged people usually need a year or two of feedback training to recognize their habit of tensing, and then to rid themselves of the "habit."

According to Whatmore, action potentials include the performing efforts, bracing efforts, representative efforts, minute tongue and throat efforts, and attention efforts. The performing efforts are the overt in-between movements that accompany any of our motions: between the beginning and the end result. Bracing efforts are those motions which hold the body rigid or on guard; minute eye motions to picture things are the representative efforts; and attention efforts come as we pay attention to sensory information. Whatmore works to ease unnecessary bracing efforts as we put our bodies on guard.

Biofeedback information is used to help people spot when they are tensing needlessly, to cut down on misdirected effort and the physical damage that might result. But lab training is only the first step in the treatment. Self-awareness must be practiced in daily life to monitor reactions, and turn on relaxation.

"A person doesn't have to stop what he is doing . . . he can keep right on with what he is doing, but cut down as much as he can on the misdirected effort component . . . and continue the well-directed effort component," Whatmore commented to the Biofeedback Society. But, it takes judgment and quick correction. Whatmore cautions, "If he does this quickly enough, he can abort the headache . . . if he catches it too late, the headache has a certain momentum of its own and will continue unless you take something to stop it, like, medication."

Time and again, in clinical practice, Whatmore's techniques have proved effective in "curing" psychosomatic illness with EMG feedback. But, perhaps because his patients are so "set" in their bad bodily habits, his procedure takes more time than many physicians would be willing to spend. "A year is too long to cure a backache," one general practioner commented, and continued to prescribe pain-killing drugs instead. But, what if the backache persists? Or, what if that pain-killing drug has negative side-effects?

Such "if's" might be better met by the more complex feedback training of the Greens at the Menninger Foundation. They mix feedbacks of EMG, EEG, body temperature, and a version of Luthe's autogenic training (conscious self-regulation) for relaxation. The Green method works much more quickly than Whatmore's, achieving success within a few sessions of one and a half hours each, compared to months, or even years, using Whatmore's technique.

How do the Greens do it? "For control of the voluntary system, it is necessary to use *active* volition; for control of the involuntary nervous system, it is necessary to use *passive* volition. . . . It might best be described as detached effortless volition." Green explained in a paper published in 1970.

People achieve this control by feeling what to do. Getting mental contact smacks of nineteenth-century terminology, but a housewife, who learned to raise the temperature of her hands by ten degrees in two and a half minutes merely by thinking about it, explained that she did it by "getting mental contact."

"When I first ran across that phrase [getting mental contact], I thought it was very funny," Green told the 1969 Biofeedback Society conferees. "But, after we worked with thirty-five housewives and trained them in blood flow control of the hands, and then asked them how they did it . . . they sort of described this . . . they had the feeling inside in some sort of internal representation that they had made mental contact. They have a feelingness that they've got it . . . those who had it, could do it. And those who didn't, couldn't."

People who could do it, literally "thought" the heat into their hands. Green explains it is done by visualization: "You visualize what you want to have happen, instruct the body to do it, and then you detach yourself from it. That's passive volition," Dr. Green said. "Use passive volition, and the autonomic nervous system does it. Use active volition, and the autonomic nervous system does just the opposite, usually. When you *try* to get the hands warm, the hands get cold."

Could alpha brain wave control alone give us such powers? It seems much too early to say. Relaxation is not necessary for alpha waves, but relaxation seems to be present in most high-alpha producers, and these people tend to have more relaxed and easygoing personalities. It is possible that relaxation might be extended to the skeletal musculature, and even to the autonomic nervous system.

Some scientists express their concerns over controlling brain waves like the alpha rhythm, and speak of the possible dangers that might result from interference with normal processes of the cortex. Dr. Wolf answered this objection by telling the Biofeedback Society of concerned researchers that, "All we are doing is training out interfering factors, so that the person becomes truly himself, and responds as a free individual without the interference. I don't think that by removing interferences you can harm anybody. . . . I think that if there are dangers of any kind, that they [the subjects] would be too lethargic, too placid." He, and other feedback scientists, pointed out some of the negative processes that have resulted from autogenic training.

Biofeedback training to treat stress problems would have to be learned from a skilled therapist or physician. The long history of autogenic training records disasters and hazards in cardiovascular dysfunction, and other complications brought on by improper use of the methods (like strain to the heart, resistance, and damage to organs). It is possible to produce a blister by hypnotic suggestion. Such localized effects can be either positive or negative.

Another researcher pointed out: "If this tool [biofeedback] is as powerful as we seem to think it is, it can do harm. Some of the things we are doing might possibly induce excess passivity in certain patients with a problem of passivity to begin with." For this reason, feedback use for medical reasons would have to be directed by a qualified scientist or physician.

Biofeedback training could be a potentially powerful weapon, and the scientists' concern is understandable. Surprising changes seem to be indicated by research findings.

Biofeedback might radically alter the physical and psychological being of individuals. The possibilities are not to be taken lightly, or dismissed as a parlor trick, or just one more fad. If feedback is handled wisely and well, it could provide dramatic help to anyone who wanted to relax away stress-induced problems, pains, and complications.

Motivation is a prime ingredient in learning to control bodily functions and brain waves. "If people have confidence, then they can do it," Dr. Johann Stoyva reminds us. Somehow, when people believe they can make their muscles relax or think they can make theta or alpha brain waves occur or know that they can turn on the brain "spindles" of sleep and turn them off again at will, it happens, and they are successful. And the results may last the rest of your life. A former student of Miller's, Dr. Leo Di Cara, worked with Dr. Jay Weiss; he taught some animals to accelerate their heart rates and other animals to slow their pulse rates. Later, the animals who had accelerated heart rates simply could not handle shock situations, and squealed pathetically at the experience of shock. The animals who knew how to slow pulse rates quickly learned how to avoid the impact of shock by lowering their heart rates.

Di Cara's experiments hint at the possibility that habitual emotional responses, like increased heart rate from stress and shock,heighten anxiety and increase stress impacts. On the other hand, the ability to control body functions would seem to help in handling stress more efficiently, and to help individuals get out of that vicious circle of stress-uptightness-pain and more stress.

Stress is a tenant of our daily lives. For most of us, events happen quickly. Earthquakes wipe out thousands, in moments, in South America. Guerilla warfare spreads across continents. A great plague sweeps over Africa. Our government overflows with new directives reaching into everyone's life. In two short days, from dawn to dawn, you could fly completely around the globe on metal wings far beyond anything Icarus imagined. And this great chaotic influx of challenge and response to stressful information flows on and on. Media overkill. Somehow, the painful death of a young soldier becomes distant as you watch it on the evening news, and your mind begins to blank out as it suffocates the unpleasantness in a blanket of unreality. But your human body recognizes its animal nature, and knows and reacts to the distress in ways so subtle you cannot even detect them consciously. People can't relax, because things happen too fast. Although you tense for the onslaught of the stress, the battle never comes as it is washed away in a plastic sea of transistor tubes.

Perhaps another sort of machine may provide the answer. It may be that the machines of biofeedback can show you the way out of that vicious circle of stress.

Chapter 6
The Branching Tree
Applying Feedback to Psychosomatic Illness

You've just got to learn to relax a little, They tell you . . . but how does that advice help the decent hard-driving man, who's holding down two jobs, as he tries to make enough money to keep his family fed and clothed and warm under that heavily mortgaged suburban roof?

You mustn't let little things upset you so much, They tell you . . . but how does that comment ease the throbbing migraine headache, of the working mother who must somehow, anyhow, in any way, cope with a monotonous typing job by day, and race from cooking to dishes to laundry to sewing at night?

It's all in your mind, They tell you . . . but that's little comfort to the thousands of insomniacs who lie awake each night thinking and concentrating upon problems as they desperately wish they could fall asleep.

And tomorrow promises more of the same. For some, tomorrow means high blood pressure, as they join the ranks of the more than twenty-five million people in the United States already suffering from hypertension. For others, tomorrow brings crippling ulcers, and no chance to enjoy that rich food they've earned with the sweat of their minds and muscles and painful compromises.

Many of us can't say "chuck it," and take to the road as hippies. Instead of fleeing from the pains of civilization that cause such psychosomatic illness, we stay. And work on. And, in increasing numbers, we begin to ache, or bleed, or cough from the varied distresses of psychosomatic illnesses.

Biofeedback training just might hold the answers for some of these ailments. First came the idea that alpha brain waves could be trained with biofeedback techniques. That seedlike theory has now grown, as lab after lab has tested it in clinical situations. Like a branching tree, the theory matured and expanded. There is something exciting about the idea "whose time has come," and biofeedback seems to be in this category. In a few seasons, the clinical experiments that have shown such amazing success in licking psychosomatic problems may be available to everyone all over the country.

In Baltimore, Dr. Bernard T. Engel, a psychologist, has taught patients to speed, slow, and narrowly regulate their heart rates. Dr. Engel, in experiments with Theodore Weiss, M.D., and Dr. Eugene Bleecker, a cardiovascular specialist, used audio and visual feedback to help patients learn how to control irregular heart rhythms at the Gerontology Research Center of the National Institute of Child Health and Development. Most of Engel's patients suffered from P.V.C.s, premature ventricular contractions, a common and dangerous irregularity of heartbeat concerned with the main pumping chamber of the heart.

How did they control their hearts? Dr. Engel once told a *Newsweek* reporter that the process is "like an athlete who does something well. He's grooving." His patients actually "think" their heart rates faster or slower with biofeedback, and gain personal mastery. You cannot do this without biofeedback and, if you just tried to use your mind without the machinery, you could actually cause damage to your heart.

One of Engel's patients was a thirty-six-year-old woman who had an eight-year history of documented P.V.C.s, and was somewhat overweight. She told of "a big thumping feeling" in her chest that occurred whenever she was angry or excited. She learned to speed her heart by thinking "about arguments with her children, and about running through a dark street." To slow her heart, she "thought about swinging back and forth in a swing." After her training, the P.V.C.s still returned occasionally, but she was able to stop them at home by turning on her slow-down swing thoughts.

Another of Engel's patients, a sixty-two-year-old man with a history of one myocardial infarction (the stoppage of a canal or passage resulting from coronary thrombosis). He had occasional angina upon exertion, and P.V.C.s on many occasions. He learned to speed his heart by thinking about "pushing or forcing" his heart to the left, and by being conscious of its rapid beating. To slow his heart, this man concentrated upon feeling as if his heart was "slowing down and stopping." After training, he still had some problems, but he could stop his P.V.C.s after fifteen to twenty minutes at home. How did he do it? By thinking about it! When his angina worsened, Engel readmitted him to the center, and began more feedback training, plus prescribing a drug, quinidine. The P.V.C.s were substantially reduced.

These, and other patients, were able to speed up or slow down their heart rates by as much as twenty percent over a set base rate. Acquiring this skill allows people to even out irregular beats. Scientists do not know why it happens, but, once someone learns to change a heart rate at will, his heart rate will smooth out and no longer be characterized by great dangerous irregularities.

"Their training and ability to lessen the number of premature beats makes their probability of sudden death statistically less," Dr. Engel commented. Heart-rate control is a learned skill. Dr. Engel compares this skill of controlled heart rate to the learning of a practicing golfer.

Mistake after mistake is made as the golfer slices away. Finally, he slams a ball perfectly down the middle of the fairway. The golfer may not "know" exactly what he did right, but he usually says that "it felt good." And, somehow, the next perfect hit down the fairway follows. And the next. And the next. This happens because the golfer has acquired the skill to perform the job. The golfer may give up golf then, and abandon the sport for years. Years later, he decides to join some friends for a game of golf, and he's amazed to learn that he hits the ball straight down the fairway. Once we learn to do it correctly, certain kinds of skills, like skating, swimming, tennis, and golf, seem to stay with us for life.

It is thought that controlling one's own heart rate is just such a skill. Once a heart patient learns how to do it, it seems that he can continue to do it throughout his life. For example, one of Engel's patients could still control his heart rate two years after Engel had trained him in the task with feedback. Why does this happen? A cardiovascular specialist speculated that biofeedback activates an unknown or primitive body perception in the mind, and this act completes a loop within someone, giving him the skill to monitor his visceral functions at will.

Engel and his associates first tested the feedback training method on people with normal heart rates, before they began to work with patients with heart-rate problems. All patients had been referred to them by private physicians in the Baltimore area.

In the pioneer experiment, Engel worked slowly. A handful of volunteers underwent thirty training sessions in his tiny windowless training room. Each session lasted about eighty minutes, and the first ten sessions dealt with speeding up the heart rate. The next ten sessions were devoted to slowing down the heart beat. In the last ten sessions, volunteers tried to alternate from fast to slow heart rates upon command. Finally, each one attempted to regulate his heart rate without any feedback, to prepare himself for living needs removed from the laboratory situation. Normal volunteers did well. Later, eight heart patients with severe arrythmic problems, heart-rate irregularities, did almost as well as the normal volunteers. Four heart patients learned to alter their heart rate and totally control beats at home, without drugs. Some managed to get twenty percent speeding and slowing rates. They could increase or decrease their heart rates by about sixteen beats a minute from an eighty beat per minute base rate.

A typical training session began in Engel's dark sound-proof chamber at the Baltimore City Hospital. All patients continued their regular heart medication before the testing began, and fully documented EKG's were obtained on all patients. Each patient would lie upon a bed with two electrodes glued to his or her chest. The electrodes were connected to a cardiotachometer which electrically signaled the heart rate, and was connected to a light mechanism sitting on a table near the foot of the bed. This light device had three lights: yellow for "the right thing," green for showing increasing heart rate, and red to warn someone to decrease heart rate. The goal was to keep the yellow light shining for longer and longer periods. Next to the light was a meter that gave a percentage reading for how long someone had successfully kept the yellow light on, and done "the right thing."

After learning the skill, Engel's patients were delighted at the feeling of personal mastery they had acquired. This positive reaction is common in people who've used feedback-gained skills to defeat psychosomatic problems. Engel cautions that his method is still in the clinical experimental stage and points out that "some patients who are improving actually get frightened because their (newly acquired) more normal heartbeat seems so strange to them. They think they're going to die." With time, people grow used to their irregular heartbeats, and think of the abnormality as normal.

One of Engel's patients was frightened as she "reported that her heart was functioning in a dysrhythmic fashion, when actually it was beating quite regularly. Her cardiograms were shown to her . . . after her misconceptions had been clarified, she subsequently learned to recognize correctly the presence of P.V.C.s."

Another feedback researcher, Dr. Peter Lang, research professor of pyschology at the University of Wisconsin, has also reported success in teaching people how to control their own heart rates. Lang used a video feedback screen to show projected lines of a person's own heart rate. Lang confirms that he taught people to "drive their own hearts." To master heart rates in Lang's test, people had to "shorten the lines," shown on the screen. As they shortened the lines, they slowed their heart beats, and most had no problem learning the skill.

Successes, such as those of Engel and Lang, cause some

scientists to predict that feedback training will lead to the possibility of helping correct a wide variety of cardiac irregularities, tachycardia, auricular flutter, extra systoles, bradycardia, and, possibly, psychologic anxiety and fear reactions.

Hypertension, a special form of high blood pressure, is rampant in this country, but may also be amenable to biofeedback training. Hypertension brings headaches and dizziness, but can be even more ominous with enough time. For unknown reasons, hypertension sometimes leads to strokes, kidney damage, and heart attacks. Psychological factors are suspected by some scientists.

Some time ago, Dr. L. A. Plumlee trained monkeys to increase their blood pressure in an avoidance-task situation with instrumental conditioning. But this success might have been only a skeletal response instead of real control, if criticism by scientists like Dr. R. M. Church is correct. In 1969, Benson, Herd, Morse, and Kelleher managed to teach three squirrel monkeys to increase their arterial blood pressure to hypertensive levels through instrumental training and an avoidance schedule. By reversing the schedule, the animals learned to decrease their blood pressure. Other investigators reported equal success with human beings. The Brener group in Tennessee, the Lafayette Clinic in Detroit, Dr. Neal Miller at Rockefeller University in New York, and investigators in Canada claimed that they were successful in using biofeedback techniques to lower blood pressure for hypertensive human beings.

Physiology and psychology merged methods and knowledge at Harvard Medical School, and the results were that hypertensive patients learned to lower their systolic blood pressure easily. Operant conditioning with feedback made it happen, thanks to a team of ingenious scientists—Herbert Benson, David Shapiro, Bernard Tursky, and Gary E. Schwartz. Before this experiment, the men conducted extensive studies and found that normal people could control both heart rate and blood pressure. In less than an hour, a student group of volunteers was trained to slow heart rates by an average of nine beats a minute. The scientists decided to investigate further to see if hypertensive patients, with long histories of blood-pressure problems, could learn the same skill as well as the normal people had.

Seven patients were chosen for the test after careful evaluation of their complete medical records. The average age of the hypertensive patients in this experiment was about forty-seven, and both men and women were included in the study. All but one of the patients was taking antihypertensive medicines of various types, and all medication was continued during the training. The patients were naive about biofeedback, and they were all told that their blood pressure would be measured automatically for about an hour, while they sat quietly. Scientists added that the "procedure might be of value in lowering their blood pressure." No other information, or instructions, were given.

For each patient, the experience was the same, and it was a daily event for two to three weeks for each one. The familiar wide blood-pressure cuff was wrapped about each person's left arm, and inflated with a regulated source. The cuff was connected to a pressure transducer, and the reading from the strain gauge was fed to a polygraph for interpretive measuring. Under the pressure cuff was a microphone which was also connected to the polygraph device. A third channel recorded the EKG for each person, and the cuff was inflated and deflated for readings. The first five sessions were like a "dry run," with no feedback, so the scientists could determine base lines. After the five sessions, patients received a tone and a light signal and were told that these signals "were desirable, and that they should try to make them appear." A reward, a photographic slide representing a payment of five cents, was shown for five seconds after every twenty presentations of tones and lights to let each one know that he was being successful. The slides pictured pleasant scenic landscapes, but they also reminded patients of money earned for the work.

Without the light and tone feedback, the scientists found that blood pressures did not change. But once feedback was added, five out of seven showed that they could decrease their blood pressure at will. There were two people who did not do well in the experiment. One was a thirty-year-old man who did not have elevated systolic blood pressure, and may not have been interested in learning the skill. The other was a man who had a disorder of the arteries, which may have blocked his progress.

Although the results seemed very successful, Dr. Benson was cautious and pointed out that such training is not ready for public application yet because, "the decrease in systolic pressure was measured only in the laboratory, and no consistent measurements were made outside the laboratory, [so] the usefulness of such methods . . . remains to be evaluated."

His study does demonstrate just how complex hypertension can be. By merely thinking about it, patients could boost their pressure to great heights as they sat in that experimental booth. Mental reactions and emotional feelings would appear to be powerful forces in the body's functioning. And, in contrast, just by letting the feel of relaxation flow, patients were able to lower blood pressure (systolic) to "normal" levels. Some people told Dr. Benson how much more at ease they felt when they learned how to decrease their own blood pressures. Dr. Benson suggests that maintaining a normal blood pressure might, in addition to biofeedback-learned skills, also call for the addition of behavior therapy, or even a change in style of life and the characteristic ways people meet challenging situations.

Another practical application of biofeedback techniques took place in Topeka, Kansas, at the Menninger Foundation, where the method was used to cure migraine headaches. Migraine headaches are blinding pains, often accompanied by nausea and dizziness, that wash over the suffering person, temporarily crippling him and keeping him from work. Migraine headaches come and go, mysteriously, and are thought to occur because the main artery that supplies blood to the neck and brain (involving the face, tongue, and external parts of the head), swells up.

Dr. Joseph Sargent, an internist, took the feedback theories of the Greens, and applied them to migraine sufferers. He managed to reduce or eliminate the pain of chronic migraine in a number of patients by teaching people how to pump less blood to their heads, and thus reduce the swelling of that main artery supplying blood to the head area.

Of twenty-eight migraine patients in Sargent's study, fourteen were able to learn to control their body temperatures. All but one of the migraine patients were women. Most learned from the machine how to raise their hand temperatures higher than their head temperatures. Beeps, burbles, and wavering needles acted as electronic monitors for them, telling them what their bodies were doing. These fourteen reported "fewer and less severe headaches." Of the others in the study, six were still learning, three could not do it, and five dropped out of the program before completing the training.

In the experiment, subjects sat in easy chairs in Sargent's laboratory. Temperature sensors were taped to volunteers' foreheads, and they were told to "think your hands warm." At first, not much happened, but, after a few tentative tries, a change occurred as volunteers watched the electronic monitors.

"At first, when I tried to warm my hands, they immediately got colder," Mrs. Stannie Anderson recounted in the Topeka *Capital Journal.* "But, by watching the meter, I was somehow able to relax, and let it happen all by itself. It's been six months now since I've taken migraine medicine, and nine months since I've had a severe migraine headache."

Another of Sargent's patients, Mrs. Lillian Petroni, is a Phoenix housewife. She found the biofeedback treatment so effective that she stopped taking headache medication, and has been free from migraine headaches for about three years.

No one knows quite why the biofeedback trained hand-warming control works, but it seems to be effective in Sargent's experiments. The pain of migraine comes from pressure on the nerves, as the blood is pumped into those distended blood vessels in the brain. The standard medical treatment is a drug to constrict the blood vessels. Scientists speculate that the head-hand temperature control reversal duplicates this drug effect.

"The idea is to learn to manipulate the body's control system," explains feedback theorist Dr. Elmer Green, whose ideas were used in Sargent's work. External warming of the hand will not reduce migraine headaches. Just putting your hand into hot water will do only one thing for you—get your hand sopping wet. To eliminate migraine problems, the hands seem to have to be "willed" warm, and this doesn't happen without biofeedback training, or other training techniques like autogenic methods. If you tried to make your hands warm without one of these techniques, the possibilities are that your hands will actually get colder.

The electronic monitor used in the Sargent experiment helps because the meter tells you the difference between the temperature of your hand and your forehead. Such monitors aid in learning.

"Your hand will feel very heavy. It will tingle, and it will feel warm," Sargent's volunteers were told. Then each person tried to move the meter needle to the right, showing that they had actually warmed their hands. With this information, a "feel" for the skill developed, and the housewives could halt migraine headaches in their daily lives. It is speculated that "willing" the warmth by sending the message through the middle brain, affects the central nervous system. Home practice was encouraged in Sargent's tests, and integrated into the learning techniques.

Not everyone succeeded in controlling migraine problems in Sargent's experiment. What about the failures who were unable to get rid of their migraine headaches? Dr. Sargent told a reporter that, "I don't think they were psychologically ready to give up the headaches."

As has already been mentioned, motivation is important to biofeedback learning, and some migraine sufferers may find that their painful headaches are a wonderful way to avoid threatening or challenging situations. "They may say that they want to be cured of migraine headaches," a Chicago doctor commented, "and, on a conscious level, they mean it, but subconsciously, they're not about to give up this defense and have to face life."

If a person really wants to learn voluntary control of a body function with biofeedback, it would seem that he has a good chance of learning how to do it. Feedback offers the individual a unique chance to filter out special skills from the welter of internal existential cues common to everyone. Different kinds of feedback—temperature, EKG, EMG, and EEG for alpha and theta brain-wave control—seem to work best for different pyschosomatic illnesses. Only insomnia seems to respond to many kinds of feedback training, ranging from temperature feedback to muscle relaxation and alpha feedback.

"Think your toes warm," a woman was instructed by researcher Dr. Elmer Green, and she learned to raise her foot temperature with electronic temperature feedback methods. After that, she was able to go to sleep quickly, and sleep deeply.

Sometimes, just turning on strong alpha waves with an EEG machine, or a meditatively learned skill, helps some people drift quickly and gently off to sleep. Marshall, a pre-med student at a northwestern university "turns on the pictures" in his mind when he wants to go to sleep. In minutes, he manages to fall asleep, and sleeps heavily. Before he learned to enhance his alpha waves, Marshall would lie awake for hours as he tried to figure out his many problems, and, on too many nights, never managed to fall asleep until dawn began to lighten the sky. With eight o'clock classes, he knew something had to change or he would flunk out of school. Learning to relax with alpha wave enhancement gave him the key to better sleep.

Learning to produce alpha brain waves also seems to help people to relax in the daytime, and be less tense at night. An early study by Dr. Maurice B. Sterman dealt with cats, but might help to explain why this relaxation happens in human beings. Sterman trained cats to produce alpha brain waves while they were awake, and saw that this training also produced longer periods of undisturbed sleep in the trained high-alpha cats. They were more rested, and carried the learning into all aspects of their lives. Perhaps, this carryover is also what happens in human beings.

Dr. Marjorie Kawin-Toomim, of Toomim Laboratories, reported that subjects who were not insomniacs had learned to deepen their alpha waves and go to sleep at will. Dr. Kawin-Toomim also noted that other people used enhanced alpha brain waves for short rest periods during the day, and found that they returned to work refreshed. It has already been reported that turning on alpha brain waves can produce a feeling of drowsiness. Unlike meditators, who try to suppress the drowsiness that occurs as brain waves go lower, insomniacs would want to ride with such drowsy feelings to go to sleep more quickly.

The alpha experience might also be useful in cutting down our need for sleep. Clyde Allen of the Neuropsychiatric and Brain Research Institute, U.C.L.A. Medical Center, was reported to have speculated that the "need for sleep could be considerably lessened if individuals were in the alpha state more often . . . [and] if people with sleep problems were to train themselves to stay in the alpha state during waking periods, they would arise refreshed as if they had slept."

An interesting experiment conducted by Dr. David Hord, Paul Naitoh, and Laverne Johnson, with the assistance of Drs. Joseph Barber and Don Irwin, for the U.S. Navy Medical Neuropsychiatric Research Unit, deals with enhancing alpha brain waves to aid the sleep deprived person. Although the tests are still in progress, positive results have been reported and would seem to substantiate Allen's idea that alpha refreshes.

Training in producing alpha brain waves also showed dramatic results in a study by Budzynski and Stoyva in their Denver laboratories. For example, one man participating in their experiments, used to need four hours to fall asleep. After biofeedback training in an enhanced alpha brain wave state, the man found that he could drift into slumber twice within a twenty-minute laboratory experience.

Budzynski and Stoyva have completed a number of "insomnia" studies using increased alpha through EEG feedback, and are now at work setting up a more complex long-term sleep project with Dr. Pola Sittenfeld from the University of Dusseldorf. As planned, the Stoyva-Budzynski-Sittenfeld sleep project will begin with building up alpha waves, then turning to deep muscle-relaxation techniques by means of EMG feedback and, finally, theta brain-wave enhancement with an EEG auditory feedback. Home practice, with taped messages on cassette tapes, will probably be included in the program. As a volunteer improves at turning on instant drowsiness progressing to slumber, Budzynski, Stoyva, and Sittenfeld will "shape" the skill by gradually increasing the difficulty of the job.

Gradual enhancement of a skill by shaping is an ancient revolutionary process. Relaxing in his compact Denver office, Dr. Budzynski leans forward as he speaks of their lab use of the shaping process, and reminds you of nature's method of teaching by "shaping" responses through gradually raising the goals to be met. Budzynski speaks of elks, and how they teach their young to swim. "First, the mother elks splash water on the young ones, beside shallow pools where they are drinking. It's fun for the infants, and learning begins. Soon, they all move to deeper pools, and all wade into the water together. In a few weeks, the young elks can swim across a deep river," Budzynski explains, and adds quietly, "And, as soon as that happens, the whole herd moves across the water and heads straight for the high country."

Such shaping of skills is used in Budzynski and Stoyva's work as they teach people how to fall asleep quickly. Lessons in how to fall asleep? Most of their students learned quickly as they rested on a comfortable couch in a quiet room with three electrodes attached to their forehead muscles, and then connected to a nearby EMG machine for feedback purposes.

The forehead muscle (frontalis), was chosen because it is a good indicator of tenseness level, and control of this important muscle leads quickly to overall tension relaxation. Often, when you think you're relaxed, tension is actually wrapped about your forehead like a constricting band. Relaxing this forehead muscle lets you go on to relax your scalp, neck, and shoulder muscles.

Besides the connecting electrodes, "sleepers" also wore earphones with a signaling tone warning of increased tension. The tone rose to a high pitch when tension rose and fell to a softly pleasing low pitch as tension lowered. Keeping that tone down to low levels worked fast, as most volunteers halved their original tension after only twenty minutes practice of simply lying and listening to the control sound. The relaxation worked best when people just "let go," but they failed when they forcefully "tried to relax."

Once they had learned how to "let go," volunteers were wired to EEG machines to practice turning on their alpha brain waves. Since they already knew how to relax by letting go, alpha brain waves came easily and, soon, deeply. From that point, *all* had no problem in quickly drifting off into slumber whenever they wished, away from the laboratory machinery.

Based upon this success, Budzynski predicted, "I think doctors are going to lend [insomniac] patients an EMG machine, instead of handing out sleeping pills, in the near future."

It may take some time before the average physician is ready

to use the Budzynski-Stoyva method to treat insomnia, and we can't all fly to Denver to spend weeks learning how to go to sleep. In the meantime, Dr. Stoyva offers some "notes for an insomniac" that might help the average person troubled with sleeping problems:

1. The room should be as quiet as possible.
2. Surroundings should be darkened.
3. The bed or couch should be medium to firm.
4. "Let go," and allow your muscles to relax deeply.

"Deep relaxation" figured heavily in Budzynski's and Stoyva's tension-headache experiments. (Also assisting them on this study was Dr. Charles Adler.) "Deep relaxation" is a profound calm to most people. Side effects, like body image changes, are common because you go from a high to a low muscle-tension level in a relatively short time. You might feel as if your legs are floating away, or your arms have become as heavy as bags of cement. In this consciousness change, images, reveries, and long-forgotten memories are apt to float into your mind as relaxation deepens. As the tension eases away from your chin, and the back of your neck, you may feel "as if your face is dripping off." Sometimes, you may feel "too open and vulnerable" from the experience, but as you grow accustomed to relaxing deeply, this fear fades away. Most people describe deep relaxation as a "pleasant, warm, drowsy state" making them feel "temporarily passive."

Budzynski and Stoyva induced deep relaxation with EMG feedback training. Their goal was to ease tension in the scalp and neck muscles because chronic clenching in these areas is the factor that causes intense tension headache. In addition to EMG feedback, Budzynski and Stoyva recommended daily home practice at relaxing.

In the initial headache study, Budzynski and Stoyva worked with healthy individuals and gave three sessions of relaxation training with EMG feedback. Their results indicated that normal individuals aided by EMG feedback could learn to relax very quickly.

Denver newspapers soon carried an advertisement looking for "tension-headache sufferers," a notice placed by the two young psychologists. Five patients were selected, the first five people with established tension-headache problems who were available for the testing time schedule. All were initially examined by Dr. Charles Adler, a psychiatric resident physician in the Denver area, to rule out the possibilities of neurological or other organic disorders, and to confirm the "tension headache" diagnosis. The volunteers were a middle-aged housewife; a dynamic middle-aged businessman; a young high school teacher, married to a medical student; a thirty-three-year-old housewife, and a married research technician with no children. Training time varied from four weeks to two months, with two or three half-hour feedback sessions each week. The difference in training time was determined by the severity of each person's own tension-headache problem.

For twenty-three years, the research technician had lived with the ache of her tension headaches. Those dull pains stretching across her forehead began when she was only nine years old; starting each morning it grew progressively stronger as the hours passed. For the study, she was asked to keep a headache diary listing the progression of pain and noting what outside events coincided with her headaches. She soon noted that her headaches were strongest on Monday and Thursday, and weakest on the weekend. Two o'clock in the afternoon was the highest peak of daily pain, and it usually happened after she had met with her supervisor to review her work. To a lesser degree, her headaches were also triggered when she lost her car keys, forgot a shopping list, or prepared dinner for company.

On her first two visits to the lab, Budzynski and Stoyva asked her to relax as well as she could without getting EMG feedback. They carefully monitored her tension levels in another room. Although she was supposedly "relaxed," the scientists discovered extremely high levels of tension. On her third lab visit, she donned earphones, and was told to keep the sound of the tone she heard low. "Low" signified low tension levels. As she progressed in the two or three half-hour training sessions every week, the gain knob was gradually turned up, increasing the difficulty of her task by shaping her progress to increasing levels of skill. Occasional "silent runs" were periodically interspersed with the feedback tone, so that she could practice maintaining a willed relaxation without the help of the EMG machine.

Between sessions, she practiced relaxing at home every day, and was also asked to try to relax in her chair at the office for ten or fifteen minutes during her lunch-hour break. Her headaches began to disappear, and her personality became more cheerful. When Budzynski and Stoyva checked back with her three months after the training period had ended, they found that her tension headaches had virtually disappeared. She had learned to spot tension coming, and could turn on relaxation whenever she needed it.

Others in this study were also able to shed their tension headaches for the first time in years. The middle-aged housewife used to "fly off the handle at small frustrations" and then get tension headaches. EMG feedback training calmed her, and she was able to relax and live with minor upsets over which she had little or no control—and her headaches all but disappeared. With the training, the high school teacher was able to rid herself of tension headaches, but when she left the city for a challenging new job, the headaches soon returned to plague her again. She spoke with the scientists, and they found that she had forgotten to practice daily home relaxation because she was so busy getting herself organized in a new situation. On their advice, she returned to those daily relaxation breaks, and her headaches faded away. The children in her classes benefited, too, because she was no longer uptight and anxious about teaching.

The thirty-three-year-old housewife was quick to learn how to relax and almost completely eliminated all headaches. She enjoyed turning on deep relaxation and discovered a side effect of the skill that delighted her. For years she had had trouble falling asleep and, once asleep, would start up to wakefulness at the slightest noise. After her training, she was able to fall asleep rapidly, and slept soundly without being bothered by minor sounds like a dog barking in the neighborhood.

From the time he was fourteen years old, the businessman had suffered frequent severe headaches whenever he was faced with stress. During the first part of his feedback training, his headaches decreased dramatically. Then he took a five week vacation and returned to Denver to find himself bogged down in accumulated business. Because he "had to get things back in order" the businessman neglected the daily relaxation periods and his headaches soon returned, more severe and painful than ever before. Two extra feedback-training sessions and a return to daily relaxation eradicated his headaches again.

Pilot studies with "happy endings," like the Budzynski and Stoyva headache experiment, throw the spotlight on the possibilities of biofeedback. But science and medicine demand complex control studies of any new treatment before a new method can be made available to the average person. Budzynski and Stoyva are now working with Dr. Adler on a controlled outcome tension-headache study to further test their theories. Eighteen tension-headache patients, with verified medical diagnoses, are involved in this experiment. The experimental group receives EMG feedback training similar to the sessions given in the earlier pilot study. One control group receives irrelevant feedback information, and a second control group gets no training at all. Preliminary results show dramatic headache reduction for the experimental group getting feedback work, and no significant changes in either control group. Because of this success, Budzynski and Stoyva optimistically are planning, in the near future, to set up a public tension-headache clinic in the Denver area, offering EMG biofeedback treatment. At this clinic, headache sufferers could quickly learn how to "relax away" their headaches.

In all of their work, Budzynski and Stoyva have not noted the development of any substitute symptoms as people shed psychosomatic illness. Budzynski did note a side effect that sometimes accompanies deep muscle relaxation with EMG feedback. The relaxation is a rapid transition for the body, and he found that in the early stages of his own training, he sometimes had a feeling of mild indigestion. With some people, stomach acidity increases immediately after the exercise due to the intense body change from high arousal at high tension to low arousal at relaxation. Dr. Elmer Green predicted this problem for about two out of fifty or sixty people, but it seems to disappear after continued relaxation practice because the body's arousal changes decrease.

Budzynski's and Stoyva's deep relaxation techniques may

have other applications. Their methods are currently being tested at two hospitals in Denver to see if these techniques could help asthmatic patients fight off the suffocating asthma attacks. Both the National Jewish Hospital and CARIH, the Children's Asthma Research Institute and Hospital, are using EMG feedback to see if the training can aid asthma patients to spot impending attacks before they begin to struggle for breath. Perhaps, these feedback techniques will help them relax away the strangling contractions.

Another sort of biofeedback training is being tested by Dr. Louis Vachon in the battle against asthma. Working at Boston University School of Medicine, Dr. Vachon measured the waxing and waning of the nonvoluntary muscles in the bronchial tree. He used a light cue to signal dilation of the muscles of the bronchial tubes and diminished airflow. His experiments are still in the preliminary stages at last report, but show promise. When he spoke of his initial findings to the Biofeedback Research Society, Dr. Vachon also cautioned, "Asthma is a somatic disease. If you have it, you have a disposition, and that will be true all your life. You may diminish the number of attacks. . . . From a small percentage to a large percentage of these attacks may be caused from emotional rises, but, if you have the disease, you have it. . . . If you meet the allergens, whether you are in perfect mental health and euphoria, or not, you'll still choke up. Possibly helping somebody to control trauma, those attacks that are centrally determined, is a help. But it's not a cure for the disease."

In New York City, EMG feedback was used successfully to help a young man with facial tics, those nervous facial tremors that plague many uptight people. Erik Peper treated the man's twitching by training him with a portable EMG machine devised by Budzynski. Standard therapies had failed to solve the young man's tic problem, but the tics vanished after just a little feedback training in relaxation.

First, the man relaxed his back, and then began to concentrate upon the sound of the clicks from the biofeedback machine that warned him when his tension was rising, and slowed to a soothing tone when his tension was drifting away. He soon told Peper that he felt a "whole new world . . . a deep warmth," and "a very heavy feeling of sinking into the bed." To his delighted surprise, he added, "I, for once, controlled my body movements. They did not control me . . . I cried for happiness because I never felt I could conquer my bodily movements. I told myself, 'Don't tic'—and I didn't.'"

Migraine headaches, asthma, tension headaches, hypertension, cardiac irregularities, epilepsy—the list is long but promising. Tomorrow's medicine may be revolutionized by today's actual lab applications of biofeedback techniques. Two clinics are already open to the public in New York City and in the Midwest, and the Denver headache clinic is due to open soon.

In the near future, feedback researchers predict clinics in all major cities. These clinics will be statted by psychologists and trained feedback technicians. In such a clinic, you might sign up for a training session after you'd been examined and the diagnosis had been confirmed by a medical physician. Various types of biofeedback would be used to cure your stress-related illness. Tomorrow's medicine may be waiting just around the corner. With its dazzling array of dials and lights and buttons and wires, biofeedback "medicine" seems an eternity away from the world of the old-time country doctor, and would have the benefit of freeing physicians from treating the pyschosomatically ill to devote themselves to cases of organic damage.

Chapter 7
Alpha
and Relaxation
Alpha's Role in Tension Reduction

R-e-l-a-x . . .

L-e-t g-o . . .

L-e-t y-o-u-r b-o-d-y d-r-i-f-t a-s t-e-n-s-i-o-n m-e-l-t-s
a-w-a-y . . .

With an idle smile, the tall woman listened as the words of
the scientist floated over the intercom system, and she let her
arms fall to her sides. Her tension level lessened; the couch felt
hard and firm under her lean body, and she opened her eyes
slowly in the dim room to look about her.

Immediately, the soft tone she had heard in the earphones
she was wearing rose abruptly and screamed in her ears, the
siren-sound warning her of her increased tension. Like the wail
of a hungry baby, the feedback siren tone demanded her
attention. Again, she let go. "I'm a cloud in the summer sky.
My arms are floating away to the sunset," she told herself. The
siren sound softened as the home tone came back on to signify
the deep relaxation occurring in her mind and guided her home
to a more relaxed world.

In the dark chamber, a figure of a man shown on the screen
in front of her flickered with a green light. She tensed her jaw

as she peered at it and, suddenly, a red light, warning of anxiety, replaced the green light. Again, she let go, and the green light returned. She drifted, floating in space, and deep, deep in her bones, she recognized a profound relaxation that she'd never felt before. It was almost a déjà vu sensation, and she wondered if she'd known that feeling as a child. Or, perhaps, was it something she'd always somehow known? She couldn't explain it, but the sensation was strangely familiar. Her mind relaxed, and her body eased as she drifted in serene peace.

The next day, she started to yell, "Don't do that!" to one of her fourth grade students. But, abruptly, she paused as she recognized the tension beginning to build up in her mind and her body. "Green light," she thought, "it's a green-light day." She searched mentally, and found that sense of deep relaxation that she had discovered the day before in the relaxation lab. Green light. Let go.

Like this Detroit schoolteacher, tension rides with all of us in our journey through life. The harried soul. The uptight person. The struggling suburbanite. All of us would like to be able to let go at times, and relax from the tension of living. For many of us, relaxation is a simple need because we're not bothered by psychosomatic illness. But, sometimes, we would like to know how to let go, and biofeedback provides a new answer. The cornucopia of our culture offers various baubles as solutions, as aids to release tension. But such outs as liquor, or happy pills, or promiscuous sex carry their own negative side effects with them.

Massage, Yoga, and biofeedback offer interesting alternatives. Massage helps you relax because massage causes decreased firing of muscle units. Dr. Kenneth Gaarder suggests other possible relaxation techniques: relaxation by passive stretching, relaxation by noninstrumental methods, and relaxation by external instrumental feedback.

Yoga exercises help you to relax because you stretch your muscles, and then let go, which causes relaxation. Noninstrumental techniques, like progressive relaxation and autogenic training, help you to relax because you learn to detect the level of your own tension and, then, to control that tension.

External instrumental feedback works much more quickly than noninstrumental methods because it eliminates that first stage of detecting the level of personal tension. Instead, you receive instant communication on your internal tension, and control occurs internally as you learn.

Alpha brain wave training is instrumental relaxation, and it offers a unique solution for the harried person. EMG biofeedback proposes a second solution. Both eliminate drugs and their side effects, like kidney damage or liver problems, as they depend totally upon the instrumentation and upon individual motivation to induce relaxation. Deep levels of relaxation have been proven possible with the use of EEG and EMG, relaxing every part of your body; but, unlike drugs, it is turned on and controlled by your own mind and can be specifically focused upon one area. Again, unlike drugs, instrumentally learned relaxation, can be turned off at will when the demands of the world call for high arousal states.

A little bit of anxiety or tension may be a good thing because it activates us, makes us more cautious in dangerous situations, and energizes our bodies as it helps us function. But, like an appetizer, it's not a complete meal, and a too-abundant helping of tension is not good for anyone.

"Alpha (training in brain wave control) might be used to bring down the level of a person's anxiety to a point where he can function at his best," Dr. Martin Orne, director of experimental psychology at the University of Pennsylvania Medical School in Philadelphia, told a reporter for a national publication. But Dr. Orne goes on to warn, "We all need a little anxiety to function, and we function best as anxiety rises to a certain point . . . past that point we do increasingly worse."

Dr. Orne is studying to see exactly what the alpha state is, and how beneficial alpha is for most people. "It's not enough to know you can contemplate your navel. You have to ask what happens," he commented on the current alpha craze. Orne uses alpha training to rehabilitate his subjects.

Experiments by other alpha scientists suggest that alpha relaxation could substitute for tranquilizers. As has already been mentioned, the typical tranquilizing drug works upon most of your body, and even your entire bodily system, while biofeedback can be concentrated upon one specific area. Alpha waves can be enhanced to let you relax.

If you're up to two martinis before dinner, alpha might be just what you need. A little alpha instead of a little one for the road? A little peace instead of the frazzled student overloaded with tension as exams approach? The Golden Mean comes to mind, as all is held in balance in organic interaction of mind and body.

Relaxation experiments in the quiet Denver laboratories of Thomas Budzynski and Johann Stoyva demonstrate a way that you might change the pattern of your life-style as you learn to relax at will. Budzynski and Stoyva used a myriad number of original sources for inspiration and produced a remarkable scientific hybrid, a new insight into combined relaxation techniques that the average person could utilize.

The scientists began with Dr. J. Wolpe's unique idea of systematic desensitization. In Wolpe's system, you are taught to substitute a muscle relaxation reaction for an anxiety reaction. Formerly, Stoyva had worked with Dr. Joe Kamiya, and also had a rich background in the history and possibilities of autogenic training. Once a space engineer, Budzynski is a recycled man who brings a depth of electronic knowledge to psychological research. Together, these two men studied Jacobsen's progressive relaxation methods. This method consists of six exercises which have been applied with varying success to stress-related disorders. It begins with relaxing the arms; then the feet; then a breathing exercise to "feel" the alternate tensing and relaxation of your chest muscles as you let go and breathe in and out; relaxation of the forehead; then eyes; and, finally, of the speech organs: the mouth, tongue, and larynx.

Next, Budzynski and Stoyva worked with the system of Johann Heinrich Schultz. Shultz's technique has its own six standard exercises, beginning as you lie down upon a couch with your hands at your sides and your legs apart. You begin to repeat to yourself the phrase, "My right arm is heavy" until you start to feel great weight upon your arm. Next, you try to produce a feeling of warmth, a result of the dilation of peripheral blood vessels, as you repeat, "My right arm is warm."

The third exercise deals with the slowing of your heart rate, a dangerous maneuver without a physician's guidance, as you repeat, "My heart is beating calmly." The fourth exercise works upon molding a calm and regular breathing pattern, and the fifth Schultz step regulates the viscera, as you try to make your stomach warm. The last auto-suggestion in this series may give you slight vaso-constriction, especially in the face, as you repeat the phrase to yourself, "My forehead is cool."

Schultz's system takes two or three months, and is followed up by four to six months of practice before profound relaxation begins to occur. This is autogenic training, and physicians are divided over its benefits. Most of all, this system simply does not work for the extremely tense person who is striving too hard to relax. Such people try, but actually make themselves even more tense by overexertion.

Before devising their own system, Budzynski and Stoyva tested all of these methods. In the beginning, they worked with alpha brain wave feedback to help teach people how to relax, but they found that extremely anxious people had difficulty producing alpha brain waves quickly, and did not reach that alpha feeling of tranquility and relaxation. Their muscle tension still remained. The scientists began to wonder about the possibilities of using the bothersome tension as a cue, almost like electronic judo where you use your own anxiety, signaled by feedback methods, to fight off tension and learn to relax.

EMG feedback might promise a quicker and more thorough relaxation technique, but appropriate machinery was not available. Budzynski headed for the drawing board, and tackled the technological challenge. EMG feedback is a difficult problem because the electrical energy or power signal you're searching for is exceedingly small, and is only a fraction of the power of the EEG alpha brain wave rhythm. Frequencies for muscle tension also cover a tremendously wide range compared to the alpha brain wave frequency, ten to ten thousand Hz. for EMG, as opposed to eight to twelve Hz. for alpha brain waves. Budzynski solved the instrument problem and built the machinery that they needed.

With the adequate instrumentation, Budzynski and Stoyva managed to teach people to relax and shaped their progress at building the skill. Their results were astonishing. In one validation study, eighty people were almost instantly taught to relax the masseteric muscle as deeply as is humanly possible, and those in the feedback group learned one hundred percent better than the control groups. These people actually learned to relax in one quick lesson, combining a smattering of autogenic methods with practice with EMG machinery. Drawing upon this relaxation study, the scientists tested the technique upon areas ranging from curing of phobias to headaches. Some people were found to need more training time then others, but the methods seems to promise great possibilities. Stoyva comments that a portable EMG feedback machine might help the average person who wants to learn how to relax. He couples this suggestion with the advice to "buy a good book on Jacobsen's relaxation techniques," follow the exercises, and use the machine for feedback information on how well you're doing at relaxing.

Muscular relaxation is not necessary for alpha brain waves to flow, according to Dr. Joe Kamiya, but he did find that muscular relaxation often follows right along with that alpha brain wave experience.

Other researchers would seem to agree. "Our anxious subjects literally cannot do it," researcher Dr. Elmer Green commented on the ability to produce high-alpha. With time, the uptight non-alpha person usually can learn to increase alpha brain waves and learn to relax, but he would seem to need much more practice at biofeedback.

This inability to produce alpha may be related to how anxious people look at life. This is a literal statement and is concerned with the visual function of the uptight individual. Think of someone you know who is very uptight. Did you ever notice how his or her eyes seem to search about a lot? This is called "looking behavior," a characteristic of uptight people, and somehow this action blocks the alpha brain wave. Anxiety may be the cause of this looking and "blocking." Feedback training may erase the problem as the anxious person learns how to relax.

Once you are able to achieve high amplitude alpha brain wave activity, the lack of tension seems to follow as a matter of course, according to researcher Dr. Lester Fehmi. In explaining this phenomenon, Dr. Fehmi reminds us of the classic studies of both Yoga and Zen masters and disciples which revealed large-amplitude alpha and theta brain waves and extremely low levels of muscle tension. Kasamatsu's and Hirai's famous experiment may indicate that the ability to turn on high alpha of low frequency may be directly connected to lowered tension.

Muscle-tension feedback was also used at the Menninger Foundation where people learned voluntary control of muscle tension and reached deep muscle relaxation down to measured intermittent zero levels. In one study by the Greens, a third of the volunteers learned "to achieve low levels of single motor unit firing in about twenty minutes in the forearm muscles of the right arm." The forearm muscle was used because it seems to be the easiest to learn to relax with and, once fine control of tension is achieved in one area, it is usually transferable to other parts of the body.

At Menninger's, they used surface electrodes and an EMG machine to observe single-motor-unit firing. Again and again, once a person had learned to relax muscle activity to near zero levels in one spot, the relaxation ability soon spread quickly to other areas. With just a little practice at EMG feedback, individuals can learn to let one area of the body completely rest, while other areas of the body may be tensed up at will.

The most successful students of relaxation at Menninger's reported body image changes. One person said he felt as if he were floating above the chair. Another said, "My arm felt like a bag of cement," a common body-image reaction. A third told the scientists that, "My arm felt as if it were moving away from me, just out into space."

Biofeedback of information about your own specific muscle tension might help you to relax. Many of the new EMG machines use surface electrodes attached with a paste that is easily applicable and quickly washed off with plain water, in contrast to earlier mechanisms requiring actual implantation of electrodes into the skin. Surface electrode attachment is easy enough for most people to accomplish once they've learned exactly where to place the electrodes to record tension levels.

What kind of information feedback is best for learning how to relax? This seems to depend upon two factors: whether you are a visually-oriented personality, or an auditory person, and the type of feedback learning involved. As investigators like Kamiya discovered, EEG alpha relaxation feedback is most apt to occur with eyes closed, so a visual signal would not seem to be of much aid. EMG muscle feedback occurs when your body is relaxed, regardless of your mental state, and visual feedback works best for this task in most experimental situations.

In Craig Cleaves' work at Northern Virginia Mental Health Institute, the visual feedback group were given dials and colors to signal levels of tension, and were the best at learning how to relax muscles. Auditory EMG muscle feedback was given to another group, but the tone did not help them to learn any more quickly than a control group of people who were taught to relax with the autogenic theories of Jacobsen and Schultz.

The amount of time it takes to learn how to relax with EEG or EMG feedback depends upon your own personality and level of usual tension. Kamiya discovered that many people are able to find their alpha brain rhythms and turn these waves on within thirty minutes of biofeedback experience. Walters' students often managed deep relaxation within twenty minutes. Brown found that people could increase their alpha brain waves within forty to fifty minutes if they had a period to mentally try out strategies before beginning to work at specific brain-wave enhancement.

Biofeedback learning is instrumental learning, and, unlike conditioning, seems to last and last with no reinforcement indicated for most people after the skill is acquired. "It is already possible to teach people to feel happy and serene," Dr. Abraham Maslow recently wrote. Perhaps biofeedback learning could speed up that teaching and aid the average man or woman to relax quickly and easily.

Chapter 8
Organic Learning
Education Applications of
Alpha Research

Where others walked, Keith ran to his own melody. Chasing a cloud, reaching for a dream, Keith tumbled through his tousled nine-year-old life. In the classroom, he wriggled about on the hard chair, and stared out the window as his grey-haired teacher droned on, *"Three times two equals six, three times three equals nine, three times four equals twelve, and now repeat after me, children, three times two . . ."*

Later, on the playground, Keith raced about with his classmates, but he made them anxious with his too-quick laughter and sudden showers of tears. Jiggling. Singing. Jumping. Hopping. Keith was an intelligent sensitive boy who was aware of everything around him—except "assigned school tasks." Perhaps he was tuned to more extreme waves of feeling than other children his age, or perhaps the monotony of discipline jangled his creative bent. Whatever the reason, Keith was a hyperactive child. His story might have had an unhappy ending with disciplinary problems, delinquency, and rebellion.

But Keith was one of the lucky ones.

In Beaumont, Texas, an imaginative educator, Miss Angie Nall, chose Keith for a unique test at the Angie Nall School-Hospital. Miss Nall decided to try teaching alpha brain wave feedback to Keith in hopes that it might help him control his own mental states. In many areas of the country, hyperactive children like Keith are sedated with tranquilizers until they become passive enough to submit to the discipline of the usual educational situation. Wholesale distribution of such drugs to calm the hyperkinetic child has alarmed parents and created controversy among a number of educators.

For some time, Miss Nall had wondered if there might not be a better way to handle the problem. Upon admission to her school, all children are given EEG examinations. When she spotted a correlation between lack of clear alpha brain patterns and the inability to "get down to work" in numerous EEG recordings, she began testing the hyperkinetic children in alpha brain wave training. Keith, and seven others with the same hyperkinetic problem, improved dramatically with biofeedback training in increasing their alpha brain waves. The sessions were given for half an hour a week, for a month's period. Keith found the electrodes pasted upon his head an interesting experience, and eagerly tried to "turn on his Alpha Wave" in the experimental sessions. Soon, he began to change from an uncontrollable wave of energy to a "highly-together" youngster who could walk through life happily, and begin to benefit from his education. Instead of rolling and rollicking before bedtime for an hour or more, he was now able to grin happily as he "turned on his Alpha Wave" and immediately drifted off to sleep. Each morning, he woke up by himself, and his cheerful good spirits were noticed by everyone because they were such a contrast to his old gloomy attitude.

Miss Nall's school, specializing in children with learning difficulties, is now using alpha brain wave training through portable feedback machines on a broader basis in a controlled project with many more children than the original study. Miss Nall's work is only one of the many ways alpha brain wave training is being used in education, and only one of many areas where alpha feedback could alter standarized educational methods.

Many research scientists believe that high-alpha people, who can turn large strength alpha brain waves on and off at will, learn in a more efficient manner than other people. It is thought that they can absorb larger gestalts, and can be more aware of relationships between objects, events, and facts. Alpha control always implies completely *suppressing* alpha for fuller attention to more difficult fact collection.

When you are "in alpha," you are more easily aware of both internal and external events in an alerted relaxation state. This allows you to absorb great chunks of data effortlessly in a nonlinear fashion. (Some types of learning are linear, like memorizing the multiplication tables, and would not appropriately occur in alpha states.) This "alpha learning" state of consciousness has caused one educator to call it "organic learning," implying a natural use of the mind's resources for large information intake.

Current theories of learning do not take brain waves into account. Yet, scientists have shown that brain waves differ and such factors as attention are definitely linked to brain-wave states. One rhythm may be best suited for memorizing the multiplication tables, while another brain rhythm may be best suited to creative outpourings like writing poetry, or painting a landscape.

Most contemporary education is based on the response-reward theory. For example, you got an "A" for memorizing the fact that Heraclitus was a Greek philosopher who lived from the sixth to the fifth century B.C. Academically, repetition acts as a constant reinforcement of the learned data, particularly on the elementary level, and the punishment of an "F" awaits failure to remember the facts. But alpha learning could be a different experience presenting a new world of thinking and possibilities of instant insights. Response, stimulus, and reinforcement are merged in the biofeedback mental loop, and could be teamed with teaching machines for some startling innovations.

Jimmy is a blue-eyed charmer with blond hair and a smile like sunshine, but his IQ measures only 85. In the standard schoolroom, he must fight the desperate battle of the low IQ child, as he tries to keep up with the brighter students. Often, he gets tired, and gives up in frustration. His conscientious teacher would like to give him special attention, but she doesn't have time to tutor each child individually. Jimmy gets left behind, and doesn't like it. Sometimes, his desperate educational journey becomes too difficult for his young soul, and he wearies of running twice as fast as the others, just to keep up. When that happens, Jimmy wraps a piece of paper into a tight ball and, with careful aim, lobs it at the boy seated at the desk in front of him. "Stop that, Jimmy," his nervous young teacher demands, but anxious insecurity edges her voice, and Jimmy senses it. For the moment, he's the star, and he grins as he scuffles up the aisle. And, in that classroom, the learning stops for awhile as Jimmy stalls with his repertoire of antics to grab some breathing time.

But Jimmy's dilemma (and his teacher's dilemma, and the time lost by all the other children in that classroom) doesn't have to happen.

If the educational processes could be perfectly tuned to each child's own capacity for each lesson, each one could learn at his or her own pace, and develop as far as he wished. Idealistic teachers may push themselves to the limit, but they cannot stretch themselves far enough to individually educate each youngster. Obviously, the American public school system cannot afford personal tutors or machines for each child. Science may have an answer—computer-assisted teaching machines tuned to individual brain waves—that would be private educational universes custom-designed for the individual student with learning difficulties, in need of specific educational aid.

In the southern San Francisco area, first steps are already being taken in this direction. These children already have the opportunity to think for themselves, and go where they wish with teaching machines. They learn in a specialized experimental situation designed to lead to more open attitudes. Gestalt-therapy-trained teachers guide children's education in several California school districts in this program designed by Dean Brown, of the Stanford Research Institute. This avant-garde study uses both nonverbal imagery and verbal material on the elementary school level, as well as selected work with older students.

In these classes, some of the children are average, some have high IQs, and some low IQs; they are mixed together in the typical nonsegregated scholastic situation. On the elementary level, they enjoy courses in botany, music, physics, math, and art, and do amazingly well. Nonverbal material predominates. The average child "develops an intuition, develops concepts, without being constrained by the words," according to program director Dean Brown. When the words are added, the "verbalization is done after the fact. It's a style of learning and discovery. . . . We keep finding evidence of latent knowledge. The child will do things no one can understand how he knows, and use concepts no one can understand how he knows." The third grader with a deep knowledge of physics is surprising, and the fourth-grade composer is even more unusual. And the fifth grader who can fully explain the "laws of genetics"?

The old chalk-and-blackboard schoolroom is light years behind Brown's mechanical educational environments. Students move a single spot around on a cathode-ray tube screen to get nonverbal information. Years ago, Dewey proposed that learning is doing, and doing is learning; Brown's technological system is based on "learning by doing," with the aid of the machine.

Imagine learning to read music by placing notes upon a sheet of music drawn on the machine's screen by turning a knob; imagine pressing a button to hear your song played, then turning a dial to let the tune whisk from waltz time to march time; and, shifting again, hear the composition in another key. Or imagine learning about the effect of gravity by drawing a room on that machine screen with the "learning spot," then placing a ball in the room wherever you pleased. Set the velocity and gravity, and watch how the ball moves. Shift again, and see what happens when you add negative gravity. Such technological innovations speed up the learning process, but feedback could make it even more efficient.

Recently, Brown conferred with feedback experts Kamiya, Criswell, and others in the San Francisco area to evolve possible feedback controls for these teaching machines. Such machines could be directed by brain waves with EEG biofeedback, to use brain waves to move that information spot about on the teaching machines. The result would be information working about a hundred times faster than the current machine control by manually revolving the dial.

"Brain wave studies may help educators define the times

when children are most receptive to learning," Dr. Donald B. Lindsley, of the University of California at Los Angeles, told a reporter recently.

Dr. Thomas Mulholland goes even further. He suggests teaching machines controlled by EEG recordings. These computer-assisted teaching machines would include warning and waking signals. When concentration is high, signified by low alpha, the machine would zip along at a fast pace for the student. When high-alpha brain waves warn that the student's mind is wandering, the machine would slow down and flash waking indicators.

Dr. Barbara Brown once suggested that the teaching machines could be teamed with biofeedback, and also include color-changing display screens. Her idea was that the screen might be green to signal "go" when a child's brain wave showed that attention was high, and the screen could shift to red to suggest "stop" when brain rhythms indicated that attention had wandered. Since children's attention span seems to be short, Brown's warning device idea would also increase the effectiveness of the teaching machines by better time utilization. Such "pay attention" signals are, ironically, similar to the method used by Zen monks in meditation. Distracted dozing disciples are rapped to reawaken them to their meditative goals by revitalizing their attention. Another suggested attention-catching device is to use exciting pictures with the teaching machines. Wool-gathering students' brain waves would signal the machine to turn on interesting pictures geared to their age level. Does this mean nudes for older students, hot rods for teeny-boppers, and cowboys and Indians shooting it out at the pass for the youngest ones? The theorizing has not yet been translated into technological reality, but anything could be possible at this stage.

A more mundane possibility is to use brain-wave-controlled teaching machines to allow for resting periods between learning times. Some scientists suggest that learning occurs in intervals, interspersed with "resting periods," as subconscious grasp of information takes place. According to this idea, standard educational practices are incorrect because they do not take the natural brain rhythms of the learning process into account. In the usual system, material is simply presented, and the student either grasps it and passes, or loses it, and fails.

Biofeedback expert Brown criticizes the conditioned quality of society and education. She disapproves of the great influence behaviorists have had. "The world of human beings doesn't benefit from the Skinners, but rats might," she quips, then smiles as she softens her words by adding, "I hope our biofeedback discoveries lead to assisting the individual to discover more of himself and aid him in recognizing that he is responsible for his own thoughts and actions."

Dr. Brown has received more than 2500 letters asking for more facts about alpha brain waves and biofeedback techniques. Many of the inquiries came from educators, psychologists, and professional people. In 1971, she wrote and published a comprehensive booklet to meet the general inquiry about alpha brain waves and biofeedback techniques. In her paper, she pointed out how feedback learning differs from commonly accepted learning theories which are based on stimulus-response.

According to Dr. Brown, the "feedback signal" stands for desirable events, but is "neutral, except for its potential." She continued her comparison by citing one of the differences between instrumental learning and conditioning as feedback: the "involuntary transference from a specific response to a response in which the interaction between subject and environment is generalized." Two active processes are involved, desynchronization and voluntary control of alpha which causes the desynchronization to happen. Both discrimination and enhanced alpha brain wave production are abrupt happenings. Dr. Brown concludes her analysis by reminding us that the feedback response, "whether it is the feeling state or the alpha activity, can be elicited or recalled voluntarily in the absence of stimuli or reinforcement."

Alpha brain wave control would seem to promise a unique learning process that merges reason and feeling together for Gestalt-type education. This broadly based event is called for by revolutionary educational philosophers who claim that today's education is in need of revitalizing.

The controversial educational theorist, George Leonard, first challenged contemporary schools in *Education and Ecstasy,* in which he called for adding joy to learning. His new work, *The Transformation,* blasts the old dualism that separates flesh from spirit, and reason from feeling. Leonard proposes a unified theory of life and society and educational enhancement. He writes that opacity is a condition of our present limited perception, and a Transformed Society is necessary to take shifting consciousness into account in all areas of life. Such perceptual awareness he believes is to free man from a singular cultural consciousness. Of course, such transformed awareness would be a hefty challenge to the fixed learning situation.

Alpha might provide the tool for this broadened awareness. Feeling states are important building blocks in biofeedback techniques, and consciousness is a changing event open to alteration. Perceptions are internalized and vary from person to person, relatively free of externalized dictates. For most people, the alpha state leads to passive awareness. This is a form of relaxed, non-critical consciousness. This broad-scale awareness of a passive nature is also a common trait among trained speed readers. Kamiya examined EEG recordings for a number of speed readers and found they were "producing lots of alpha in strong amplitude." The power reading process is based on a relaxed flowing, and turning on alpha gives a similar state of mind.

Biofeedback training might also aid in learning difficulties ranging from the hyperkinetic child to the slow reader who subvocalizes. Feedback methods have already had outstanding results with slow readers troubled by subvocalization, or silent mouthing of words.

Subvocalization is common, and slows down many children and adults when they read. It is an overlearned response, and is an electrical activity occurring in the laryngeal muscles of the Adam's apple, as the reader literally "reads aloud" on inaudible levels. Many such slow readers actually know how to read well, but, in spite of courses in remedial reading, they are unable to read any faster than 150 to 200 words per minute. Subvocalization also causes fatigue because it uses unnecessary energy, but this reading hangup is difficult to spot with standard diagnostic reading tests.

In the past, subvocalization was checked with the Faaborg-Anderson method. In this technique, needle electrodes were inserted directly into the Adam's apple muscles. While someone read, recordings were made to see if such excess activity was taking place. Not too surprisingly, the slow readers of the world did not all race off to have electrodes poked into their Adam's apples to see if they subvocalized. This technique can be both painful and, possibly, hazardous, if done inaccurately.

Unfortunately, just being warned that you silently mouth words as you read is not enough to do away with the habit. Speed reading courses and other special reading training also cannot get rid of subvocalization because it's an ingrained "habit" that begins in the first years of elementary school. This extra muscle activity in the laryngeal muscles continues to drag you down, much like a sprinter who tries to run the one hundred, with fifty pounds of chains dangling from his legs.

It appears, however, that a new feedback method can liberate the slow subvocalizer from his habit in just one or two sessions. Psychologist Curtiss Hardyck, at the University of California in Berkeley, and Dr. Lewis F. Petrinovich, Chairman of Psychology, at the University of California, Riverside, tackled the slow readers' subvocalization problem with the tools of biofeedback on both the high school and college level. They reported success as they found that subvocalization was eliminated for most students.

Drs. Hardyck and Petrinovich began their studies with seven subvocalizing students who were enrolled in a reading improvement class at San Francisco State College. The student volunteers had surface electrodes pasted upon their throats on each side of the Adam's apple. The electrodes were connected to an elaborate Honeywell data acquisition system, and a Beckman oscillograph to show individual EMG patterns.

The student was then asked to choose a light fiction book that interested him from a crowded bookshelf nearby. After picking a book to read, he sat down in a comfortable chair for an undisturbed half-hour of reading, while the scientists studied the recording charts to check EMG levels.

The choice of light fiction was deliberately made by Hardyck and Petrinovich. During reading of difficult material, everyone subvocalizes to some degree in working to comprehend and absorb material. Only habitual subvocalizers show evidence of this "silent mouthing of words" activity when they are reading interesting light fiction. Also, Hardyck and Petrinovich hoped that the light material might help the students become so engrossed in stories, that they could ignore the strange situation of sitting in an unfamiliar room with electrodes taped to their throats while scientists observed them.

As the students relaxed and read, Hardyck and Petrinovich watched the EMG activity record to filter out any artifact peaks caused by a swallow, a head movement, or any other inadvertent energy-producing action.

A week later, the students returned, and were retested to be sure that the machine recordings of muscle tensions were caused by subvocalization and not by nervousness at the novelty of the experience. When EMG patterns of extra tension levels again appeared, the students were told that subvocalization was taking place from silent mouthing of words. The havoc that this habit causes during reading was explained in detail.

After the electrodes were pasted on again, each student settled down once more to read. Again, wires from the electrodes ran to the EMG machine, but a new device was added, an instrument that sang with a pleasant amplified tone during relaxation—and a hideously rasping 500 cycle per second sound when tension reappeared in the laryngeal muscles. Silently mouthing a word tightened the larynx and triggered that unpleasant noise which then blared through a loudspeaker. No one liked that 500 cycle noise and, within one hour, every student was able to completely abandon the subvocalization habit.

Further testing of this biofeedback method was set up at the University of California at Berkeley, and at Emery High School, in Emeryville, California. Hardyck and Petrinovich found that the Berkeley students eliminated the subvocalization problem within one lesson. All of these college students had fairly high IQs, and were highly motivated to learn as they had responded to notices promising them possibilities of improving their reading speed.

The Emeryville high school students were another story. Their IQs covered a broad range, and ages ranged from seventh graders to twelfth graders. Regardless of grade, the below average IQ students did not respond as quickly to the biofeedback methods and, at a later rechecking, were found to have returned to their subvocalizing habits. But all of the average and above average IQ students learned quickly and completely eliminated slow reading habits caused by subvocalization. At a later check, none of these students had retrogressed to their previous reading problems.

Slow reading due to subvocalization is one educational area where biofeedback theories are of practical use. Another educational problem is the hyperkinetic child and, earlier in this chapter, mention was made of the Angie Nall School's pilot study using alpha biofeedback to reduce hyperkinetic activity. The original alpha-enhancement training project has been expanded to include fifty-four children. Gary Laird, a research therapist from Lamar University in Texas, is directing the controlled experiment. Alpha feedback devices will be used in half-hour sessions each day to increase the strength of alpha brain waves in the experimental group. Control groups will not receive the biofeedback training.

The opposite approach to aiding hyperkinetic children was taken at Green Valley School in Orange City, Florida. Superintendent George von Hilsheimer used biofeedback training to teach hyperkinetic children to suppress their alpha brain waves. These children learned to detect alpha brain rhythms and to turn these waves off during learning situations. Von Hilsheimer reported that alpha brain wave suppression helped children in his school improve their attention spans significantly.

Alpha brain wave control might also be of use in increasing such learning skills as attention, recognition, recall and visualization. One experimenter was reported to have found that learning is improved when biofeedback training has taught a person to control the difference in brain wave activity between the two cerebral hemispheres.

Attention, or the lack of it, is believed to show up in the patterns of your brain waves. A study by Mulholland indicated that brain waves are faster when you're paying attention to something specific and alpha rhythms are blocked. Mulholland's experimental work suggests that the absence of alpha brain waves pinpoints "an alert orienting attitude." Mulholland's findings on alpha blocking seem to show that brain-wave blocks of the alpha rhythm occur when you have visually fixed upon something, or when you track a moving object with your eyes. He trained people to decrease their alpha brain waves with feedback techniques, and suggests that the absence of alpha waves (and presence of beta?) could reveal higher attention levels.

To test his theory, Mulholland and Runnals invented a slide-projector system linked to a brain-wave-filter computer. When alpha brain waves were suppressed, pictures flashed upon the screen. When alpha brain waves returned, the pictures would automatically disappear. To hold the image on the screen, alpha waves had to be turned off. Learning to hold an image on the screen helped build attention spans through brain-wave control. However, EEG brain-wave recordings may not be the complete answer to gauging individual attention. Mullholland pointed out that movement of the eyes can alter EEG records. For example, oculomotor activity, like rolling your eyes upward, is a quick way to change your wave pattern, but is not related to your level of attention. (A standard yoga practice is to roll the eyes upward to look at the "ajana" or "third eye.")

A related experiment by Erik Peper tested the correlation of attention with brain waves. Brain-wave activity was used to check attention payed to slides of nudes and flowers. Pictures of voluptuous nude females surprised male volunteers, who quickly paid attention and peered at the sensuous scenes. By paying attention, they flipped off alpha brain waves for beta brain waves. When their alpha ceased, the nude immediately disappeared because only alpha production controlled the showing of the slides. The men had no trouble sustaining alpha brain waves, and signifying nonattention, during the slide depicting flowers. This result would seem to prove the relationship between alpha brain waves and attention and show that strongly directed attention shuts off alpha—except for one male volunteer whose reactions were the reverse of all the others.

Peper wondered if his experiment had failed until he questioned the young student who produced alpha easily during the nude picture, and shifted into beta brain waves when the flower slides came on. The student was a newlywed, oversaturated with nudity in his new marital relationship, and he could easily ignore the nude. But he was a horticulturist, and the flower fascinated him. He concentrated upon that slide because he'd never seen that species before and was trying to figure out what it was.

The nature of attention is a mysterious land only newly open to exploration by biofeedback researchers. The distinguished phenomenologist, Maurice Merleau-Ponty, proposed that attention might really signify "intention." Paying attention to an object or event by giving it a name also gives the object or event reality through recognition of it. This reality is said to come from our attachment to the object or event. Merleau-Ponty's definition of attention sounds like a Western version of Lao Tzu's comment in the *Tao Te Ching*, "The named is the mother of all things." Attention is linked to attempts at identifying objects or events in our minds, and cultivation of particular brain-wave states may aid in increasing attention spans.

The nature of visualization is another unknown educational area. Many scientists have speculated that visualization is the key to creativity, or, at least, one of the important factors in creativity. Visualization activity is thought by some researchers to happen within a narrow band of brain waves, twelve to thirteen Hz. It is placed, by other researchers, at about five to seven Hz., in the low-alpha to theta brain-wave area. People have learned to turn on each of these brain-wave areas at will, and increased imagery is said to result.

The Greens' work at Menninger's used brain-wave feedback to train people in the low-alpha and theta rhythm area. This technique might be useful in recall, and bring an end to the all too familiar mental blocks during examinations. The poised nondrowsy state that is generally associated with a high percentage of alpha brain wave production, appears to aid in increasing recall powers, according to the Greens' findings.

The Greens have been fascinated by the nature of the creative process. Increasing alpha and theta wave production can skyrocket creative possibilities, if the Greens' theories are correct. The noncreative person would like to become more creative and try to unlock unknown talents; the creative artist or writer or musician would like to enhance his present creative abilities. But, until recently, most thinking on creativity saw it as a fixed quantity. This may be incorrect.

To most people, creativity means presenting a new concept in a unique or artistic way. To be creative one need not necessarily be an artist: The conscientious housewife mixing chocolate-cake mix with cherry-cake mix to create a new flavor is being creative. The fourteen-year-old boy who uses his stack of abandoned comic books and decides to paper his walls in a colorful collage of comic fantasy is being creative. The Philadelphia artist who gathers scrap from trash cans and welds the discarded metals together into a massive abstract structure of a figure of a woman is being creative.

Creativity comes in many forms and finds outlets in areas ranging from a practical cake to sublime sculpture. In little ways, creativity lets the average person put some joy into a mundane existence. And, once in a great while, that creative energy bursts forth in genius, and mankind is enriched by a *Last Supper* by Da Vinci, or a *David* by Michaelangelo. Multiple factors, like talent and application of disciplined skills, determine just how "good" the results of any creative endeavor will be. Creativity can give us new ways to handle our life-styles and challenges, but, until recently, most people felt that their creativity ended with finger painting in nursery school.

Perhaps the deepest factor in creativity is its nonverbal aspect, its presence when the intellect is least apparent and the subconscious is free-flowing. One of the first steps in the creative process as delineated by G. Murphy, is:

> . . . the long immersion of the sensitive mind in a fulfilling medium with the world of color, of images, of social relationships, of contemplation, etc. Secondly, experiences are acquired in "great store-houses" by this immersion and consolidate themselves into structured patterns. From these great storehouses of experience comes an inspiration or illumination such as Archimedes leaping from the bathtub shouting, "I have it!" upon conceptualizing the law of specific gravity. Finally, the creative act is

sifted, tested, "hammered out," and integrated into the individual's other experiences with which it combines to produce the new poem, painting, invention, or other creative product.

Alpha brain wave states could be of help in this first stage of the creative process. The alpha experience results in a passively alerted state which is ideal for immersion. Davidson and Krippner found that this state is usual in alpha experiences. Once immersion has begun, the doors to the next creative steps are open to you. The Greens found that the stage of synthesis of images and thoughts and the recall of past experiences or facts, is commonly a low-alpha and theta state. Imagery and recall enhancement might open the doors to your locked creativity, and could be controlled at will with alpha and theta feedback training.

In 1964, Dr. Robert R. Holt studied imagery and recall, and wrote, "I want to mention briefly one specific implication of the work on imagery, which, to me, opens the most exciting vistas. . . . Several lines of evidence are beginning to suggest that the capacity for an astonishingly complete recording of experiences may be virtually universal, and that the problem is primarily one of getting access to the traces . . . the vehicle of the extraordinary recall is imagery . . . the indirect means of imagery may furnish the key to the fabulous storehouse of memory."

Imagery, the ability to think in pictures, is a creative mental happening. The vivid symbols flash by quickly behind your closed eyes, and you choose what you wish to work with. Another door to creativity may be found in reverie, defined by the Greens as a state of inward-turned abstract attention, or internal scanning. Simplified, what happens in reverie is that you internally sort through a great selection of visual symbols, and then put them together in a new alignment to create original relationships and, sometimes, concepts.

According to the Greens' research, low-frequency alpha and theta rhythms are definitely linked to both a state of reverie and hypnagogiclike imagery. They cite many outstanding thinkers whose most valued ideas came to them in such states described as "the fringe of consciousness, the off-consciousness, the transliminal mind, and reverie." These stages can be turned on at will with feedback training in the appropriate brain waves, and the Greens have trained numerous people to regulate these brain waves. Drowsiness, characteristic of these stages, is avoided with Greens' ingenious mercury-switch finger ring.

If feedback explorers like the Greens are correct, the untapped riches of creativity may lie just ahead for everyone within that "fringe of consciousness."

Chapter 9
Inner Awareness
Alpha and Meditation

The body is like a mountain . . .
The eyes are like the ocean . . .
The mind is like the sky . . .

The Siberian shaman chanted. His eyes glittered like stars, as he glanced at the men and women swaying on the cold dull earth in front of the tents of the Tungus. A-a-a-a-h, he breathed, like a shout, and his wrinkled hands slammed against the celestial horse drum to summon the spirits.

Shattered pillars bore mute testimony to bygone pride, but the Sufi dervish ignored the message of the past, as he whirled ever faster. Around and around, he danced in a swirl of motion, as he sought union with his God.

The air was moist and flat in the catacombs hidden deep below Roman eyes. Candles flickered, reflecting tiny spots of light along the earthen floor, but a great shadow swayed behind the Christian priest as he raised the blessed Host for everyone to see. The transformed Host signified the spirit of God for early Christians praying nearby.

Some mountains are like women, soft and curving, but the mountains in Mexico's Sonora are like rugged men, as they stand stark and militant against the thin air. Huddled inside a smoky hut, the Tehuamara Indians swallow the sacred mushroom in hopes of mystic experiences as they join with God. Looking disturbingly out of place in his levis and drip-dry shirt, Hal Jenkins dutifully chews upon the wrinkled brown button. As he gags at the bitter taste, he feels his stomach muscle clench with the grip of nausea, but fights down the sensation. He hitch-hiked 2500 miles from Cleveland, Ohio, to find expanded awareness in the mushroom ritual.

Satori, fana, union with God, transformation, cosmic awareness. Mahanand achieved through *samadhi.* Mystical experiences. Eigenwelt world. Dozens of words in dozens of languages preserve the religious experience of heightened awareness. Methods to alter consciousness and reach that mystical experience range from drugs to dances to meditation and fasting. Most of these techniques have their own particular drawbacks; the new biofeedback instrumentation may offer a more rapidly controlled pathway to internal exploration and expanded awareness in mystical experiences without side effects.

Through the ages, men and women have put themselves through astonishing contortions and self-multilation to reach mystical experiences. Why they have done so may be answered by Dr. Abraham Maslow's theory equating mystic consciousness and the peak experience. Maslow wrote that, "What has been called the unitive consciousness of the mystic is often given in peak experiences. That is, the sense of the sacred glimpsed in and through the particular incident of the momentary, the secular, the worldly . . . the fully human person in certain moments perceives the unity of the cosmos, fuses with it, and rests in it, completely satisfied for the moment in his yearning for oneness." Maslow's definition of peak experiences lists those timeless, egoless moments that happen spontaneously to all of us and are characterized by serene joy, and gives life validity despite its briefness. Such moments are so intense that they outweigh months of tedium without meaning. Examples of peak moments are the feeling you might get when you suddenly solve a problem you've worked upon for days and feel almost as if you had "given birth to the answer"; or, the feeling of ineffable joy when you touch the tiny fingers of your newborn child; or, the feeling of quietly watching the sunrise with a loved one and feeling yourself flow and merge with the enveloping colors.

Psychological researcher Dr. Arthur J. Deikman, tells us that the mystic experience results from an unusual state of consciousness, and may be beatific, satanic, revelatory, or psychotic, depending upon the predominating stimuli. Mystic experiences would tend to be states of internalized perception characterized by a unity of perceptivity and sensations. This concept often looks upon life as being enveloped in a cloak of unity, similar to that described by Wordsworth:

> There was a time when meadow, grove, and stream,
> The earth, and every common sight,
>   To me did seem
>   Appareled in celestial light,
> The glory and the freshness of a dream.

Meditation is a classic path to mystical insight. Practice consists in quietly paying attention. This calm and contemplative state allows you to be aware of your experiences. Even the agnostic can find positive value in meditation, as it tends to increase sensitivity and empathy, or openness to the feelings of others, in daily living situations. A unique experiment by Terry V. Lesh in *zazen* sessions of meditation, whose aim is to reach all the layers of human consciousness—from conscious to pre- and unconscious—suggests that meditative training might help a person "to be in tune with himself, and more openly effective in relating to others." *Zazen*'s goal is to allow all the human layers of consciousness to come to the surface by way of the normal senses in a wide-awake, alert state. Lesh studied a group of graduate students in psychology who were not very empathetic with their patients. They practiced a meditative exercise under scientific direction for a half-hour each weekday for a month. Significant improvements in empathetic ability were reported.

The quality of empathy, according to psychologist Katz, is a process known as "adaptive regression." This is a conscious attention to the more primitive layers of mental processes, a letting-go of logic and defensive attitudes, with increased access to preconscious states. It leads to an openness to experience, inner and outer, allowing us to identify with the feelings of others. Identification with others' needs comes first, as you remember when you felt similar sensations. Then you begin to incorporate the other person's experiences into your own gestalt, feeling the sensation as if it were your own when your best friend tells you of his shattered marriage. The feeling that you absorb echoes in your mind and reawakens a new understanding of others, and of yourself. "There, but for the grace of God, go I" is the cliché, and this is the experience that takes place. Finally, you withdraw from the feeling, and use psychic distance to think about the event, analyze it, and perhaps apply the experience to your personal life.

In the Lesh study, the most successful meditators enhanced their empathy and were the more self-actualized individuals, who depended upon their own feelings and value systems instead of the opinions of outsiders. Lesh concluded that *zazen* meditation appears to be an effective means of assisting people to self-actualization. Biofeedback alpha training can be used to speed up the meditative process.

Another type of meditation, transcendental yoga, is also amenable to the biofeedback alpha techniques. Just a few years ago, the tangled grey hair and glowing eyes of Maharishi Mahesh Yoga sparkled upon page after page of newspapers and magazines, as he carried the idea of his system of transcendental meditation to the world. This form of mantra yoga swayed the minds and souls of thousands, including such celebrities as the Beatles and Mia Farrow. Transcendental meditation seeks to allow the mind to "transcend" the subtlest activity of thinking, and reach a state of pure awareness in the source of thought, giving pure creative intelligence.

Physiologist R. K. Wallace investigated numerous transcendental meditators and found a number of physiological changes that happened as they meditated. Meditators' metabolic rates were reduced by an average of 20 percent, although blood analysis showed that a normal balance of oxygen to carbon dioxide was maintained. Their rate of anaerobic metabolism did not increase, but oxygen consumption, carbon-dioxide elimination, cardiac output, heart rate, and respiratory rate decreased in every case. Skin resistance increased, and EEG's of brain waves showed specific changes in certain frequencies. Alpha waves predominated, and were regular and stronger in amplitude. In a few cases, low-voltage alpha brain waves, and trains of the slower theta waves, appeared. Repeated sound and light stimuli had no inhibiting effect upon the alpha waves, although this reaction is common with the average untrained person.

Peering into the minds of these meditators by use of the EEG showed Wallace that their brain-wave patterns were extremely different from those in a sleeping stage. During normal sleep, slow delta waves, or sleep spindles, appear in the brain-wave pattern. No such patterns were found in the recordings for transcendental meditators. Their usual brain-wave pattern was characterized by strong alpha brain waves.

The most famous examination of meditators' minds was made by Dr. Akira Kasamatsu and Dr. Tomio Hirai, who studied EEG recordings of Zen masters and disciples in Japan in the 1960s. They discovered a distinctive energy signature of increasing alpha brain wave amplititude with a decreasing frequency, climaxed in some cases by a rhythmical theta train of these slower brain waves. This characteristic pattern was found in electrical brain signatures for all of the Zen meditators and has led Kasamatsu and Hirai to suggest that the meditative experience influences both the psychic life and the actual physiology of the brain.

Kasamatsu and Hirai investigated brain-wave patterns for forty-eight Zen priests and disciples from both the Soto and Rinzai sects. These Zen practitioners ranged from twenty-four to seventy-two years of age. Some were beginners with one to five years experience at Zen meditation, while sixteen were priests with over twenty years practice at *zazen* meditation. The scientists recorded meditators, EEGs, pulse rates, respiration rates, and GSRs for skin response for a week during a Sesshin session, an intensive Zen religious retreat that includes as many as eight to ten meditative periods a day.

These Zen Buddhists practiced *zazen*, a religious exercise

consisting of a sitting meditation devoted to concentrated regulation of the inner mind. Practice of Zen meditation aims at emancipation of man from the dualistic bondage of subjectivity and objectivity of mind and body, and of birth and death; freed from consciousness of one's self, there is an awakening to one's pure, serene, and true self.

Silver-coated disc electrodes were attached to the shaved scalps of the monks in the Kasamatsu and Hirai experiment. Electrodes were placed upon the frontal, central, parietal, and occipital regions in the middle line of the head. (This would be equivalent to running a line from the middle of your upper forehead to the very back of your head just above your neck.) Before meditation began, the monks' EEGs showed beta activity. Then they sat down on round cushions, crossed their legs, and looked downward as the *zazen* session began. Within fifty seconds, their EEGs had changed and showed alpha brain waves, even though all of the monks kept their eyes open while meditating. Throughout the sessions, all of the monks were able to respond to click stimuli, and yet maintain their brain patterns.

As meditation continued, their EEGs showed alpha waves beginning to increase in amplitude, making steeper "mountains" on the graphs. Finally, the alpha waves peaked at high amplitude levels, but began to decrease in frequency. The most experienced meditators then showed a rhythmical theta train. There was a direct correlation between years spent in Zen training and the variety of EEG changes. The Zen master evaluated his disciples' proficiency at meditation for Kasamatsu and Hirai, and confirmed the correlation of high proficiency and vast EEG changes.

The *roshi*, a rank in Buddhism equivalent to an abbot, showed extremely strong amplitude alpha brain waves, and more even brain patterns than the less experienced monks. The EEG changes of a Zen priest, with twenty years experience at meditation, showed pronounced brain-wave changes. Within a minute of beginning meditation, 40-50 microvolt strength alpha waves began. About seven minutes later, these alpha waves had increased to 60-70 microvolts, and the alpha wave presence was almost continuous from electrodes in all regions of the brain.

Alpha was especially dominant in the frontal and central regions. After about a half an hour, low alpha and theta waves appeared, and were soon followed by theta waves at six to seven Hz cycles.

Kasamatsu and Hirai recorded these dramatic changes in brain activity during meditative exercises. The outside observer would not be aware of these massive brain changes and would only see shaven-headed monks wearing colorful robes as they sat cross-legged and stared at the floor. These meditators try for an alert poised inner awareness and they "look for enlightenment with open eyes."

Erich Fromm wrote of enlightenment (in relation to psychological phenomena) and called it "a state in which the person is completely tuned to the reality outside and inside of him, a state in which he is fully aware of it, and fully grasps it. *He* is aware of it—that is, not his brain, nor any other part of his organism, but he, the whole man. He is aware of *it*, not as of one object over there which he grasps with his thought, but it, the flower, the dog, the man, in its or his full reality. . . . To be enlightened means the full awakening of the total personality to reality."

Yogis call such enlightenment *mahanand,* a state of ecstasy reached through their meditation, or *samadhi.* Yogis who practice Raj Yoga claim that they are oblivious to external and internal stimuli during their meditation. Stories of stupendous feats of mind over matter by Eastern yogis are old news. Indeed, 150 years ago, British colonists returned to England from Indian duty, and told those stories to wide-eyed children and adults in front of countless fireplaces. The yogis were said to be able to walk on fire without blistering, lie upon nails without wincing, raise and lower their blood pressure, drive sharp objects through their flesh without bleeding, and even decrease their body temperatures and heart rates to such a low low that they could be buried alive for days.

Three Indian scientists, B. K. Anand, G. S. Chhina, and Baldev Singh, decided to study the brain-wave patterns of yogis to learn what happens in the mind during *samadhi.* Two types of yogi practitioners were examined: Raj yogis during *samadhi,* and yogis with raised-pain-threshold skills. One of the yogis in the study also practiced the exercise of "pinpointing of consciousness," where attention is supposed to be concentrated upon different points of the vault of the skull. Raj yogis meditate with closed eyes.

All of the yogis showed a great deal of alpha activity in their normal and resting brain records. During meditation, their alpha waves were persistent, and had well-marked increased strength. A strong light affected the meditators enough to block their alpha rhythms and lower the voltage of their brain waves when they were resting. However, when the yogis were meditating, nothing disturbed their brain-wave patterns of strong alpha. The experimenters shined lights on them, made loud banging noises, and even touched them with hot glass tubes and vibrating tuning forks. When they were in meditation, no outside stimulus had any effect upon their brain waves.

The yogis practiced at raised-pain threshold showed copious alpha brain waves in EEG recordings both before and during the time hands were immersed in cold water of 4 degrees centigrade (39.2°F.) for almost an hour.

Both the Kasamatsu-and-Hirai Zen study and the Anand-Chhina-Singh yogi study, demonstrate that brain-wave functions are affected by meditative exercises. With enough practice and experience (as the Zen masters' EEGs showed), the changes become even more pronounced. Eyes-open alpha is rare in the average untrained person, but all of the Zen monks produced eyes-open alpha easily. The Zen monks did initially react to the stimuli, but adapted to it, reflecting the external and internal unity of their meditative philosophy.

The yogis' brain waves, showing no response to any stimuli from the external world, is equally unusual. Yogi meditative philosophy is internalized, and aims at shuting out the outside world.

Dozens of experimenters have shown that most people can learn to produce alpha brain waves quickly with biofeedback machinery. Now, it has been suggested by some meditators that these instruments could aid in meditating. Within a short time, many people can turn on persistent alpha waves, and increase alpha strength to high amplitudes. People who have had some experience with meditation have been shown to find turning on alpha an easily accomplished task.

When Kamiya learned of the Kasamatsu and Hirai study in Japan, he searched for individuals in the San Francisco area who meditated. When he tested and trained these American meditators in biofeedback at his laboratory at the Langley Porter Neuropsychiatric Institute, he found that meditative experience was a definite factor in biofeedback learning skill. Meditators learned faster and better than the average person, and could easily produce strong, prominent alpha waves.

In another feedback test at the Toomim Laboratory in Los Angeles, two experienced meditators learned to raise and lower the frequency of their brain waves in a matter of moments as they followed the pacing device of feedback instruments. Both meditators were found to have well-established high-amplitude alpha rhythms in tests made before they began their religious exercise. They were also just as quick to learn how to move into the highest ranges of alpha brain wave frequencies, around twelve cycles per second, and quickly control these waves. Alpha biofeedback training could give neophyte meditators a tremendous head start towards the more sublime states of meditative consciousness. Most forms of meditation and alpha control seem to flow best from passive alertness and relaxed attention states. Biofeedback alpha training has been used to extend inner freedom and powers by increasing self-awareness which are also the first steps in meditative awareness.

Serious religious meditators also practice elaborate exercises in breathing, thought direction, posture, and other rigors. Alpha brain waves are not the only physiological characteristic of meditators. As Wallace noted, a variety of physiological changes take place during meditation, many more extreme than those sometimes noted in alpha states. Turning on alpha waves does not necessarily turn on all those other physiological changes accompanying meditation and altering conscious states. Alpha brain waves are only one parameter of the meditative experience. However, a high alpha state is common in meditative minds and is achievable with instrumentation, in just a few hours. It might save a great deal of meditative time, and move the wishful meditator along in his task, if accompanied by other practices in the chosen meditative procedure.

"But it would only be a first step," Sessue, an old Zen monk commented. "Yes, you may get the same brain states with the help of these machines. It is possible if science says it is so. But it is like the burglar who breaks into the upstairs window to get into the house. Isn't it better to go in the front door?"

The front-door entry takes many years, too long for impatient Western personalities. Biofeedback-induced alpha is a beginning to speed meditative progress, and it may turn out to be a uniquely Western meditative discipline, an original meditative exercise of its own, that seems uniquely suited to our national characteristics.

Electronic meditation could be the technological society's answer to Western man's current quest for inner awareness. McLuhan tells us that electronic circuitry is orientalizing the West. Biofeedback does that by extension of the microcosm inside each of us and completing the loop between mind and body. Like the microscope, it enhances our sensitivity to the environment, but this environment is internal instead of external.

Feedback techniques bridge our awareness and "form a loop, and allow you to get information to a place that it's not normally available, or, if it is, it's an extraordinarily difficult thing," Dr. Robert Ornstein told the Biofeedback Research Society. He pointed out parallels between feedback techniques and meditative exercises, ranging from the Eskimos to the Zen masters to peoples in the desert, that work to illuminate the possibilities that lie within each human being. Instead of a prayer wheel spinning while you repeat various phrases, or a concentration upon breathing, or a focused awareness upon a word like "Om" or a picturesque mandala (graphic symbol), the feedback experience is its own meditative exercise.

Just exactly how could you use the biofeedback process for meditation?

You could let the feedback tone act as a mantra as you concentrate upon centering your self in nonjudgmental awareness upon that sound. You would let the sound cue guide you to self-awareness as you block out all movement and concentrate upon flowing with the signal.

Or:

You could use the tone like a koan in Zen. The harder you struggle to find the answer to the unanswerable question, the less apt you are to find it. Finally, you let go, and find there was nowhere to go all along. The same thing happens with biofeedback. You can struggle and struggle to reach alpha or to increase the amplitude of your alpha waves, and nothing happens. Yet, when you relax and let go, the alpha comes unforced.

Or:

You could use the light feedback on the machine as a mandala, and let that visual signal be your position of single-pointedness.

Or:

You could relax with the tao of your mind, and let the alpha waves flow until a warmth seems to glow in your brain, and nonjudgmental awareness ripples upon your consciousness. The essence of relaxation is not to cling, and the essence of naturalness is to make no effort.

Or:

You could pretend to be a Tibetan and stand by the river of your own mind as the feedback creates an image of your brain waves with tones and lights.

Clearly, biofeedback could be used as just another meditative technique. There is a danger for the neophyte meditator if the technique becomes an end in itself. This would be equivalent to the spiritual athlete, like the yogi who becomes so interested in body manipulations that he neglects the spiritual enhancement for which the exercise were created.

One West Coast based nonsectarian organization, the Bio-Meditation Society, already uses feedback machinery in meditative experiences. They adhere to no one meditative discipline, and also sell feedback EEG machines. Led by Jack Gariss, the organization has taught feedback meditative methods to some 800 people including artists, students, teachers, hippies, and parole officers.

Gariss is a grey mountain of a man and his words are reminiscent of the Greens' feedback philosophy as he speaks of self-regulation, instead of control, of alpha brain waves. He quotes Anthony Wallace's comment that depressives turn to meditation, while schizophrenics turn to the occult. Gariss was an avant-garde radio commentator on KPFK-FM for four years, and is articulate in explaining why so many people have turned to meditation. He says they become meditators, "Because they hurt. Because it hasn't turned out. Because they're on drugs, and want to get off. Or because they heard about meditation from someone else and the idea touched a curious nerve." He calls biofeedback meditation, "Meditation in the Year One."

During a recent weekend, he encouraged his meditator students to bring their feedback machines for a consciousness expansion trip in an inflatable environment. It simulated the "womb experience" for some, and the "mountain experience of choiceless awareness" for others. Spending the weekend in a huge inflatable environment like a translucent rainbow bubble is startling enough, but it was coupled with feedback machinery producing a cloud of tones signaling alpha brain waves. The wild sound of numerous tones flowing at once is almost orgiastic in the sensory bombardment that is produced.

Sharon is an eighteen-year-old student majoring in fine arts at a California college. She participated in one of these feedback meditative sessions and found the experience mind expanding. Her apple cheeks and sunshine yellow curls are reminiscent of a Rubens milkmaid, and her shy eyes reflect her sincerity, as she tells of the experience.

She recalls Gariss's confident voice, telling her to dial in and block out the irrelevant and concentrate on a nearby object.

She stared at the pattern of the tattered prayer rug she had brought with her, and felt the abstract patterns washing back and forth like a stream. She remembers being told not to strain, and to observe with a sense of joy as she related to the object. Soon, she felt vibrations from the colored patterns radiating to her body and her mind. The feedback tones for alpha sounded around her, and she believed she was losing her "self" as she let go and tried to flow warmly into the very atoms of the sinuously curving flowers on her rug. For a moment, she believed she could feel the flowers reach out. Her muscles felt soft and weakened in a strange but pleasant way. She imagined that her mind flew through space, skipping past the stars, and quietly speeding past weird gaseous clouds. Time melted, like Dali's limp clock.

"I can touch the universe. I am the universe. The universe is me," Sharon believed, and then grinned with joy. Loud and clear, the feedback tone rang alpha, and her amplitude meter pointed to sixty microvolts.

Working long enough with alpha feedback might lead to altered states of consciousness and mystical experiences like Sharon's. Altered consciousness has not occurred in all feedback experiences, but many of the lab reports deal with a few sessions, and people who are already adept at alpha wave rhythms often are blase about the experience and uninterested in continuing the work. However, a long-term experiment by Dr. Arthur Deikman, University of Colorado Medical School, produced some startlingly different results from most short-term feedback experiences. Dr. Deikman began to study meditators and had a scientist's curiosity as to why meditation brings on a mystical experience. He gave instruction in Pantanjala Yoga to naive subjects without telling them what the practice was and without emphasizing posture or breathing exercises. Alpha feedback training was added to see if expanded consciousness might result. Deikman gave up to fifty sessions, of about forty minutes each, in biofeedback training to each person in his study group. This is about five to ten times more sessions than the average feedback research experiment.

Unlike Zen meditators, Deikman's volunteers did not build up the strength of their alpha waves noticeably beyond a peaking point. But they did reach altered states of consciousness in many cases. For some, time condensed or expanded so that five minutes seemed like five hours. Body-image changes were reported, particularly detachment of limbs and great weight in legs and arms. After lengthy experience in feedback alpha, shifting consciousness was documented, but Deikman points out that "alpha feedback per se, as a way of training in meditation, has very definite limits."

Alpha brain waves seem to be most interesting to people

excited by inner-awareness potential, according to many investigators. But, once alpha wave production is mastered, people want to use it in some way. If this doesn't happen, they get bored and often drop out of laboratory experiments. Noting this phenomenon, Dr. Joseph Hart suggested that, "Alpha seems like a getting into a receptive background state, and then, from there, they can use things to emerge," but he added that "volunteers who were not given challenging chances to use the 'alpha' in productive ways dropped out of the studies."

Dr. Hart, who has examined the brain waves of the hypnotized, discovered that alpha feedback training enhanced hypnotic suggestibility. In a study by Dr. David R. Engstrom, Dr. Perry London, and Dr. Hart, the professed stability of hypnotic suggestibility factors was found to be incorrect. Until this study, science believed hypnotic suggestibility to be a constant characteristic that could not be altered or increased. Engstrom, London, and Hart used auditory feedback signals to teach increased alpha waves and discovered increased hypnotic suggestibility in the subjects after training.

Hart has also studied EEGs of swamis, yogis, tantra practitioners, autogenic training devotees, and transcendental meditators. He reported that everyone who had practiced any form of meditation for at least six months to a year, showed the same EEG pattern of high, base-line alpha, when they were not meditating. After meditation began, individual differences appear. Hart found this pattern was also true for hypnosis EEGs, which he calls "meditation for the common man." Hart once compared Eastern and Western meditation and said Eastern meditation had implicitly spiritual goals while in "Western form of meditation, hypnosis, those goals have dropped out, and what remains is the goal of control. Control and more power."

The spiritual goals of Eastern meditation are taught in a class called Yoga Psychology at Sonoma State College by Dr. Eleanor Criswell. This is one of the first American college credit courses in the theory and practice of Raja Yoga and also examines the psycho-physiological states of Yoga meditators. Dr. Criswell reminds us that Yoga and liberating disciplines have used a form of feedback from experience for centuries.

She invented a contemporary version of the Tibetan prayer wheel using visual stimuli on a cylinder placed upon a turntable. Within five minutes of watching it, altered sensory awareness begins. EEGs recorded from individuals using the wheel showed desynchronization followed by enhanced alpha of increasing amplitude.

Another parameter of the meditative EEG was studied and reported by Dr. Lester Fehmi, of the State University of New York. Dr. Fehmi has explored consciousness, attention, awareness, concentration, and focus, and he is interested in both feedback and meditation. Fehmi told of a karate expert who had spent ten years learning how to send all of his attention into one simple movement, a karate punch that was his prime act among a number of other karate blows. Fehmi examined the EEG of the karate expert, and found that, as the man waited to respond to a command to act, his brain waves were in fairly strong alpha with amplitude around seventy microvolts. When the signal to act came, he responded in a multiple of the alpha frequency, with amazing strength, ranging around 200 microvolts. Such concentrated awareness or mobilization of presence is about ten times greater than the average person produces.

The Yoga masters perform equally astounding feats in the areas of bodily control. In addition to being pioneer researchers, Dr. Elmer and Mrs. Alyce Green are at home with yogi theory and have practiced yogi exercises for a long time. Swami Rama, a genial Yoga master, volunteered to work with them in 1970, so that they could study the physiological nature of a virtuoso yogi. Swami Rama has trained in Yoga since he was four years old and is now in his late forties. Not too long ago, he held the rank of an associate Shankaracharya, about the highest degree of yogi rank possible.

Through sheer concentration, Swami Rama easily demonstrated his heart-control powers. For seventeen seconds, he stopped his heart from pumping blood.

Utilizing EEG feedback, the Greens signaled the Swami to enter into states they wished to investigate. Swami Rama meditated and easily entered theta of four to seven cycles per second. He could turn on stronger theta and maintain it with no difficulty and called it "a noisy state" where shards of memory from his deep unconscious erupted to the surface of his consciousness. Usually, such deep theta is present only during sleep, except in pathological cases. Surprisingly, the Greens subsequently trained a number of normal people to produce abundant theta brain waves easily, with no evidence of pathological activity. This evidence caused a Chicago psychologist to wonder if the current brain-wave definitions for pathology and psychological disturbance needed alterations.

Alpha brain waves have been discovered in the recorded brain patterns of meditators of varied disciplines. Alpha biofeedback techniques can teach you to enhance your own alpha waves and replicate the brain patterns of experienced meditators, providing a meditative shortcut along the long road of spiritual evolution. But alpha is only the beginning of meditative mental states, and further mental exercises would be necessary to allow us all to enjoy the spiritual ecstasies of a roshi or a swami. Alpha will open the door for you, but you must walk further along that path by yourself.

Chapter 10
The Dark Side of the Mind
Alpha and Psychotherapy

Speeding through the dark night, the grim man hunched over the wheel of his car, gripping the wheel with hands paled by tension. Trees and brush loomed past as he tried to outrace his fears. "This time, I'll see it," he thought, and turned his head quickly to peer at the back seat.

But there was no one there. Nothing unusual was visible. His car swerved, and he turned back to watch the highway in front of him. "Mustn't let it get to me," he thought, and forced himself to drive on toward home.

But the thought began to build again, as fear crept on lizard feet into his mind. *Death was his passenger. Death was riding behind him through the night. There was a body in the back seat of his car.* Again, he warned himself not to get frightened, knowing it was imagination playing tricks upon his anxiety.

Weeks later, he lay quietly upon the couch as he told the psychologist of his mental experiences. Funeral houses, graveyards, coffins, and corpses peopled his mind and filled him with dread. His fear of the dark, and what it might hold for him, had grown so strong that he was physically unable to enter the dim basement of his own home. Standard therapy had had no effect upon his deep-rooted fears.

"Lie still," he was told, "and just let go." Electrodes were attached to his scalp, and feedback cues were flicked on. Alpha brain wave states might help the man relax enough to allow the psychologist to explore the dark side of his troubled mind. The idea was that the alpha state might work as an anxiety counter-conditioner to desensitize the man. Nothing else had worked. After two biofeedback sessions, he managed to raise the strength of his alpha brain wave level from twenty percent to eighty percent.

In a separate session, Dr. Budzynski asked the man to list his special fears, and he named such items as sleeping in the attic and a cemetery nearby. Then he was asked to visualize each item he'd named as a fear. His alpha rhythms disappeared and he moved into beta whenever he visualized a frightful scene. It was soon seen that visualization of pleasant scenes had the same effect on his alpha brain rhythms. The presence, or absence, of alpha brain waves could not be used to indicate the level of anxiety in his case, so a finger signal was added and used to indicate feelings of increased anxiety.

Alpha feedback was used between each visualization of a fearful image to soothe the man's mind. He found that the feedback helped him banish negative scenes quickly and aided him in rapidly reentering states of deep relaxation. In this deeply relaxed state, he was able to gradually confront his phobias, understand them, and slowly eliminate them. The deep relaxation experience also aided in recall. Several hours after his first desensitization session, the man remembered that his grandmother was buried in the cemetery he had visualized. Other recalled memories explained his fears of basements and attics, and his phobias began to vanish with his increased understanding. At a check six months later, all of the man's phobias had been completely eliminated.

Alpha states are relaxing to most people. In another study by Dr. Lester Fehmi, with EEG feedback and associated states of awareness, only a few people were unable to produce and control their own alpha brain waves. The great majority learned quickly and found the experience gave them "an increase in smooth-flowing energy, a release of tension, and a spreading of attentional focus." Other alpha researchers report similar results, stating that most people find the alpha experience relaxing and pleasant.

The relaxation aspect of alpha has been used with remarkable success by Dr. Thomas Budzynski and Dr. Johann Stoyva. They combined deep relaxation methods with feedback for desensitization treatment of phobias in a number of cases. Deep relaxation is a long-accepted psychological technique, first utilized around the turn of the century by other psychologists. Systematic desensitization has a time drawback, as it takes many sessions prior to fear confrontation. The psychologist must first teach the patient a series of exercises for deep relaxation. Once that deep-relaxation state has been achieved, the therapist must slowly and systematically lead the patient on a journey to understand his anxieties. Budzynski and Stoyva introduced EMG biofeedback for quickly achieved relaxation, and drastically cut the treatment time necessary for systematic desensitization.

Systematic desensitization without the objective monitoring and relaxation properties of the EMG feedback usually runs the risk of attempting desensitization when the patient is not relaxed. Budzynski and Stoyva first trained the patient in deep relaxation with biofeedback and then used the feedback machinery to help the patient remain relaxed during the therapy.

In one of their cases, a forty-five-year-old woman had tried conventional behavior therapy methods but still could not relax. At parties, she was so nervous that her right hand shook dramatically. Due to her trembling hand, she could not even hold a glass or shake hands with someone introduced to her. Her therapist referred her to Budzynski, who taught her deep relaxation with EMG biofeedback training. He began with her forehead muscle, the frontalis, but that proved to be too frustrating. Training treatment was shifted to her forearm muscle. When she achieved that, they progressed onward until she was able to relax her frontalis muscle when she wished. After she learned deep relaxation, she returned to her regular therapist, and confronted her fears in an intense desensitization session. Her tremor soon disappeared completely.

Budzynski used a similar muscle feedback technique to free a twenty-two-year-old girl from a huge collection of phobias, including fear of heights, fear of crowds, fright over riding in cars, claustrophobia, and panic attacks.

Another feedback success was reported in the case of a young member of the Alpine ski team. He was an excellent skier, who froze before races from incapacitating leg cramps due to anxiety. Budzynski used muscle feedback to teach the skier how to relax his leg muscles before a contest began.

In another case, a middle-aged management consultant had become so afraid of facing people in public that he'd refused to accept several lucrative public-speaking jobs. EMG feedback training by Budzynski taught this man how to relax and systematic desensitization sessions followed. Today, the management consultant can address large crowds with only occasional twinges of anxiety.

Other scientists have tried feedback to help anxious people relax. A New York City psychoanalyst, Dr. Charles C. Dahlberg, reported his professional experiences to the Biofeedback Research Society. Dr. Dahlberg used a portable audible GSR machine for EMG feedback in an attempt to help an extremely tense patient relax before analytic sessions. Prior to the experiment, Dr. Dahlberg noted that the patient was a wave of motion, jerking and bending even while sitting in a chair. The man simply could not sit still, and twisted his arms around, cracked his knuckles, and even burped and gurgled as his extreme tension overflowed.

Dr. Dahlberg obtained a small GSR machine and gave the feedback instrument to the youth, instructing him to train himself for about ten minutes before each analytic session was scheduled to begin. The young man's relaxation came sporadically, but his overall tension lessened to some degree. Sometimes, the patient could not let the relaxation state come, and sometimes he just refused to do it. He explained to Dr. Dahlberg, "If you can let it happen, it's fine. You can't always let it happen." On at least one occasion outside of the doctor's office, he was able to turn on the learned relaxation in a distressing situation, and the experience helped him greatly. When the patient relaxed in the office, visual images floated vaguely into his mind, with drifting pictures of the water, or the beach.

This bubbling up of images could have therapeutic value. Dr. Elmer and Ms. Alyce Green have worked in this area and use a unique biofeedback approach to produce willed reverie in individuals. Usually, the reverie stage is of little use to therapists because the individual cannot communicate well, but the Greens' feedback-induced reverie is so self-controlled that people are able to answer questions intelligibly while maintaining the reverie experience and corresponding brain waves. In the Greens' technique, alpha waves are slowly lowered and theta waves are increased. If their lab successes at producing reverie are amenable to transplantation in the broader outside world of psychotherapy, treatment time could be dramatically reduced. The Greens hope this will be true.

"Psychiatrists," they propose, "will be able to develop in many patients a deep reverie in a short period of time through the use of feedback technology for a deep relaxation and, if they use EEG feedback during interviews with selected cases as we have done with each experimental subject, an increased amount of normally unconscious material should be recoverable."

EEG recordings of alpha activity might also be useful in measuring changes in psychotherapy. Dr. Marjorie Kawin-Toomim suggests this possibility. She reported the experience of a clinical psychologist who used one of the portable alpha pacers designed by Dr. Toomim, to test levels of alpha brain waves while she worked with her clients.

When she was working, the clinical psychologist found that she was producing copious alpha and experienced an "accepting non-judgementally flowing feeling of merging with a client's thoughts and feelings." Yet, when she was quietly alone, her alpha brain wave levels dropped. Dr. Toomim believes checking alpha waves of both therapists and clients could help gauge levels of corresponding sensitivity and openness and provide a measure for psychotherapeutic changes.

Biofeedback training may also lead toward a science of introspection. Each feedback-trained individual learns about his inner being and knows how to look at the physical nature of himself through the nature of the feedback learning process. This instant inner knowledge is necessary for the learning loop to be completed, and it presents a challenge to contemporary science.

Carl Rogers wrote of the "possibility of universal human value directions emerging from the experience of the human organism" as man discovers values from within, instead of relying upon those imposed from outside forces. Biofeedback comes from this kind of internal discovery and is a technological key to help the individual open himself to himself in an introspective journey into his own inner reality.

Drs. Davidson and Honorton wrote of the implications of biofeedback discoveries, and the possible effects this perceptual science may have upon psychological science. As more people learn how to use feedback to utilize "volition" and "will" in controlling their own psychological processes, challenges will occur. They theorize that the self-actualization process would appear to be immediately speeded up as men exercised their "free will" in a more liberalized fashion than has ever been possible before.

In the early 1960s, Maslow praised the self-actualized man for his ability to resist "rubberization," the end result of civilization's processing of human beings. Maslow's ideal self-realized individual could resist the onslaughts of cultural biases or societal conditioning. In the decade since Maslow expressed his ideas, more and more people have come to resent being processed and are seeking such "self-actualization." Drs. Davidson and Krippner predict that the biofeedback innovation will help "large numbers of people evolve into more integrated beings who are less subject to manipulation, and more inner-directed."

"Know thyself," Plutarch counseled centuries ago. Davidson and Krippner suggest that Plutarch's maxim could be realized in unprecedented ways with feedback techniques. They wrote that, "With the self control of a variety of internal parameters, individuals may be able to function in new psychological states, as yet unidentified, permitting them to explore latent and undeveloped aspects of their beings." According to their ideas, current instrumentation could be used to create new states through regulation of varied internal parameters and might even "help people attain states that have been known to Zen and Yoga practitioners for centuries."

Individual therapeutic application of feedback techniques is also suggested by Dr. Barbara Brown. Her numerous laboratory tests would seem to indicate that individuals can spot subjective activity through perceiving, isolating, and identifying aspects of the inner self with the aid of brain-wave feedback. Dr. Brown concludes that this feedback-aided awareness of the self "also provides the visual recognition (and hence validation) of the individual ability to produce and sustain a useful, enjoyable, and confident effect," which is an essential factor in both psychiatric and psychosomatic treatment techniques.

Feedback could also be used to give a new dimension to group-therapy and consciousness-raising sessions. Dr. Thomas Mulholland proposed such brain-rhythm training for groups. The participants would be hooked up together to biofeedback equipment and would use brain waves tied to a group-reinforcement system. A reward would be given when all members of the group managed to produce alpha in their occipital recordings. Mulholland speculates that the alpha state might occur coincidentally among members of the group more often in a linked setting.

At first, the idea of a group of people wired with electrodes as they try to "home in" on a feedback tone sounds as fantastically bizarre as a science fiction writer's midnight fancy. But, the beginning laboratory proof for the effectiveness of such group wave control has already been accomplished. In 1969, Dr. Joseph Hart studied "yoked control" possibilities for alpha brain wave training. He reported that most subjects in his experiment doubled their alpha production when they received taped feedback tones from a training subject adept at producing alpha brain waves. Perhaps, just as you can "learn" how to play golf from a golf pro, you might also be able to "learn" alpha brain waves from an alpha pro.

Group experiences in alpha states might also increase sensitivity levels. Recently, Kamiya suggested feedback training increases sensitivity and relaxed awareness and might have beneficial effects upon group-therapy sessions.

It may also be possible to use brain-wave recordings to diagnose approaching neurosis or psychosis. Feedback scientists, like Fehmi, are now studying nervous circuits in the brain to learn how patterns deviate from their optimal and normal activation patterns to bring about behavioral disturbances.

Recently, Dr. M. A. Bruck investigated both phase and frequency aspects of brain-wave recordings for hospitalized schizophrenics, nonschizophrenic patients, and normal people. The normal person's patterns were used for controls. Schizophrenics were found to show less synchronization in wave patterns taken from various areas, and also had faster wave activity.

The in-phase score, a measure of how relatively synchronous the activity from the different areas is, was found to be more similar in normals. The average person had brain-wave patterns that were more integrated, and had more of an overall agreement or synchronization. Bruck then attempted to train subjects to control this phase relationship between wave production with biofeedback. He reported that voluntary control over phase relations, between occipital recording sites, was achieved.

On the basis of his study, Bruck concluded that schizophrenics could be distinguished from normal and nonschizophrenic patients by checking both phase and brain-wave amplitude. In a related area, Fehmi suggests that enhancement of amplitude and phase agreement through biofeedback techniques might have beneficial effects on psychotic patients.

In another study, Drs. Thomas Mulholland and Frank Benson found that large recurring bilateral mismatches in brain-wave recordings were "a pathological sign, even if the individual wave forms of the EEG are not clearly pathological." The Mulholland-Benson experiment took place at the Perception Laboratory of the Veteran's Administration Hospital in Bedford, Massachusetts. Previously diagnosed aphasia patients' brain patterns were contrasted to recordings from normal people. Aphasia is the loss or impairment of the power to use or understand speech resulting from brain lesion or, sometimes, from functional or emotional disturbance. Recordings were made in a dim room, with electrodes placed on the parietal and occipital areas on both the left and right sides of the brain. To reduce the difference of "noisy" variations in alpha and no-alpha periods, visual feedback was used and included slides with pictures of a house and a policeman, and words like broom and bitch. Aphasia patients' recordings showed bilateral mismatches and led Mulholland to conclude that such recordings could be used for more efficient diagnosis of brain pathology.

Extreme alpha asymmetry, with great differences in patterns of alpha from different brain regions, is believed to be present in cases of brain pathology. Extreme asymmetry is rare in normal people's brain-wave recordings, although it may sometimes be found.

In a pilot study in the spring of 1971, Erik Peper trained normal people to voluntarily control alpha asymmetry, through biofeedback training. Electrodes were placed in the parietal and occipital regions of volunteers' scalps and a tone was used as the feedback cue. Some of the volunteers learned to optimize the conditions under which asymmetry and symmetry happen, and Peper is setting up a more extensive experiment that might show that biofeedback can aid in voluntarily controlling alpha asymmetry for possible use in treating brain pathology.

Alpha feedback promises to do many things to aid in psychological therapy and may even institute a new science of introspection. Alpha states relieve tension in many anxious, uptight people. Alpha feedback might also be used to present a relaxing atmosphere for confrontation of minor fears or stress-producing factors. Many scientists are convinced that alpha training helps the individual know himself better and aids him in interacting with other people. Biofeedback of brain-wave states has produced states of reverie in one recent experiment, and such reverie at will could facilitate therapy. Alpha feedback could be of use in systematically desensitizing people with anxieties and phobias. Finally, some experts have conducted studies that suggest alpha brain wave patterns could aid in diagnosing brain pathology and schizophrenia.

Part Three:
The Individual
and Alpha

Chapter 11
Buying
Your Own Piece
of Alpha
Home Biofeedback Machines

Ravi Shankar's music dances upon the air as you enter the mod factory of Aquarius Electronics, a simple wooden shelter in northern California, 170 miles above San Francisco. Inside, colorful electronic trinkets are strewn across handmade wooden tables beside a beckoning fireplace with its crackling fire. A screen device and a wooden box gleaming with dials and buttons stand in front of a large window revealing ancient trees.

Tim Scully, primary owner and director of Aquarius Electronics, typifies many of the feedback-machinery manufacturers. Located near the picture-postcard town of Mendocino, his electronics firm is operated in a candidly casual manner, and instruments are assembled by counterculture citizens on a part-time basis. *Life* magazine credited Aquarius Electronics with being the first biofeedback firm offering portable alpha instruments for sale to the public. They began in the late sixties and have sold nearly 1000 instruments. The owner, Scully, once handled sound details for a famous rock-and-roll group and, like most biofeedback manufacturers, has a broad background in engineering. He became interested in biofeedback after serving as a volunteer subject for an alpha researcher and soon built up an extensive library of biofeedback research materials.

His patented invention, the Alphaphone headset, is one of many types of home feedback units available on the market. Other manufacturers offer sets ranging from do-it-yourself assembly kits for $29.85 to elaborate laboratory quality instruments costing thousands of dollars. His original instrument was a headset, a battery-operated device with metal electrode tabs held in place by a headband which relayed brain waves to black boxes transmitting the sounds in the earphones. They now manufacture a more elaborate feedback instrument, boxed in a fine wooden case, with complex filters to avoid artifacts (spurious signals) of background noise. A photon coupler is also available and functions like an adapter so that the battery-powered instruments may be linked to AC powered equipment like repeating lights, music synthesizers, color organs, amplifiers, and chart recorders. They have worked with researchers Drs. Davidson and Honorton, and are now constructing an environmental brain-wave device designed by Dr. Jean Houston.

Scully's feedback instruments have been sold to purchasers from Kansas City to Ontario, Canada; Bangkok, Thailand, to London, England; and Johannesburg, South Africa, to Pontiac, Michigan, through direct mail and advertisements in publications like *Psychology Today.* Pleased purchasers send him letters with comments that range from "Wowie, Zowie," and "Right on," to "Your efforts are greatly appreciated. God bless you all!"

Many types of feedback instruments are manufactured by men like Scully, and are for sale for home use. Instrument quality varies from bad to merely mediocre to good, although, because of the expense, none are of complex laboratory quality. With some forty-eight manufacturers, it is no surprise that potential feedback purchasers feel marooned in an electronic jungle. Immense rivalry exists among manufacturers, and many denigrate others' products. Today, there are no industry standardization criteria, although some manufacturers, like Scully, have corresponded and are hoping to set up an industry-wide code of standards. There are no government standards on feedback machinery at this writing.

Most available machines are EEG biofeedback for alpha or

for alpha/theta. A dozen manufacturers produce headphone battery sets based on the electroencephalophone principle, costing from $50 to $200. Next come the portable boxed instruments, with or without earphones, costing around $200, and featuring more elaborate technology. The better EEG machines are sold with a warranty, a repair agreement, and a thorough booklet and/or record of instructions on machinery use and electrode placement. Most manufacturers sell by direct mail and many begin and end their business careers within a few months. A few EMG feedback machines are available, including the Bioelectric Information Feedback System model, designed by researcher Dr. Thomas Budzynski.

One of the biggest problems with home use is background interference or other artifact interference from improper electrode placement. Many research scientists disapprove of portable home instruments. Dr. Thomas B. Mulholland recently presented a report to the Massachusetts Psychological Association in which he warned that ". . . for the true believer, any sound from the alpha kit is welcome news even if it is produced by scalp twitches, or amplifier noises. Ignorance can be blissful. There are technical problems when recording the EEG, which become more difficult when the recording is done under uncontrolled conditions, with improper techniques, and with no knowledge of the various kinds of spurious signals which can be recorded from the scalp . . . when an amateur is using a do-it-yourself alpha feedback kit." He added, "Of course, it is possible to make reliable, accurate alpha amplifiers and to learn the proper technique of recording. It is unlikely that this package would be inexpensive."

Recognizing the problems involved, another researcher cautioned the first annual conference of the Biofeedback Research Society to set up guidelines, and warned of the ease with which almost anyone with a smattering of engineering knowledge could obtain a circuit diagram, and replicate his or her own home-made alpha pacer, or individual EEG, EMG, or GSR machine. GSR machines are of particular interest to the Food and Drug Administration, because actual skin penetration is often involved in the procedure. Electronarcosis instruments, with needle implantation into the scalp, are also under investigation. A number of "implantation instrument" manufacturers have reported informal visits from F.D.A. inspectors, but the EEG and EMG field is still wide open. The proliferation of home feedback units has caused a controversy among scientists because some of the machines are of good quality, and others are quickie concoctions which have small chance of recording anything except background electrical noise. The more "chancy" firms also tend to be the most grandiose in their advertising claims, and promise quick cures for everything on the way to the Promised Land. The more responsible manufacturers are less expansive in their claims and offer all kinds of aid to the beginning feedback enthusiasts, including free literature, drawing accurately and heavily upon respectable research material. They also tend to impose controls of advertising by distributors.

Dr. Barbara Brown commented that the proliferation of home feedback units was bound to happen because people have such a strong interest in the field. She has urged scientists to devise some kind of standards before problems occur. As a simple example of possible hazards, eye blinks are picked up on many home machines, and the amateur trying his hand at feedback could easily think these eye flickers are alpha. Before he knew it, he could train himself into a blinking squiggling eye pattern.

Even more serious dangers could occur, with machines giving inaccurate feedback. Dr. Brown employs a number of laboratory assistants who are carefully instructed to watch EEG's on each subject, and instantly halt any experiment when an irregularity begins to appear. But she tells of another scientist's study where a woman was suddenly spotted as mistakenly learning to produce epileptic spikes because of inaccurate machinery. Improper machinery might not discriminate between two such wave patterns, and produce problems.

The home trainers are all battery operated, and types of available electrodes vary from steel to silver and even gold. Filter circuits range in ability to exclude frequencies. Of economic necessity, all inexpensive instruments must be mechanical compromises. This is similar to the difference between a transistor pocket radio sold at $9.95, and an $150 AM/FM radio receiver with exceptionally fine tuning.

Home feedback instruments are sold with a wild assortment of extras. One manufacturer lures you in with training tapes and a mind-power personality integration course. Another offers a mind globe, so you can watch the colorful patterns of your own thoughts. (The globe is a simplified color organ, also available at lower cost from mail order scientific suppliers like Edmond's.) A third device uses a "white noise" generator for a blocking effect and, as a modulation carrier, a rather surprising electronic combination. And, if none of these technological tidbits tempt you, then you might wish to purchase your feedback instrument from the manufacturer who offers you one free computerized analysis of your brain waves.

What's wrong with this proliferation of home feedback instruments, multiplying overnight like the brooms in the tale of the Sorcerer's Apprentice?

"Some persons in need of medical attention may be led into relying upon methods which *must* still be regarded as experimental," warned Leonore Morrell, Stanford University School of Medicine researcher, in *Science News*. "The premature commercial exploitation of biofeedback technology raises serious questions of ethics, the presumed benefits remain to be substantiated by serious research." Other researchers add to her caution the advice that, when all benefits have been investigated and proven, the medical training should still be supervised by experienced technicians following thorough medical diagnosis. Scientists point out that home machines for do-it-yourself alpha could lead to medical problems. Many machine manufacturers have strong electronics backgrounds, but no training in neurophysiology. Diagnosing your own illness is dangerous enough, but treating yourself could be even worse. The use of home instruments to treat your own possible psychosomatic illness is *not recommended* by research scientists or by this writer. For example, you could attempt to train yourself in heart-rate control with a home feedback instrument and actually produce "resistance" by adding stress to your overtaxed heart.

In the not too far distant future, feedback clinics should be available throughout the country. Such clinics would feature elaborate finely calibrated machinery that could give specialized training in a particular control after outside specialists confirmed diagnosis of an ailment. Electrodes would be properly placed and programs would be shaped to a particular need. Improperly placed electrodes give you a recording of jaw clenching, mouth movements, eyeball movements, or eye blinks. If you do plan to buy your own feedback instrument, have a qualified EEG technician teach you how and where to attach electrodes to receive appropriate brain waves. You would be best advised to buy a machine recommended by one of the legitimate scientific researchers.

Most researchers feel that the portable EEG feedback machines are best suited for meditative use. Portable EMG instruments would seem best for learning how to relax. However, the machines are not overnight wonder workers.

Hopefully, a qualified scientific organization, like the Biofeedback Research Society, will soon formulate a list of standards for home feedback instruments available for public use. Such public guidelines undoubtedly would include necessity of warrantees, available repair service, good filters, thorough manuals on operation, guarantees on parts and workmanship, good artifact rejection or filtration, and fine sensitivity.

Other possible factors to consider might be: both amplitude moderation and frequency modulation, output jacks and a real time output dial, a percentage indicator, and a reasonable price. Whatever the factors, however, a good guideline is necessary to aid the public in choosing a good machine. Such guidelines are necessary from qualified scientists before some overly enthusiastic entrepreneurs create public harm and give the biofeedback field a tarnished reputation. In addition to the responsibility owed to the public, scientists owe it to themselves to create machine standards before public opinion sours on feedback and public money for research work becomes unavailable.

Chapter 12
The Alpha Sellers
Psuedo-Scientists and Public Danger

The rented hotel meeting room was overcrowded, and there were no vacant seats beckoning the latecomers to rest. A few people sat on the floor near the speaker in the front of the room, or in the very back, fringing the crowd of seventy-five expectant men and women with their positive smiles and aura of practiced hope. All of these people had paid two to five dollars each to hear an advertising pitch from an "alpha seller." Alpha sellers are the pseudo-scientists now riding the lecture circuit, like old time travelin' men who roamed about the country selling bottles of Dr. Crock's cure-all elixir. But the present-day elixir is "alpha," bottled and packaged in a commercial version that seems like a strange step-sister to legitimate alpha feedback scientists because *none* of the current "alpha sellers" use any feedback machines. Alpha feedback without the feedback machinery just isn't possible.

Ah well, never mind, the alpha sellers tell the crowds of desperate, or curious, or superstitious, or naively hopeful people. It's still "alpha," because they say it is. They'll gladly sell you a piece of that alpha future for $150, sans machines, of course.

Most alpha sellers (and they are legion) begin with a come-on lecture which is a catch-all version of Cayce, positive thinking power, and old time revivalist's turn-on. The alpha "lecturers" are smooth, oh so smooth, and they function like technological gypsies. All seem to make vague allusions to their own research societies, research foundations, and connections with legitimate researchers. And they all promise something for nothing, but you "get what you pay for." And the promises, like exotic baubles, are whisked away again before you have a chance to examine them in strong light and see that they may be only glass. Large expensive ads in Sunday newspapers across the land proclaim, "looky-looky-come-and-see" in a sophisticated style. But, between the lines, these ads still reek of the carny's now-you-see-'em-now-you-don't. Respected national magazine articles on alpha scientific breakthroughs are quoted in the ads—out of context, of course. Roll it all together, and you have a great tinsel ball of promises.

Through lectures alone, the alpha sellers promise to give you better grades, better memory, revitalization and healing, help with sleep and headache problems, aid in ESP intuition, better concentrative powers, spiritual and religious experiences, increased pleasure and enjoyment, prolongation of youthful vigor, problem-solving powers, and the elimination of pain. Oh, and also, help with drug and drinking problems, aid in eliminating bad habits, increased inspiration, enhanced creativity, and perfecting of your internal powers so GREAT THAT YOU ARE BOUND TO BE A PRIME CITIZEN IN THE SECOND PHASE OF HUMAN EVOLUTION ON THIS PLANET, A MEMBER OF THE ALPHA GENERATION.

These introductory alpha-sell lectures used to be free, but inflation has a long arm, and now you are charged for the privilege of hearing the pitch. Budgets are tight, and the admission price is usually collected by the lecturer's wife or a devoted "graduate." To cloak their claims in legitimacy, many of these alpha sellers distribute unauthorized reprints of articles from national magazines that tell of alpha discoveries by scientists. However, these reprints sometimes are bootlegged and give no credit to the original publication source; they are pretty, often packaged in fancy binders, and stamped with glue-on decals proclaiming it "confidential," or "restricted information."

Lecturers ride the circuit from major city to major city, but each visit is preceded by glossy ads in the local papers announcing their "important introduction to alpha." Each lecturer spends a week or two in each city, then moves on to the next, and the next, and the next. The alpha lectures always seem to be given in the same type of hotel, those homogenized plastic structures populated mostly by lonely-eyed salesmen on expense accounts. Lecturers rent a meeting room and wait for the responses to roll in. Inquiries are haphazardly coordinated by a staff of one, consisting of a paid answering service at $15 a month. But, when you're running a franchise operation, as some of these alpha-sell packages are, you've got to watch your expenses. Right?

As you pay your admission price to enter the meeting room, a sweet-faced young girl hands you a registration card and smiles innocently as she asks you to fill out the form. The card has blanks for your name, address, phone, occupation, and such assorted tidbits as: "How did you hear of the lecture?" and "Would you care to recommend a friend who should be invited to the next lecture?" These cards make a dandy direct-mail list for re-pitching you in the future, and that's just what they're used for. Turn in your card, and enter the lecture hall.

Inside the room, the walls are barren except for the harshly stark sheen of the mass-produced lighting fixtures. A thick green carpet covers the floor, and straight chairs are soon claimed by the milling crowd. The audience is a cross-section of hard-pressed humanity. In the front is the fading beauty, preening as she pats her hair. Beside her is the beaten secretary, pulling her skirt down modestly over her fattened thighs. The bald head of the pink-cheeked lean octogenarian gleams beside her. A middle-aged housewife sits behind them, resplendent in criss-cross pumps, glasses, and a home permanent. The engineer types tend to sit in the middle of the hall, and many of them studiously zip out pens and pads to take notes. The old and the young smile at each other in a nervous, quivering way, each wondering what the hell the other is doing there.

The lecturer strides to the front of the room, smiling. He

smiles a lot during the evening, especially when he quickly throws out his more outlandish statements and claims. He is tall and lean, with intense eyes, and a pair of horn-rimmed glasses that he dons like stage props whenever he "reports" a scientific discovery.

He begins to speak in a practiced, warmly dynamic voice, and welcomes you to an adventure into the inner space of the human mind. Quickly, he speaks of Taoism, Hinduism, Edgar Cayce, Norman Vincent Peale, Bernard Baruch, Franklin Delano Roosevelt, Freud, Berger, Kamiya, Brown, Mulholland, The Greens, and Jung. Somehow, with the assistance of these names, he promises aid to both the shell-shocked soldier and the housewife with migraines from stress.

"All you need to do," he says, "is orient your thought to hope, and you will develop new abilities instead of disabilities." Alpha feedback findings are recounted sketchily. A woman in the back of the lecture hall gets up, and walks out huffily. Appeals to the idea of self-aggrandisement, or ego needs, come next. The lecturer tells you that all you need to do is to change your image of yourself, and then live up to the new picture you've concocted. A fat lady shrugs, stands up, and noisily walks out of the room.

A quickly simplistic course in Psychology 101, mixed with mass panacea in liberal dollops, follows: "Unconsciousness is a misnomer . . . there is no such thing as unconsciousness . . . there are only different levels of consciousness . . . psychic phenomena are possible for everyone to experience . . . you can turn on your alpha for relaxation just by programming yourself into alpha . . . you can turn on your theta and be more creative, just by programming yourself for theta and thinking about it . . . alcoholism can be cured with a swig of alpha instead." A thin middle-aged man gets up and walks out of the room.

The lecturer continues, "Beta is nutsville, and close to Camarillo, baby . . . your sources of genius can be easily tapped if you just tune in to them by thinking of it . . . you can tell what someone's illnesses are without ever meeting them, just by getting their vibes from looking at their name written on a card . . . take yourself to alpha level and lick all your problems . . . beta is bound to get you into trouble . . . bring me cards with the names of people mentally or physically ill; just write down their names and addresses, and we'll take it from there . . . geniuses, yogis and successful businessmen we've studied all have alpha . . . alpha can be tapped because it's a prior sense and everyone turns on alpha when they're going to sleep. All you have to do is to learn how to turn it on."

And, all of this IS WITHOUT BIOFEEDBACK MACHINERY. WHERE, OH WHERE, IS THE FEEDBACK IN THE ALPHA FEEDBACK?

Just turn it on. Tune it in. Program yourself. Take somebody to level. You're your own machine. Zippity doo, and you can have the world, if you'll just sign up for our little course. Short on money? Well, you can pay as you go. No money at all? Sign on the line, and take your time about paying. No credit? Just come on, y'all, and I'll trust you on your word alone, $150 for a one-week course. Master the secrets of alpha in just seven days. Only $100 each, if two or more in one family sign up at the same time. And, after you take our course, do come back as often as you want to the lectures, free of charge, and please bring a friend. Better still, bring two or three people. Oh, and if you're so broke that you're starving, see me after the class for our scholarship program.

In a typical session of alpha sell, there will be between seventy and ninety people at the original lecture. About six will walk out early in the evening before the three- to five-hour lecture draws to its close. About twenty people will sign up for the alpha-sell course, paying $100 to $150 a head. The promotor pays about $100 a night for the hotel's meeting-room rental, and the first night of lectures pays its own way—and then some. That presell newspaper advertisement runs around $300. The alpha seller will gross about $3000 for his week's work, and nets, after paying for room rental, free coffee for the participants, telephone answering service, and publicity, about $2000. The promotors range from big city to big city, but need time to rest between performances. They may give anywhere from ten to fifty such alpha courses in a year.

With few overhead expenses, it's clearly a profitable business. An IRS agent, who refuses to be named, is now checking into the alpha sellers' income tax returns, and he estimates most alpha sellers net a clear profit of anywhere from $25,000 to

$100,000 a year. Who knows for sure just how big the net is? Only Uncle Sam, and he's not telling.

For the record, most of these alpha sellers have had no scientific training, no certifiable knowledge of feedback technology, and claimed academic degrees that, upon checking, were simply not theirs. A few do have some background in psychology but know nothing about neurophysiology or even elementary anatomy. Most are ex-salesmen of products ranging from encyclopedias to body-building courses.

One of the largest alpha-seller organizations operates all over the country. In this outfit, the director collects 30% of the student's fees from his instructors, and handles the ad campaign. Some other independent alpha sellers are on their own and are literally one-man bands, being their own "extensive research staff," administrators, teachers, promoters, and bill collectors.

"Graduates" of the course who've taken the entire series of lectures are encouraged to return with the bait of free entry to the talks and, often, free attendance or a cut rate for a refresher go-round on the full course. Nothing converts others like the newly converted, and such positive buyers have a strong effect upon the timid and the hesitant at lectures. Graduates tend to sit on the floor during lectures, very much at home in cross-legged positions reminiscent of crystal Buddhas. At break time, graduates are pleased to rap with the curious and rave about the benefits of the course.

Graduates are also told that they are "research assistants" in the study of alpha control, and are asked to report their positive experiences, perferably at an introductory lecture meeting. They are asked to bring their friends to the lectures "to help them gain the benefits of alpha training." It is not unusual for graduates to see their "experiences" included in advertisements for the course. Phone calls remind graduates to bring their friends to upcoming lectures.

And they do. Wives bring husbands. Old maids bring fellow tenants from their lonely apartment houses. Dope-plagued students round up other freaked-out fringes of youth. And they all praise the course because it relieved them of being uptight and has changed their lives by letting them "program themselves" to be positive. Again and again, they tell you how the lecture course gave them the handle on their insights into self-power.

And one man with blazing eyes continues to wipe his hands nervously on a dirty handkerchief stained with Godknowswhat as he tells you how the classes helped him gain the lightning of his God-given powers.

The alpha courses tend to offer more of the same (as the lectures), liberally sprinkled with self-help and God and parlor psychology. Much of the training smacks of self-hypnosis. For example, one group features lying upon the floor as the "leader" counts downward. When he reaches one and snaps his fingers, you are to open your eyes and turn on your peak level of physical functioning. Sometimes, a metronomelike device, with a monotonous tick-tick is used to "relax you." Another alpha seller tells students about a miraculous cancer cure accomplished by one of the members, but wisely tempers his tale with the caution that he can't assure you that you have the ability to cure and heal. He warns of the multicyed AMA, but dials off with the admonition that you should have an open mind and see for yourself just what you can do. Many alpha sellers stress the power you will have if you simply focus your will upon a task. One course even holds out the ghostly help of male and female "helpers" conjured up from the past by your imagination, helpers who will aid you in your introspective journey.

Most classes tend to culminate with a test, an exam of psychic powers. Each student tries to "feel" the problems of a man or a woman whose name is written on an index card. Mental or physical ailments are to be "felt" by turning on alpha waves.

And, it is precisely this diagnosis by long distance that worries so many of the professional alpha-feedback scientists.

One pioneer scientist commented that, "If they're really getting into medical diagnosis, it could be dangerous. These groups appeal to people on the edge of despair who are looking for aid. What if they keep someone from seeing a physician? What if someone dies because he didn't see a doctor in time as he turned to turning on his alpha waves instead?"

Another scientist's comment: "Alpha buyers are merely the lonely, the bored, and the freaked-out. Don't they know that they could buy a nicely adequate home feedback machine for what these courses cost?"

Other professionals tend to agree. "Faith" courses such as the alpha sellers' classes have been around a long time, and the only thing new about them is the word "alpha" in their promotional material. Ages ago (d. 1926), Emile Coué, a French psychotherapist, drafted the faith formula that these courses all seem to repeat: "Day by day, in every way, I am getting better and better." Coué's phrase was invented to aid stress-bothered persons, who were to repeat it in the morning before they began their daily activities.

In an article in the *National Observer,* research pioneer Dr. Elmer Green, commented that the alpha seller is "not doing anything wrong, it's just his choice of words. He should either change his advertising to delete promise of alpha training, or simply buy some biofeedback machines." Dr. Green noted that the alpha-sell technique is not brain-wave control, but is, instead, control of internal mental and emotional cues.

Research pioneer Joe Kamiya, agreed with this estimate when he commented: "Some of the things in these courses might work to help people get rid of stress. The need is understandable. Unfortunately, there is nothing available for the needy public until clinics open. Until then, people desperately want this kind of training. And they're glad to pay for the promise alpha seems to hold out."

Perhaps, in an alpha-sell course, you might actually turn on alpha by relaxing or self-hypnotizing or positive-thinking yourself into the desired brain-wave states. But, you'll never know for sure because no electronic monitors are available to check if you've really made alpha. This feedback-provided, ineffable, but certain, internal knowledge is the most important key to alpha control *and to all the benefits of alpha.* It takes a machine to give you such instant knowledge, and it takes instant accurate electronic information to know you're doing what you wish to do.

Alpha-sell without any alpha feedback machine is a logical and scientific impossibility.

Chapter 13
Pandora's Box
Future Applications of Alpha

Swirls of cobalt light stroke the theater walls, shifting into a rainbow of serene blues that seem to melt into each other, as the husky actor speaks.

"We are immigrants in the strange land of ourselves," he whispers, and sinks to the floor, as the sound of his brain waves are heard rustling like a waterfall.

In this theater of the future, Varda Jillson sits in a water-inflated plastic seat and nods, as the electrodes dangling from her head pick up her thoughts. Shades of green begin to sparkle on the walls, reflecting Mrs. Jillson's memories of a peaceful picnic in a distant woodland in her childhood. The sound of her brain waves mingle with the actor's electronically reflected thoughts, adding a tone like the chirp of crickets. This is Theater as Shared Experience in the future. Every performance will be unique because actors and audience will interact electronically with the sounds and colors of brain waves, and each show will be a mint-fresh sensory experience.

In Chicago, Martin Howard sits up in alarm. The siren screaming in his ear from his Biofeedback Alerto warns him that his heart rate is speeding up. "Time for alpha," he realizes, and begins to relax away his tension. The siren sound mutes, and fades into the soft warble of his alpha relaxation cue. "Keep the tone on," he reminds himself, remembering the horror of his heart attack two years before. The doctors had warned him that he was too tense and anxious. The pain of his attack had been an awful sensation of weight upon his chest, feeling as if an elephant had stepped upon him. Turning to his calendar, Howard scribbled a memo to himself to visit his Alpha Relaxation Clinic on Friday.

Harry Grabowski curses as he hears the dull click. A turn blinker signals electronically, and he feels the automatic brake slowing his long-distance truck. He wipes a tired hand across his forehead. Rolling along the lonely highway, he hadn't realized that he was getting drowsy but the Alertometer that he wore had monitored his brain waves and sounded the alarm to the truck's automatic mechanical functions. He gingerly steered to a shoulder of the deserted highway for the enforced rest he must take before his brain waves regained the necessary alert level that would reactivate the truck's machinery. Grumbling, he longed for the "good old days" of "bennies" and hot black coffee to see him through the night. "Progress," he complained to the evening sky.

Science Fiction? No. Prophets of the future of biofeedback predict these innovations in living could happen. Mankind stands now beside Pandora's box, with the chance to use biofeedback knowledge to enrich life. Many of the first steps for inventions, like the Futuristic Theater, the Alertometer, and the heart Alerto, have already been taken. Other prospects have progressed no further than the idea stage, ideas waiting to be born which may never come to pass.

"These are possibilities, not promises," Dr. Joe Kamiya cautions. Just what are the implications of these new biofeedback discoveries? Every thoughtful person wants to know what he can expect before he decides to lift the lid of Pandora's box.

Biofeedback technology could offer man the possibility of control of involuntary body functions, and a panoramic insight into individual mental processes. Aware and self-regulated humans of the future might be able to control their feelings and physical functions and play the instrument of the brain like Zino Francescatti might play on a fine Stradivarius violin. Clinics operated by therapists could reinforce our aware control of ourselves, and the fiber of our lives might be altered by science's loom.

Narcotics addiction and drug abuse could be left behind in the Neanderthal Age as brain control replicates drug sensations without bodily damage. Therapists and social workers might aid the maladjusted to organic introspection with feedback training. The creative arts could be revolutionized, as everyone plays their own kind of music in *1984* fashion, and new brain wave entertainment centers open for business. Unique schools might revitalize education as teaching machines are triggered by brain waves for attention. The nation's health might soar to Olympian levels as psychosomatic diseases fade away with diminishing stress and doctors are freed to treat the functionally ill. Industry might schedule alpha relaxation breaks instead of coffee breaks, and athletes might set new records due to their totally integrated mind and body activities. Alcoholism and cigarette smoking would be a relic of past crude cultures to be replaced by controlled mental states. And people could enjoy the Golden Age of the Mind at last.

These are only siren songs, some observers comment. But the vivacious biofeedback pioneer, Dr. Barbara Brown, predicted that, "In five years, there will be biofeedback centers all over the country, in which people can learn all manner of mind and body functions. As has happened with every discovery, some will use it well, and some will ill-use it."

Dr. Brown and many other scientists foresee substitution of the pleasant effects of the alpha experience for dangerous narcotics and addictive drugs. She predicts that some individuals will relate to the pattern feedbacks of their own brains and find the consciousness alterations a satisfactory drug substitute. She has projected her own possible research in the areas of drug problems.

Although alpha experiences are not psychedelic, enhanced alpha supplies many people with a multiple number of "drug effects," including expanded awareness and consciousness alteration. Drs. Davidson and Krippner have already pointed out the similarity between subjective reports of subjects in the alpha high state (Kamiya, 1969), and reports made concerning marijuana effects (Tart, 1970).

Many researchers are already experimenting with biofeedback training as drug substitutes. In 1971, Wolverton, Bokert, and Markowitz used a combination of Yoga, meditation, and the Schultz-Luthe autogenic training techniques to successfully decrease drug needs for heavy drug users. Inclusion of feedback for immediate learning might cut treatment time and help in withdrawal. With alpha feedback, most people can produce desired brain-wave states of alpha, and seemingly duplicate the consciousness alterations of drugs. Relaxation is easily achieved with alpha enhancement, and the alpha experience is as relaxing as tranquilizers. Alpha suppression and beta enhancement give the mental stimulation of an "upper," or that cigarette and coffee break.

Dr. Budzynski predicted that "the exploration of biofeedback-produced experiential states will probably become as commonplace as Yoga is today." He also mentioned that seekers of new inner experiences might give up LSD and other "heavy" drugs for the inexpensive and harmless legal highs of twilight stages achieved through biofeedback.

Biofeedback training could revolutionize physical rehabilitation, as lightweight units, powered by the mind, replaced bulky devices of the past for paralyzed or injured people. These feedback units are already in existence and work by utilizing minute residual muscle-power that lurks unknown to us in the muscles, even when we seem to be paralyzed. Dr. Worden Waring, University of California at Davis, has applied feedback muscle ideas successfully for some neuromuscular disorders caused by diseases, spinal injuries, and trauma. He noted that these new bioelectrically-powered units are unsuccessful only with cases when a muscle is totally enervated and devoid of feeling.

The first steps in this new rehabilitation field were taken a few years ago, when Litton Systems designed a fine motor arm powered by five sources of EMG signals to individual motors. Quickly, people learned to drive the five motors serially, reach down and pick up an object like an orange with the device, and place it in a basket. Some learned better than others to perform with such fine control, just as some people are better than others at hitting a ball with a bat.

Then Dr. Waring added the elements of biofeedback to the basic idea. He worked with electrico-mechanical assistive devices, like braces and supports instead of false arms. Waring was able to extend the use of injured or paralyzed parts of the body for numerous people. In many cases, he found that a limb or hand or foot was injured and "unfeeling to normal perception, (but) minute quantities of feeling remain, and can be spotted with biofeedback acting as an extra pair of senses for us." Dr. Waring attaches electrodes to the injured area, then visually displays the hidden muscle action on a scope, so that the subject can see it, sense it, and strengthen it. This hidden potential is used to power the assistive devices.

In extreme cases, where potential is so low that visual feedback from the subject's own body, would not help, Waring uses a color wheel. This painted wheel is rigged to coincide with the desired motion for the device, and whirls around in the same direction as the device should move. Watching the wheel, subjects learn how to turn and move the rehabilitation device in spite of the fact that sensation is missing from an injured limb.

Biofeedback has other social implications in rehabilitation and therapy. A middle-aged parole officer in Southern California already offers his charges the chance to learn how to relax with his own biofeedback machine, and most find the alpha experience a serene and refreshing oasis in their struggle to survive. Another socially viable opportunity was suggested in an interview with Dr. Budzynski, who proposes that feedback might provide "low-cost, short-term therapy for the masses." His idea calls for the production of libraries of cassette tapes for home training of patients. Such carefully worded tapes would suggest ways to "increase self-esteem, confidence, and possibly assertiveness" for gradually controlled personality changes, as the patient keeps himself in a hypersuggestive state through biofeedback training techniques. This idea suggests that you could literally program yourself to be serene and happy.

Long time commitments of psychotherapy might be

dramatically reduced as patients learned to relax into a reverie state with feedback techniques. They could remember long-hidden pains, or free associate in more spontaneous streams of thought, as was tested by Bertini, Green, and other researchers.

Mapping the realm of your own reality is another alpha possibility. Biofeedback offers you instant information on your own introspection. Devices could be designed to aid you in awakening after each dream, so that you could enjoy and interpret your own subconscious. Instant information on your mental and physical universe might make experiences clearer to you, as you enhance your generation of hypnagogiclike images, to gather information on your inner being.

Dr. Jean Houston called biofeedback, "a tool which is open-ended in all directions from the most hardware scientific physiological physical substratum, to the most mystical ecstatic form." Such a tool could be used for pure amusement, or for introspection, as each of us comes to understand inner natures and create consciousness as we choose.

A more vocal integrated type of person might emerge with a wide use of feedback, as personalities change from regularly repeated alpha experiences. According to observations by Kamiya and by Foulkes, definite positive personality alterations do occur. Alpha subjects become more sensitive, relaxed, and aware than they were before biofeedback practice.

The creative arts could warm with a Renaissance of creativity, as artists revel in the expanding images. Each of us could enhance our own creative gifts by using theta or alpha biofeedback for imagery visualization, or problem solving conducted in a more organic manner. You might choose to produce your own light-and-sound show for "your own kind of music," as suggested by Barbara Brown. Such a device would translate brain signals into visual art forms and, additionally, signal when you were "getting out of tune with yourself." Most home feedback units are already available with couplers for attachment to color organs.

The Greens investigated imagery and brain wave biofeedback in college students. Dr. Green suggests, "Even though such an aid is merely a door opener to internal awareness, and even though individuals can be expected to eventually leave all such tools behind, short-term use is expected to be highly significant, especially in learning how to combine conscious and unconscious processes in the creative shaping of ideas." The pioneering Greens have already experimented with playing "biological music" as brain-wave signals were filtered through auditory feedback systems.

For the nonvisualizers, such experiences could enrich their lives. Dr. Brown once confided to interviewer Rasa Gustaitis, "When I was six, I was sitting with two friends under a mulberry tree. One of them asked, 'How do you think?' and the other said: 'Oh, I just close my eyes, and I see all those bright colored pictures.' But I ran home crying because when I closed my eyes, I just saw grey." Dr. Brown has speculated about setting up a coast-to-coast biofeedback hookup by way of satellite, where an artist and a musician would work together to paint pictures and mind-music for everyone's enjoyment.

Other technological supershows already exist in experimental laboratories around the country. You cannot pay your admission price and sail off on mind-expansion feedback experiences yet, but the future may see these "feedback environments replicated as mass entertainment centers a la *1984.*"

Lights danced about a surrounding screen in a hallucination-inducing environment designed by Dr. Elmer Green. Volunteers' hands were thrust into loudspeakers pounding with white noise. They wore stereo earphones filling their ears with white noise of about 120 decibels in volume. After about fifteen minutes, volunteers began to hallucinate. In Chicago, there was an amusement park named Riverview and, after the experience, one volunteer remarked to Dr. Green, "Riverview never had anything like this."

Strobe lights and loud music in discotheques are mild compared to the sensations people experienced in Dr. Honorton's experimental environment for psi experiences. He describes it as an "audio-visual womb." The hallucination-inducing environment was created for the Dream Lab at Maimonides Hospital in Brooklyn, New York. If you were to enter this environment, you would find yourself surrounded by a 180 degree screen showing pictures dissolving from mood to mood. As you doze off, the program comes on for twenty minutes and can range from schizophrenic art combined with preverbal speech patterns to Egyptian mythology. Within a few minutes, the environment is fully experienced on an internal basis and you begin to hallucinate.

Dr. Thomas Mulholland thinks that tomorrow's theater will be one of shared experiences as each artist produces his own "novel sensory patterns to evoke more intense psychological and emotional" responses. Artists would control the theatrical environments with physical responses. Dr. Mulholland adds that, as the artist "learns to control these by feedback training, he may then attempt to achieve a control of the stimulating environment which would result in patterns of light, sound, and movement (to) add a new means of achieving control over physiological processes by higher nervous functions." We would pay our admission money to attend a theater where we would watch the "beauty of someone's brain patterns, and the sound of a uniquely different brain," and, perhaps, we might have to show our personal EEG cards to attest to our stability before we could jointly participate in more emotionally taxing dramas.

Schools could shift into "environmental learning centers," where computer-assisted teaching machines would give forth new information only when brain-wave attention level signaled receptivity. As has been suggested by Lindsley, Brown, Mulholland, and other scientists, the teaching machine's pace would be controlled by mental receptivity monitored by brain-wave signals. Much material is best assimilated during drowsy or light sleep stages, according to a study by Dr. F. Rubin in 1970, and Budzynski suggests a biofeedback trained subject could turn on a "special hypersuggestible learning state" whenever he desired without the problem of losing sleep, improving technologically over the sleep learning practices of many of the Russian schools.

During school years, an overt response and brain-wave-pattern card could be made up for each pupil and fed into teaching machines. Dr. Krippner suggests that this idea would give each student "an individually adapted program based on each person's learning curve, short-term memory strength, changes in consciousness while learning, special skills and disabilities, and his perceptual and cognitive styles."

A new subject—the inner knowledge of your own mental and physical functions—could be added to the school curriculum, beginning in kindergarten. According to Dr. Mulholland, these guides to your inner landscape would enhance your understanding of yourself and increase your ease in getting along with others. At the end of the school years, you would have continuing psychological records and a chance to shape your own emotions and moods to fit your own ends with internal understanding. Applying the same idea to physical problems would give the child with a cardiac disorder due to rheumatic fever the ability to control her heart system at an early age, and avoid long-term physical or psychological damage. The epileptic boy could run and play like everyone else and be secure in his own internal knowledge of how to control threatening seizures, thanks to feedback training.

Medically, biofeedback holds out the promise of relief for stress-related illnesses, leading the patient to become responsible for his own recovery. Patients who prefer sugar pills and soft words to self-regulation would need longer training time to learn to master themselves.

Many drugs prescribed by physicians are all-or-nothing compounds and act upon the entire body. Serious side effects are tolerated when major disease necessitates the use of the drug, but biofeedback techniques offer an alternative. According to Davidson and Honorton, biofeedback has the positive trait of being quite specific in its effects. If your head hurts due to tension, you could use biofeedback training to alleviate that harsh localized pain, a procedure already used successfully by Budzynski and Stoyva. The feedback method would seem preferable to anesthetizing yourself into total oblivion when a localized headache occurs. The efficacy of specifically directed biofeedback application has been demonstrated in dozens of experiments, including the work of Shapiro, Tursky, and Schwartz, in 1970.

For the adventurous person, in the future biofeedback may mean self-regulation and control of all physiological processes.

Through feedback-trained self-awareness of the internal system, a mental monitor could warn you when better maintainence is necessary.

Feedback information could also be used in diagnosing neurological conditions. Mulholland's experiments indicated that variations in patterns signal possible brain damage. Baker reported, in 1971, that the two hemispheres of the brain differ in alpha production. By training sections separately as well as together, it might be possible to determine the type, degree, and location of the damage by determining how patterns react to training.

According to Green, warts and other skin growths could be starved away. People with cold feet and related circulatory problems have already used temperature feedback training to successfully increase the heat in their limbs at will. In another instance, *The New York Times* published an account of the successful application of temperature feedback to cure a case of Raynaud's disease, a circulatory dysfunction.

When we don't get enough sleep, we feel "cottony" and our reflexes are much more gross than usual. Biofeedback techniques might provide an answer to this problem. Initial tests have demonstrated that alpha states often refresh the mind and the body. Preliminary studies by the U.S. Navy's Medical Neuropsychiatric Research Unit hint at the possibility that a person deprived of sleep could rejuvenate himself by turning on an alpha state learned through feedback techniques.

Other vast uncharted areas of health offer possible golden rings on the merry-go-round of living. Two researchers published a paper that suggested, "If a disorder has a specific psychological component, it is potentially amenable to self control. This can be extended to quite subtle responses, such as the ph (acidity) level of the stomach. In ulcer patients, with the aid of biofeedback processes, control can be gained over the fluids in the stomach, and thereby heal the ulcer."

Yogi's no-pain feats may be duplicated with biofeedback. At New York University, Ramon Torres, a lean angular man, demonstrated no-pain qualities to EEG feedback researchers, using his own version of South American Yoga. He stuck a sharpened bicycle spoke through his cheeks without feeling any pain. Researchers watched the EEG machinery and saw that he did, indeed, generate a high amplitude alpha, signifying a blank mind, similar to yogi and Zen-master EEGs. These no-pain brain levels would allow someone to undergo serious surgery without the debilitating effects of anesthesia. The fear and pain of dentistry might also become a relic of the past, as we tune on our headphones and listen to the alpha tone while the dentist works on our teeth. Kamiya suggested that natural childbirth methods could benefit from the addition of brain-wave control through feedback. Women could deliver children without sedation as they turn on alpha waves to relax during childbirth.

Business and industry might even be revamped. Can you picture yourself stepping into an alpha chamber at the office, and attaching electrodes for your alpha break? Or lying down with an EMG machine for a rest period? Both the Xerox Company and the Martin Marietta Corporation are already watching research findings to decide if they could someday use biofeedback machines to relax their executives and spur creative thinking. McDonald's Hamburgers, Inc., have installed an executive "think tank" in their Chicago, Illinois, quarters, where executives actually hook up electrodes to their scalps in a supersonic-type capsule and turn on alpha for creative relaxation breaks. Martin Marietta Corporation also "considered biofeedback training for Skylab astronauts on the theory that space travelers could learn to control functions, thoughts and physiological functions." In the future, these corporations might brave the research trails and introduce a new concept into industry—the feedback break. In *The New York Times Magazine,* Budzynski predicted that there would come a time "when frenetic corporations, law firms, and television studios will have a cot and an EMG machine to permit quick naps and preventative medication for harassed workers during the day."

The serene long-haired owner of an incense factory in Los Angeles is already setting tomorrow's business fad. He roams about his firm with attached electrodes dangling from his head, and connects himself to his biofeedback machine every few hours for relaxing "alpha breaks." He neither smokes nor drinks and finds the breaks refresh him and make him sharper when he goes back to work.

Another industrial feedback use would be the "Alertometer," proposed by Dr. Mulholland. This device would turn off dangerous equipment when the operator's brain waves fall below alert levels to signal drowsiness. Throughout the country, such devices could signal alarm and deactivate trucks or cars when drugs, alcohol, or sleep deprivation lower alert levels.

Another research scientist suggested rigging up future astronauts to prevent low performance due to drowsiness. A *Wall Street Journal* article carried the report that United States intelligence agents might someday be taught how to "turn on alpha, monitor other body processes, and be immune to any lie detector."

Traditionally, lie detectors monitor your heart rate, breathing, pulse, and GSR. Lie detectors may soon be obsolete because these "visceral responses can be shaped in the same way as any other behavior, and are no sure route to emotional truth," according to Dr. Peter Lang.

Controlling visceral responses through biofeedback training could also revolutionize athletics. The classic book, *The Zen of Archery,* advises total relaxed mental states and organic integration into an action for superior performance. Echoing this philosophy, Dr. Brown was quoted in *Look* magazine on athletics: "Perfection in athletic accomplishments is acquired largely through mental concentration to produce an optimally integrated physical sequence of events. The individual can just as easily practice the mental state away from the practice area, using the feedback signals from his brain waves and muscle states to signal moments of optimal preparation."

For the distant future, scientists suggest trying biofeedback techniques to help compulsive eaters and smokers. Even alcoholics might be helped if they can train themselves to recognize their "compulsive drives" and counter their drinking by turning on appropriate brain waves. Kasamatsu and Hirai discovered that the acutely intoxicated person shows large amplitude and slow frequency alpha waves. Researchers suggest that, once the corresponding brain state for a compulsion has been recognized, subjects could turn that brain state on at will with biofeedback training, and substitute the brain state for smoking, drinking, or overeating.

Researchers have even suggested using biofeedback techniques to enhance orgasm, banish frigidity, and as the ultimate in birth-control techniques. Most gynecologists believe frigidity comes from tensing of the vaginal muscle and an inability sensually to let go. Orgasm is a sensual peaking and release dependent upon a flowing forth of energy. One alpha researcher suggests that male and female orgasms are experiences accompanied by strong alpha patterns. Orgasm and frigidity would respond to deep relaxation in high-alpha states. Temperature feedback is proposed for birth control by Kamiya.

And would you like to slow down your aging process? Or even cure cancer? Conscious control over cell death might halt the ravages of aging. Many cancer experts are puzzled by the fact of spontaneous remission of the disease when cancer rampant in metastases, suddenly disappears. Dr. Brown posed that question to the Biofeedback Research Society: "What kind of a state is this person in? What does he approach to be able to do this? It is highly conceivable that we have the tools to tackle this kind of problem today." Could biofeedback be extended to cell control to halt such cell processes? Only time, and serious research application, will provide clues to the outcome of these momentous possibilities.

What about ESP and telepathy? Some research scientists believe brain-wave control can make it possible for us to communicate instantly with each other without uttering a sound, even over vast distances. In an experiment by Simonov and Velueva in 1956 in Russia, subjects learned to control their GSR with GSR feedback and sent Morse code messages to each other with GSR responses. Davidson and Krippner believe that such psi abilities are "potentially amenable to change with the application of feedback." In another Russian experiment by Ostrander and Schroeder, in 1970, two telepathic persons actually transmitted messages to each other over a distance of 1200 miles. The messages were sent in Morse code, and the receiver was monitored by a government investigator who stated that the man's EEG actually picked up the messages accurately.

All of these biofeedback promises would seem to indicate a Golden Age ahead for man, but biofeedback is like Pandora's box. Pandora discovered the world's ills flying out of that ancient container, and many thoughtful scientists urge cautious use of the gift of biofeedback learning. New scientific knowledge always brings its own responsibilities and challenges. Atomic energy discoveries led to the horror of Hiroshima, but they also brought new cheap power to deprived areas of the world, with nuclear reactors helping to improve life. Biofeedback researchers are the first to point out the negative implications of biofeedback training. Dr. Jean Houston, of the Foundation for Mind Research, spoke up at the first meeting of the Biofeedback Research Society, and cautioned against science playing God to desperate people. She imagined people saying, "Oh, boy, you can program yourself against anxiety, to euphoria, to love, to whatever it is you ought to be. This is what, in cultures, has traditionally been performed by sacramental functions. And there is this emergent sacramentalism with regard to the feedback processes that I am sensing here. . . . There are emergent shamans in your group."

Dr. Barbara Brown, who is credited with the discovery of five important drugs in her prior research as a pharmacologist, cautions, "Whenever we developed a new drug, we said, be sure you try to develop the antidote for it. And I think we are going to run into some problems, and some of us should be thinking about how we are going to prevent some of the disasters that might occur. In autohypnosis, for example, they've had a great deal of disaster. People carry this too far with inadequate information. . . . We are going to have to develop an antidote."

Improperly placed electrodes pick up muscle "sounds" like jaw clenching, and flickers like eye movement. This could also lead to biofeedback problems. Dr. Kamiya cautioned, "A hysterical person could be greatly alarmed at such sound pickups and conclude that the artifact sound is the sound of brain damage. Remember a certain percentage of people tend to hysterical symptoms." Drugs sometimes cause paranoid or hysterical reactions.

In one frightening case, a biofeedback scientist was working with subjects who were using drugs. He reported on one man, "I don't know what he was taking but he came in most of the time straighter than new money. But he had a panic-stricken experience in the apparatus, and he didn't come back for a long time. He said, 'all I could do was get together with the light, and I wanted out, out, out!' Apparently, he got into some kind of little intellectual game with that light, or some emotional game, and it scared the hell out of him." Drug users, especially of the major narcotics and psychedelics, could have freak-out sensations, and inadvertently turn on past panic reactions.

Illnesses would have to be diagnosed by a physician before biofeedback treatment, or dangers could result. As Dr. Stoyva has pointed out, you would want to know, is your "tension headache" in reality, caused by brain damage? Is your "stomach cramp" caused by stress, or is it really appendicitis? Improper feedback for medical use could be hazardous.

Unsupervised biofeedback experiences present other hazards. Home users do not have the scientific knowledge to stop sessions when unusual waves appear, such as epileptic spikes, and often have inadequate monitors to detect similar dangers.

There may also be dangers in relaxing too deeply. A physician was shaken by a woman patient who was unusual in her ability "to relax in a very profound way, without feedback other than my presence, and [who] was able to virtually anesthetize herself from her growing carcinoma of the bowel. It was my chief concern, while we were preparing her for surgery, that she would perforate, and no one would know."

Put very simply, there are reasons for pain, particularly in cases of muscle injury. Recently, the sports world has revealed many cases in which injured football players get shots of novacaine or other pain killers in the damaged muscles, and go on to play—and irrevocably damage the muscles.

Biofeedback training could hold the same dangers as autohypnotic techniques. In some autohypnotic incidents, would-be mystics have played with breathing exercises to bring on "visualization of the gods," and accidentally trained themselves in labored breathing patterns. Also in the medical area, in heart-rate control, unless training is carefully done there could be reactions of additional cardiac problems. Schultz's autogenic training methods stress that all corrective exercises be held until the end, or patients can actually produce a counterresistance that is harmful.

The thoughtful scientist, Dr. Thomas Mulholland, pointed out "the possible danger of conditioning or training heart rate down below a certain level." He added another word of warning about seizure patients with petit-mal history. There is a high-powered training technique for epileptics that uses bright strobes to bring on seizures. Mulholland spoke of one of these subjects whose brain recordings showed that he suddenly broke into "large, synchronous waves, two or three times as large as usual, and, at the same time, there were spike discharges which triggered a pathological sign of activity." Although the experiment was instantly halted, feedback might increase possibilities of such experiences.

Many medical doctors are pessimistic about biofeedback training techniques. The training involves much more time than is required in prescribing a pill, and a network of clinics is not yet available. Psychosomatic illness occurs for many reasons, and is often a symptom of deep-rooted psychological problems; some people would simply substitute a new illness or symptom if the original problem is untouched. Since their problems hadn't really been erased, they might trade their ulcers for another ailment. "Substitute symptoms" don't happen in every case, but they do happen. In addition, there are always the patients who don't want responsibility for their own health, and would rather leave medicine to their doctors. Although all the facts are not yet available, there is also a possibility that some people cannot be trained, and don't generate any trainable brain waves. A balding overworked Seattle physician sums up his feelings about biofeedback, "I went into medicine because I wanted to help people, and we already have too many machines in medicine. I don't need another gadget to come between me and my patients. I want to cure their bodies, not play God by changing someone's personality, or life pattern."

Is it necessary to have government control of biofeedback machinery? There are as many views on this question as there are research scientists in the field, but it seems that government controls would be almost impossible to enforce. With circuitry designs, readily available in many manufacturer's brochures, any first-year engineering student could build his own biofeedback machine from easily obtainable circuitry parts. The Biofeedback Research Society is a young organization, but its members have pointed out possible dangers. Manufacturers may set up their own industry council to form instrumentation standards and voice ethical responsibilities. To date, there is no group providing guidelines, and no policing organization to supervise standards and use, to avoid dangers.

Clearly, an answer is called for, or biofeedback could be "popularized out of existence" through abuse by the public, and by charlatans and quacks. This fate overtook hypnotism, orginally a scientific technique showing great potential. Freud experimented with hypnotism decades ago, and other legitimate scientists followed suit. But "mesmerism" became a parlor fad, and a "golly, gee whiz" auditorium exhibition on the Chautauqua circuit. Europeans were unaffected by this faddism and scientists continued their hypnosis research. It took forty years before hypnotism shed its "fad" reputation, and again became an area of scientific study in America. LSD was first discovered by a Swiss scientist and promised enormous therapeutic potentials, but the faddists moved in for easy thrills, government controls were imposed, and LSD research efforts all but died in this country.

Is biofeedback going to be a fad, or a fantastic opportunity for mankind? If we want to collect on biofeedback potentials, public responsibility is imperative. If we're wise, we may fulfill a prediction made by Dr. Elmer and Ms. Alyce Green, and Dr. Dale Walters. They wrote that, "The most significant thing that may be facilitated through [biofeedback] training in the voluntary control of internal states is the establishment of a Tranquility Base, not in outer space, but in inner space, on, or within, the lunar being of man."

Chapter 14
Questions and Answers About Alpha and Biofeedback

In Boston, in a chilly auditorium high on a hill, a young psychologist spoke about alpha waves. Afterwards, came the questions.

At California's Esalen Institute, another research scientist talked about brain-wave control against a backdrop of wind-sculpted trees and waves. Again, people voiced similar concerns.

In New York City, an experimental psychologist explained his experiments in altered consciousness through feedback to a crowded lecture hall. And, again, the public had questions that repeated others' inquiries. These are the most common questions about alpha and feedback, and tentative answers collected from the experts in biofeedback science:

What is alpha? Who discovered it? Was it always there?
"Alpha" is the name given to the wave length of one pattern of electrical activity produced by the brain. It measures eight to twelve cycles per second, according to most authorities. (Note: A few scientists chose to chart alpha waves from seven to thirteen cycles per second.) The alpha brain wave varies in amplitude, or strength, in each person based upon individual

MODEL WEARING HEADSET.
PHOTOGRAPH BY DON DOUGLAS, COURTESY AQUARIUS ELECTRONICS.

differences and on past training. Hans Berger, a German psychiatrist, is generally given credit for discovering alpha brain waves in 1929. Although alpha waves have always been produced by the brain, the discovery of this characteristic brain wave had to wait until the 1920s because adequate measuring machinery had to be developed before it was possible to detect this subtle energy. It is measured in microvolts.

What does alpha feel like?

"Relaxed alertness" is Dr. Joe Kamiya's description of the feel of alpha, adding that his volunteer subjects have also said that alpha is "a pleasant letting go . . . a drifting."

Although most people enjoy the feel of the alpha experience, Dr. Maurice B. Sterman's findings indicate that some people have a "blah" reaction to alpha and a few people find alpha states unpleasant or irritating.

Dr. Lester Fehmi describes the alpha experience as a relaxed but alert and sensitive into-it-ness.

How can I control my alpha brain waves? How do I get into an alpha state?

Practice in meditative exercises for at least six months to a year builds alpha, according to Dr. Joseph Hart's tests. Dozens of investigators have found that training in EEG biofeedback enhances alpha brain waves for most people. Feedback of a color or a tone cue, to check your progress, aids in alpha wave generation and control.

The quickest way to turn on alpha waves is to roll your eyes upward, as is called for in many esoteric religious practices. Scientists do not recommend this method of alpha production. Kamiya points out that most people have some alpha when their eyes are closed, and recommends beginning alpha training with closed eyes. Mulholland notes how eye flickers intrude upon alpha production. Cutting down your flickering rate could be accomplished by staring at an object without blinking profusely. Concentrated staring is a common feature of many meditative disciplines.

Other aids to alpha production are monotony, relaxed breathing, and comfortable position. Watching mental images or phosphenes behind your closed eyelids has been noted as an aid to alpha enhancement by Tart, among others.

Is it true that some people have no alpha? I tried alpha and got nothing. Does that mean that there's something wrong with me?

Absence or presence of alpha brain waves varies with the individual and may be affected by numerous conditions, as innocuous as the varieties that occur in hair color or eye color. Rosenberg's study reported that 8% of people have no alpha brain waves in normal waking conditions. Many people with little or no alpha have learned to enhance the alpha rhythm with biofeedback training. It is possible that no-alpha results were due to improperly placed electrodes, inadequate machinery, or turning the gain dial too much higher than individual alpha production.

What does biofeedback mean? What is the difference between EEG and EMG feedback? BFT? GSR? EEP? EKG?

"Biofeedback is a new term for a new science. "Bio" comes from the Greek word *bios,* meaning life or living organisms. "Feedback" is a technical term referring to the giving back of the effects of a process to its source, according to Webster's *Collegiate Dictionary.* The biofeedback process occurs when you receive back information concerning your internal state through mechanical devices, known as feedback instruments.

EEG is the abbreviation for the electroencephalogram, or brain-wave-detection instrumentation. Electrical energy of your brain waves is detected by tiny electrodes attached to your skin with paste. These electronic messages travel in wires to a recorder where they are magnified about 100,000 times, and then moved to delicate pens which trace the pattern of your particular brain waves on paper that keeps moving horizontally on a drum.

EMG is the abbreviation for the electromyograph, which works on the same principles as the EEG. The EMG is used to record energy generated by the muscles.

BFT is the abbreviation for biofeedback training, or biofeedback techniques, the act of using feedback for instrumental learning.

A GSR machine detects skin reaction to outside stimulus. An EEP is the abbreviation for the electroencephlaphone, a headset EEG machine. EKG is the abbreviation for the electrocardiogram, the tracing made by an electrocardiograph which records the action of the heart muscle.

Will alpha training make me more sensitive?

Possibly. Kamiya has noted that high alpha producers tend to be sensitive and empathetic. Budzynski and Stoyva noted that some people became more sensitive and sometimes felt vulnerable as they became aware of their own alpha brain waves.

"Sometimes, people feel more open and it scares them at first because it makes life too intense. They feel vulnerable. But, in time, they become accustomed to it and enjoy their enriched sensitivity" Budzynski pointed out.

Will "doing alpha" change my personality? Will it help me get along better with other people?

Perhaps. Dr. Neal Miller's experiments with rats indicated that biofeedback-trained animals were better able to adapt and tolerate anxiety-producing situations.

What about human beings? A number of investigators have noted personality changes. Kamiya found that some trained individuals could relate better to other people, and tended to be less anxious in everyday situations.

Will alpha training help me in my meditation? Will it give me "instant satori"?

It could aid in meditation. Meditation is typified by strong alpha waves. Wallace, Anand and others in India, Kasamatsu and Hirai, and Okeima in Japan, all noted consistent alpha brain wave patterns during meditative sessions. Beginning students of meditation showed lower amplitude alpha waves, and lacked characteristic trains of the slower theta waves. Continued biofeedback practice can give most people abundant alpha. The Greens' work indicates theta may also be enhanced with biofeedback techniques.

Is biofeedback training truly electronic LSD?

You will not get psychedelic reactions. If you're looking for other mind-expansion experiences, like altered consciousness states and unique perceptions and sensory changes, you could probably turn them on and off at will with feedback training. Dr. Barbara Brown notes that, "you get what you put into the experience, and you get about what you want from it." With biofeedback, you control the experience instead of a chemical controlling you.

Isn't this more machine thinking, treating the body like a machine to be turned on and off at will?

No, it's a learning technique. Is it machine thinking to drive a car to travel somewhere? The car is a vehicle for a change in location, while biofeedback is a vehicle for a change in self control.

Doesn't the use of a machine lessen the spiritual experience in the meditative state?

Each culture tends to evolve its own characteristic meditative exercises. Ours is a technological culture. Ramana Maharshi, a "realized being," many levels above most beginning meditators, said, "The aim is the cessation of mental activities. So long as there is effort made towards that goal, it is called yoga. The EFFORT is the yoga."

Is alpha control really a form of hypnosis or self-hypnosis?

The alpha subject is passively alert, and not especially suggestible. In numerous tests, the alpha subject demonstrated different consciousness alterations from the hypnotized subject. EEG patterns for hypnotized subjects are not too different from those of nonhypnotized subjects in normal waking stages. However, Hart and London did discover that training in alpha production does make individuals more susceptible to hypnosis.

What does amplitude of my alpha mean?

Roughly, amplitude is a measurement of how strong your alpha brain waves are. Without special training, the average person's alpha brain wave would measure about 10 to 20 microvolts. With feedback training, most people peak at about 60 microvolts. Zen masters have been measured and found to produce alpha brain waves that were as high as 100 microvolts, or almost ten times the average person's strength.

Will alpha training give me ESP powers?

Preliminary results of studies by Krippner and Ullman demonstrate increases in paranormal sensitivity that seem to result from feedback experiences. Research at the Dream Laboratory at Maimonides Hospital in Brooklyn, New York, suggests a relationship between dreams, EEG for alpha, and ESP. Stanford and Levin found that alpha frequency increased from pretest to test, and was associated with the ESP ability to call cards.

Honorton's experiments indicate that people with high alpha

scores do score much higher in ESP card-guessing tests. In another experiment, Honorton joined with Davidson and Bindler and found that people who achieved almost hallucinatory effects from feedback-enhanced alpha also scored much higher in ESP testing than people who reported little or no mind alterations from enhanced alpha brain waves.

My daughter uses drugs. Could alpha substitute for her drug highs?

Leading researchers believe that drug-induced consciousness alterations can be duplicated with feedback training. For some individuals, turning on alpha has proved to be a satisfactory substitute for drug highs.

Could a government use biofeedback to control people?

This is not likely, according to Brown. The basic concept of biofeedback is self-regulation, and self control through self information. Perhaps soldiers could be taught to feel "no pain," but each individual soldier would have to turn on that feeling by himself at self-command.

Would alpha training be useful in marriage counseling or group therapy? Could it help me get along better with my wife?

Green reported that feedback-trained subjects have "a general feeling of tranquility." Toomim tells of a psychotherapist who found alpha enhancement made her "more sensitive and responsive to others."

Devices already exist for two people to hear each other's brain waves and attempt mental unity. Couples and group therapy participants might find that mental unity made them less anxious and more serene as they respond to other's thoughts in a group setting.

Can I increase my creative powers with biofeedback?

The chemist, Kekulé, devised a famous theory of molecular construction and advised his colleagues, "Let us learn to dream, gentlemen," in reference to his own dreamlike experience in conceptualizing his theoretical insight. Dr. Green uses biofeedback training to enhance the individual's imagery and reminds us of Robert Louis Stevenson's ability to dream publishable plots by commanding the "brownies" of his mind to furnish him with a story. Poincaré also described how mathematical ideas rose in clouds, dancing before him and colliding and combining into the first Fuschian functions, as he lay in bed awaiting sleep.

In the *voluntary* controls program of the Greens' laboratory, people learn how to free their thoughts, emotions, and attention, to reach creative reveries and enhanced hypnagogiclike imagery. Both alpha and theta waves are associated with creativity in different dimensions. To date, the Greens' sessions for self-enhanced imagery indicate that average people can be trained to turn on such skills.

To what extent does religious study aid in achieving alpha control?

Western religions may not help too much, but Eastern disciplines seem to be an important factor in alpha skills. "If you've had religious training in any of the meditative disciplines that practice calm and avoidance of struggle, you're more apt to find generation of alpha waves an easy task. And, you'll probably be able to learn to control them faster than other people," Kamiya comments.

Students of Zen learn to achieve alpha states with their eyes open, while Yoga students concentrate upon eyes-closed alpha. Distractions, like a dog barking nearby, tend to be less disruptive to the meditatively trained mind.

Can alpha help me relax? What about EMG?

Yes. Generating alpha brain waves gives most people a feeling of serene peacefulness, which is definitely relaxing. Relaxation is not necessary for alpha, but it often accompanies alpha states, relieving mental stress.

EMG is probably more effective for muscle stress. Budzynski and Stoyva recommend learning both EEG alpha feedback and EMG feedback with relaxation training for deep relaxation.

Could I have a mystical experience through biofeedback? How would it compare to the ecstasies of saints like St. Theresa?

That depends upon your own input. Many people report

body-image changes and other perceptual alterations during alpha experiences, according to experiments by Tart. "I felt like I was floating . . . my mind left my body . . . I was united with the universe and all living things. . . . My arms and legs seemed to melt. . . . The walls glowed like church windows," are all reports recorded by biofeedback researchers.

Mulholland has noted that "set" has a strong impact upon specific alpha experiences. If you are of a religious or mystical bent, you could experience a religious ecstasy. Is it real? What is reality but your perception of an event? And altered perceptions give you different versions of reality.

I went to a lecture given by a group that claimed they could teach me how to use alpha for all kinds of things—ESP, curing my ulcer, getting rid of my insomnia—and it sounded great, EXCEPT, they claim to do all this without using any machines of any kind. Just lectures. Is this possible?

"These groups can teach you how to be more relaxed through 'positive thinking', but, without a machine to feed back instant and accurate information on your internal states, you could not possibly have biofeedback," Kamiya states tartly. And you would have no way of knowing if your pleasant "feeling" was alpha brain waves, or just enjoyment of your lobster thermidor as you digested your dinner during the lecture.

I'm a medical doctor. What does all this alpha and biofeedback business mean to me? If it works, what about symptom substitution?

If Brown is right in her estimate that 60% of the illnesses sending patients to doctors are really psychosomatic disorders, it could mean a great deal to you, and to everyone. Better health for the nation. Physicians freed to treat functional disorders and diseases as many psychosomatic patients assume responsibility for their own ills. Decreased drug use and lessened danger of resulting side effects.

Freud mentioned the danger of symptom substitution. Kamiya commented that studies show this phenomenon does occur, but only very rarely.

Where can I get more information?

See the suggested reading list in the bibliography of this book. After you've read the more popular articles, you might want to read the *Aldine Reader,* a roundup of important scientific background documents on biofeedback and self control, or the *Aldine Annual,* a yearly collection of important scientific documents on biofeedback research. Both are available from Aldine-Atherton, Inc., Chicago, Illinois.

The Biofeedback Research Society publishes its annual proceedings, and you could purchase a copy by writing to:

Dr. Johann Stoyva, President
Biofeedback Research Society
c/o University of Colorado Medical Center
Denver, Colorado

The many forms of consciousness are discussed in Charles Tart's *Altered States of Consciousness,* a collection of research papers published by John Wiley and Sons, Inc.

Acknowledgments

The author is especially grateful to the dedicated scientists who freely gave their time and advice in aiding original research for this book. Deep thanks for their information and hospitality are owed to Dr. Joe Kamiya, and his wife, Joanne; Dr. Johann Stoyva, and Dr. Thomas Budzynski; and Tim Scully and Ms. Ethel Scully. Also, acknowledgment is due for the valuable information and encouragement I received from Dr. Maurice B. Sterman; Dr. Charles Tart; Dr. Barbara Brown, and her staff, for extra aid; Dr. John Basmajian; Dr. Lester H. Fehmi; Dr. Thomas Mulholland; Dr. Bernard T. Engel; Dr. Gary Galbraith; Dr. Stanley Krippner; Dr. Jackson Beatty; Dr. Richard Davidson, Dr. Charles Honorton, and James Scott of Dunscott Bioscope Instruments.

Also of special assistance were Dr. Neal E. Miller; Erik Peper; Gary Laird, Research Therapist; Miss Angie Nall; Dr. Leo V. DiCara; Dr. Curtiss Hardyck; Dr. Lewis Petrinovich; Dr. Joseph Hart; Dr. Perry London and his staff; Jack Gariss and Jeanette Gariss; Dr. David Hord; and Dr. Herbert Benson.

The author is also grateful to those scientists whose seminal research has been publicly reported to share their important knowledge and aid in compiling this book: Dr. Jean Houston; Dr. Eleanor Criswell; Dr. Montague Ullman; Dr. Elmer and Ms. Alyce Green; Dr. Wanda Wrywicka; Dr. George Whatmore; Dr. Charles Dahlberg; Dr. Joseph Sargent; Dr. David Nowlis; Dr. Martin Orne; Dr. Arthur J. Deikman; Dr. E. Dale Walters; Dr. Edward Bokert; Dr. Edward Wortz; Dr. John Sinclair; Dr. David Kahn; Dr. Marjorie Kawin-Toomim; Dr. Theodore Xenophon Barber; Dr. David Foulkes; Dr. David Paskewitz; Dr. Louis Vachon; Dr. Kenneth Gaarder; Dean Brown; Superintendant George von Hilsheimer; Dr. Terry V. Lesh; Dr. Akira Kasamatsu; Dr. Tomio Hirai; Dr. B. K. Anand; Dr. Baldev Singh; Dr. G. S. Chhina; Dr. V. B. Malkin; Dr. N. M. Asyamolova; George Leonard; and Dr. A. K. Kochetov.

And, lastly, personal thanks for conscientious and considerate assistance above and beyond the call of duty from the editor, Ms. Sylvia Cross; and for sacrifices and devoted encouragement from Bob Lawrence, Gregg Scott Lawrence, Marc Jeffrey Lawrence, and Ross McKean Lawrence, my long-suffering family, without whose loving care and self-deprivation this book would never have been possible.

References

General

Altshuter, H. Psychologist's 11-year study reveals you can be taught to control your brain waves. *National Enquirer* 44:2, October 19, 1969.

Buhrman, R. Liberating the mind of the '70's. *Los Angeles Magazine* 15: 36-40, January 1970.

——. The mind hucksters: riding the brain wave to profit and power. *Los Angeles Magazine* 16:38, May 1971.

Collier, B. L. Brain power: the case for biofeedback training. *Saturday Review* 10, April 10, 1970.

——. Personal mastery. *Baltimore Pink Sheet*, April 12, 1971.

Davis, F. Brain training. *Glamour Magazine* 64: 170-177, October 1970.

Dusailly, J. F. Psycho command and psycho reaction. *Radio Electronics Magazine*, 44-45, September 1964.

Edwards, B. Minds' electronic profile unlocks life's mysteries. *The News*, Van Nuys, California, February 10, 1970.

Eisenbud, J. To be or not to be . . . victim or victor? *Fate Magazine* 23: 56-57, February, 1970.

Ertl, J. P. Using speed of brain waves to test I.Q. *Medical World News,* March 8, 1969.

Ford, B. ESP in the dream laboratory. *Science Digest* 67:10, January 1970.

Green, E., and Green, A. Exploring the mind's mastery of the body. *Midway,* Sunday supplement, Topeka, Kansas, January 18, 1970.

Gustaitis, R. The alpha gambit. *Los Angeles Times, West,* Sunday Supplement, August 8, 1971.

Hallgren, D. Learning how to control one's own brain waves. *San Francisco Chronicle,* July 14, 1969.

Huxley, Aldous. Brave new world. Harper & Row, 1946.

Hess, R. EEG handbook. Sandoz, Ltd., England, 1966.

Honorton, C. Tracing ESP through altered states of consciousness. *Psychic Magazine* 2:18, September/October 1970.

James, W. The varieties of religious experience. New American Library, Inc. 1958.

Kahn, Dr. F. Man in structure and function (trans. from German). 1939, Eng. version Knopf and Co.

Kawin-Toomim, M. The alpha rhythm, its meaning and application. The Toomim Laboratories Publ. 1970.

Lang, P.J. Autonomic control. *Psychology Today* 4:37, October 1970.

Luce, Gay, and Erik Peper. Mind over body, mind over mind. *The New York Times Magazine,* September 12, 1971.

Life magazine. Turning on with alpha waves. 69:60, August 21, 1970.

Look magazine. Dr. Kamiya's work. 30:116, June 28, 1966.

McNutt, W. People can learn to control own brain waves, relax alertly. *Arizona Republic* (Phoenix) February 8, 1970.

Meyers, R. Picking the brain. *Los Angeles Times, West,* Sunday supplement, August 8, 1971.

Morgenstern, J. Lamebrains. *Newsweek,* March 29, 1971.

Newsweek (Science and Space). Making brain waves. 92, March 23, 1970.

Pines, M. Train yourself to stay well. *McCall's Magazine* 48, June 1970.

Poppy, J. Work in progress/George Leonard. *Intellectual Digest,* November 1971.

Popular Science Monthly. Machine measures thought. 52, April, 1930.

Powers, C. T. Picking the brain (profitably). *Los Angeles Times, West* Sunday supplement, August 8, 1971.

Psychic Magazine. Psychenauts of inner space. 1:9, May/June 1970.

Rorvik, D. M. Brain waves: the wave of the future. *Look magazine* 34:88, October, 1970.

Schaffer, R. A. Biofeedback. *Wall Street Journal,* April 19, 1971.

Scully, T. The alphaphone brainwave analyzer instruction manual. Mendocino, California, 1971.

The Sciences. The tutored heart. New York Academy of Sciences, 10, January, 1970.

Tart, C. Altered states of consciousness. John Wiley and Sons, 1969.

Time magazine. The body: controlling the inner man. July 18, 1969.

Timmons, B., and Kamiya, J. The psychology and physiology of meditation and related phenomena. *Journal of Transpersonal Psychology* 2:1, 1970, (a bibliography).

Trotter, Robert J. Listen to your head. *Science News* 100, November 6, 1971.

U.S. Dept. of Health, Education, and Welfare, Public Health Service, Natl., Institute of Mental Health. Current research on sleep and dreams. Publ. No. 1389, U.S. Govt. Printing Office.

Walter, W. G. The living brain, W. W. Norton & Company, Inc., 1953.

Wooldridge, D. E. The machinery of the brain. McGraw-Hill Paperbacks, 1963.

Specific

Adrian, E. D., and Matthews, B. H. C. The Berger rhythm. *Brain* 57:355-385, 1934

Albino, R., and Burnard, G. Conditioning the alpha rhythm in man. *Journal of Experimental Psychology* 67:539-544, 1964.

Anand, B. K., Chhina, G. S., and Singh, B. Some aspects of electroencephalographic studies in Yogis. *EEG Clinical Neurophysiology* 13: 452-456, 1961.

Aterman, M. B., Howes, R. C.; and MacDonald, L. R. Facilitation of spindle-burst sleep by conditioning of electroencephalographic activity, while awake. *Science* 167: 1146-1148, 1970.

Bagchi, B. K., and Wegner, M. Electrophysiological correlates of some Yogi exercises. *EEG Clinical Neurophysiology* 7:132-149, 1957, Suppl.

Barber, T. X.; DiCara, L.; Kamiya, J.; Miller, N. E.; Shapiro, D.; and Stoyva, J. editors. Biofeedback and self-control, an Aldine Annual on the regulation of bodily processes and consciousness. Aldine-Atherton Co., 1970.

Bartley, S. The relation between cortical responses to visual stimulation and changes in the alpha rhythm, *Journal of Experimental Psychology* 27: 627-639, 1940.

Bash, K. W. The alpha rhythm during relaxed wakefulness, dreams, and hallucinations, twilight stages and psychoses. *Psychiatric Clinic* 1: 152-174, 1968.

Basmajian, J. Control of individual motor units. *American Journal of Physical Medicine* 46:1, 1967.

———. Control and training of individual motor units. *Science* 141: 440-441, 1963.

Basmajian, J., and Cross, L., III. Duration of motor unit potentials from fine-wire electrodes. *American Journal of Physical Medicine* 50:2, 1971.

Beatty, J. Control of EEG activity; similar effects of feedback signals and instructional information. 1971.

———. Effects of initial alpha wave abundance and operant training procedures on occipital alpha and beta wave activity. *Psych. Sci.* 23:3, 197-199, 1971.

Benson, H.; Shapiro, D.; Tursky, B.; and Schwartz, G. E. Decreased systolic blood pressure through operant conditioning techniques in patients with essential hypertension. *Science* 173: 740-742, August 20, 1971.

Berkhout, J.; Walter, D.; and Adey, W. R. Alterations of the human electroencephalogram induced by stressful verbal activity. *EEG Clin. Neurophysiology* 27: 457-459, 1969.

Berkhout, J., and Walter, D.C. Temporal stability and individual differences in the human EEG, *IEEE Trans. Bio-Medical Engineering* 15: 165-168, 1968.

Brown, B. B. Awareness of EEG-subjectivity activity relationships detected within a closed feedback system. *Psychophysiology* 7: 451-464, 1971.

———. Effect of LSD on visually evoked responses to color in visualizer and non-visualizer subjects. *EEG Clin. Neurophysiol.* 27: 356, 1969.

———. Feedback systems for awareness and control of one's own physiological activity. *Proc. West. Pharmacol. Soc.* 12: 13-15, 1969.

———. Recognition of aspects of consciousness through association with EEG alpha activity represented by a light signal. *Psycholphysiology* 6: 442-452, 1970.

———. *Some thoughts on biofeedback.* 1971.

Brown, D. *Biofeedback Research Society Proceedings* 1969.

Budzynski, T., and Stoyva, J. Biofeedback techniques in behavior therapy and autogenic training. 1970.

Budzynski, T.; Stoyva, J.; and Adler, C. Feedback-induced havior therapy and autogenic training. 1970.

Budzynski, T.; Stoyva, J.; and Adler, C. Feedback-induced muscle relaxation: application to tension headache; a controlled outcome study. *Behavior Therapy and Exper. Psychiatry* 1: 205-211, 1970.

Bundzen, P. U. Autoregulation of functional state of the brain: an investigation using photostimulation with feedback. *Federal Proceedings Trans. Suppl.* 25: 551-554, 1966.

Chertok, L., and Kramarz, P. Hypnosis, sleep and electroencephalography. *Journal of Nervous and Mental Diseases* 128: 227-238, 1959.

Crisswell, E. Feedback and states of consciousness: meditation. *Biofeedback Research Society, Proceedings,* 1969.

Dahlberg, C. *Biofeedback Research Society Proceedings,* 1969.

Darrow, C. W., and Hicks, R. G. Interarea electroencephalographic phase relationships following sensory and ideational stimuli. *Psychophysiology* 1: 337-346, 1965.

Davidson, R., and Krippner, S. Biofeedback research: the data and their implications. Second International Invitational Conference on Humanistic Psychology, University of Wurzburg, July 1971.

Deikman, A. J. Implications of experimentally induced contemplative meditation. *Journal of Nervous and Mental Disease* 142: 101-116, 1966.

———. *Biofeedback Research Society Proceedings* 1969.

Demet, W., and Kleitman, N. The relationship of eye movements during sleep to dream activity: and objective for the study of dreaming. *Journal of Experimental Psychology* 53: 339-346, 1957.

———. Cyclic variations in the EEG during sleep and their relation to eye movements, body motility, and dreaming. *EEG Clinic Neurophysiology* 9: 637-690, 1957.

Diamant, J.; Dufek, M.; Hoskovec, J.; Kristof, M.; Perarek, V.; Roth, B.; and Velek, M. An electroencephalographic study of the waking state and hypnosis. *Int. Journ. Clin. and Ex. Hypnosis* 8: 199-212, 1960.

Eberlin, P. Alpha blocking during visual after-images. *EEG Clin. Neurophysiol.* 25: 23-28, 1968.

Engstrom, D. R.; London, P.; and Hart, J. T. Hypnotic susceptibility increased by EEG alpha training. *Nature* 227: 1261-1262, 1970.

Fehmi, L. Biofeedback of electroencephalographic parameters and related states of consciousness.

Fruhling, M.; Basmajian, J. V.; Simard, T. G. A note on the conscious controls of motor units by children under six. *Journal of Motor Behavior* 1: 65-68, 1969.

Gaarder, K. Muscle feedback theory and mechanisms. *Biofeedback Research Society Proceedings*, 1969.

Galbraith, G.; London, P.; Leibovitz, M. EEG and hypnotic susceptibility. *Journal of Comp. and Physiol. Psychology* 72: 125-131, 1970.

Green, A. M.; Green, E.; and Walters, E. D. Voluntary control of internal states: psychological and physiological. *Journal of Transpersonal Psychology* 2: 1-28, 1970.

Guttman, G. Analysis of frequency stability of the alpha rhythm based on informational theory. *EEG Clin., Neurophysiol.* 24: 390, 1968.

Hardyck, C., and Petrinovich, L. Subvocal speech and comprehension level as a function of the difficulty of reading material. *Journ. of Verbal Learning and Verbal Behavior* 9: 647-652, 1970.

Hardyck, C., and Petrinovich, L. Treatment of subvocal speech during reading. *Journal of Reading*, February 1969.

Hardyck, C., Petrinovich, L.; and Ellsworth, D. W. Feedback of speech muscle activity during silent reading: rapid extinction. *Science* 154: 1467, December 1966.

Hart, J. Autocontrol of EEG alpha. Paper, Seventh Annual Meeting of Society for Psychophysiological Research, San Diego, California, 1967.

————. Research reports: EEG feedback. *Biofeedback Research Society, Proceedings,* 1969, Pan. 3.

von Hilsheimer, G. Some simple techniques in biological and behavioral feedback. AABT Annual Meeting, Washington, D.C., 1971.

Hirai, T. Electroencephalographic study on the Zen meditation. *Psychiatlica et Neurologica Japonica* 62: 76-105, 1960.

————.; Izawa, S.; and Koga, E. EEG and Zen Buddhism; EEG changes in the course of meditation. *EEG Clin. Neurophysiol.* 18: 52-53, 1959, Suppl.

Honorton, C. Relationship between EEG alpha activity and ESP card-guessing performance. *Journal A.S.P.R.* 63: 365-374, 1969.

Honorton, C., and Carbone, M. A preliminary study of feedback-augmented EEG alpha activity and ESP card-guessing performance. *Journal of the American Society for Psychical Research* 65: 66-74, 1971 (No. 1)

Honorton, C.; Davidson, R.; and Bindler, P. Feedback-augmented EEG alpha shifts in subjective state, and ESP card-guessing performance. *Journ., A.S.P.R.* 65: 308-323, 1971 (No. 3).

Hord, D., and Barber, J. Alpha control: effectiveness of two kinds of feedback, *Psychon. Sci.* 25: 151-154, 1971.

Hord, D.; Naitoh, P.; and Johnson, L. Intensity and coherence contours during self-regulated high alpha activity. *Electro. and Clin. Neurophysiology,* to be published 1972.

Jasper, H., and Shagass, C. Conscious time judgements related to the conditioned time intervals and voluntary control of the alpha rhythm. *Journ. Exp. Psychol.* 28: 503-508, 1941.

Johnson, L., and Hord, D. Progress report: recuperative value of self-regulated states and of brief sleep for sleep loss and fatigue. 1970-1971.

Kamiya, J. *Biofeedback Research Society proceedings* 1969.

——. A fourth dimension of consciousness. *Experimental Medicine and Surgery* 27: 13-18, 1969.

——. Introduction to biofeedback. *Aldine Reader*, 1972.

——. Operant control of the EEG alpha rhythm and some of its reported effects on consciousness. Altered states of consciousness. Charles Tart, (editor). John Wiley and Sons, Inc. New York: 1969, 507-517.

Kasamatsu, A., and Hirai, T. An electroencephalographic study on the Zen meditation. *Folia Psychiatlica et Neurologica Japonica* 20: 315-336, 196.

——. Science of Zazen, *Psychologica* 6: 86-91, 1963.

Kasamatsu, A.; Okeima, T.; Takenaka, S.; Koga, E.; Ikeda, K.; and Sugiyama, H. The EEG of Zen and Yoga practicioners, *EEG Clin. Neurophysiol.* 9: 51-52, 1957, Suppl.

Kreitman, N., and Shaw, J. C. Experimantal enhancement of alpha activity. *EEG Clin. Neurophysiol.* 18: 147-155, 1965.

Krippner, S., and Davidson, R. The use of convergent operations in bio-information research, an invited lecture. Institute of Psychology, Moscow University, Moscow, U.S.S.R., 1971.

Krippner, S., and Ullman, M. Telepathy and dreams: a controlled experiment with electroencephalogram-electro-oculogram monitoring. *Journal of Nervous and Mental Disease* 151: 394-403, 1970.

Laird, G. Alpha biofeedback training as a behavior modifier in hyperkinetic children with learning difficulties. 1971.

Lindsley, D., Psychological phenomena and the electroencephalogram, *EEG Clin. Neurophysiol.* 4: 443-456, 1952.

London, P. The psychophysiology of hypnotic susceptibility, symposium on recent research in hypnosis. APA Meetings, Washington, D.C., 1969.

London, P.; Hart, J. T.; Leibovitz, M. P. EEG alpha rhythms and suseptibility to hypnosis. *Nature* 219: 71-72, 1968.

Loomis, A. L.; Harvey, E. N.; and Hobart, G. Brain potentials during hypnosis. *Science* 83: 239-241, 1936.

Lubin, A.; Johnson, L.; Austin, T. Discimination among states of consciousness using EEG spectra. *Psychophysiology* 6: 122-131, 1969.

Malkin, V. B.; Asyamolova, N. M.; and Kochetov, A. K. Classification of the electroencephalogram of a healthy subject in relation to the problems of selection in aviation. 1969.

Miller, N. Experiments relevant to learning theory and psychopathology, an invited lecture. International Congress of Psychology, Moscow, 1966.

———. Learning of visceral and glandular responses. *Science* 163: 434-445, 1969.

Morrell, L. Some characteristics of stimulus provoked alpha activity. *EEG Clin. Neurophysiol.* 21: 552-561, 1966.

Mulholland, T. Can you really turn on with alpha? Presented at the meeting of the Mass. Psychol. Assoc., Boston College, 1971.

———. Feedback Electroencephalography. *Activ. Nerv. Sub.* 10: 410-438, 1968.

———. Occipital alpha and accommodative vergence, pursuit tracking, and fast eye movements. *Psychophysiology* 8: 556-575, 1971.

———. Occipital alpha revisited. Presented at the Colloquium on the Oculomotor System and Brain Functions, Slovak Academy of Sciences, 1970.

Nall, A. Alpha training and the hyperkinetic child. 1970.

Nowlis, D., and Kamiya, J. The control of electroencephalographic alpha rhythms through auditory feedback and the associated mental activity. *Psychophysiology* 6: 476-484, 1970.

Peper, E. Comment on feedback training of parietal-occipital alpha asymmetry in normal human subjects. *Kybernetik* 9: 156-158, 1971.

————. Feedback regulation of the alpha electroencephalogram activity through control of the internal and external parameters. *Kybernetik* 7: 107-112, 1970.

————. Reduction of efferent motor commands during alpha feedback as a facilitator of EEG alpha, and as a precondition for changes in consciousness. *Kybernetik,* in press.

Peper, E., and Mulholland, T. Methodological and theoretical problems in voluntary control of electroencephalographic occipital alpha by the subject. *Kybernetik* 7: 10-13, 1971.

Scully, H., and Basmajian, J., Motor unit training and influence of manual skill. *Psychophysiology* 5: 625-632, 1969.

Scully, H., and Basmajian, J. Effect of nerve stimulation on trained motor unit control. *Archives of Physical Medicine and Rehabilitation* 50: 32-33, 1969.

Simard, T., and Basmajian, J. Methods in training the conscious control of motor units. *Archives of Physical Medicine and Rehabilitation* 48: 12-19, 1967.

Sinclair, J. *Biofeedback Research Society Proceedings.* 1969.

Slater, K. Alpha rhythms and mental imagery. *EEG Clin. Neurophysiol.* 12: 851-859, 1960.

Stoyva, J. The public (scientific) study of private events. *International Psychiatry Clinics* 7: 355-368, 1970.

Stoyva, J. and Kamiya, J. Electrophysiological studies of dreaming as the prototype of a new strategy in the study of consciousness. *Psychological Review* 75: 192-205, 1968.

Tart, C. Toward the experimental control of dreaming: a review of the literature. *Psychological Bulletin* 64: 81-91, 1965.

Travis, L. E., and Egan, J. P. Increase in the frequency of the alpha rhythm by verbal stimulation. *Journal of Experimental Psychology* 23: 385-393, 1968.

Ullman, M.; Krippner, S.; and Feldstein, S. Experimentally induced telephathic dreams: two studies using EEG-REM monitoring technique. *International Journal of Neuropsychiatry* 2: 420-437, 1966.

Wallace, A. Physiological effects of transcendental meditation. *Science* 167: 1751-1754, 1970.

Walter, W. G., Brain responses to semantic stimuli. *Journal of Psychosomatic Research* 9: 51-61, 1965.

———. Intrinsic rhythms of the brain. *Handbook of Physiology*, J. Field, editor. American Physiology Society, Washington, D.C., 1: 287 ff, 1959.

Weiss, T., and Engel, B. Operant conditioning of heart rate in patients with premature ventricular contractions. *Psychosomatic Medicine* 33: 301-321, 1971.

Whatmore, G. *Biofeedback Research Society Proceedings*, 1969.

Whatmore, G., and Kohli, D. R. Dysponesis: a neurophysiologic factor in functional disorders. *Behavioral Science* 13: 102-124, 1968.

Wortz, E. Feedback and states of consciousness: meditation. *Biofeedback Research Society Proceedings*, 1969.

Name Index

Subject Index

235